THE MARKETING REVOLUTION

THE MARKETING REVOLUTION

A Radical Manifesto for Dominating
the Marketplace

Kevin J. Clancy
Robert S. Shulman

HarperBusiness
A Divison of HarperCollins *Publishers*

Library of Congress Cataloging-in-Publication Data

Clancy, Kevin J., 1942–
    The Marketing revolution : a radical manifesto for dominating the
marketplace / Kevin J. Clancy, Robert S. Shulman.
        p.   cm.
    Includes index.
    ISBN 0-88730-481-8
    1. Marketing—Management. 2. Marketing research. I. Shulman,
Robert S., 1951– . II. Title.
    HF5415. 13.C546   1991   91-35902
    658.8—dc20   CIP

Printed in the United States of America

91 92 93 94 SWD/HC 9 8 7 6 5 4 3 2 1

To our parents,
William and Anne Clancy and
Joseph and Doris Shulman

☰ CONTENTS

≡ ACKNOWLEDGMENTS

In a February 1675 letter to Robert Hook, Sir Isaac Newton said: "If I have seen further it is by standing on the shoulders of giants." If we have seen further it is because we have been influenced over the years by many talented people. Among them: teachers, researchers, and practitioners, including Al Achenbaum, Paul Berger, Joe Blackburn, Hubert Blalock, Alice Brennan, Jamie Campbell, Ron Curhan, Thomas Dewey, Tom Dillon, Bruce Dohrenwend, Ted Dunn, Bob Goldberg, Paul Green, Russ Haley, Jim Jordan, Phil Kotler, Paul Lazarsfeld, Ted Levitt, Melanie Lenard, Sy Lieberman, Larry Light, John Little, Herbert Menzel, Tom Nagle, Dan Nimmo, E.E. Norris, Hubert O'Gorman, Al Ossman, Derek Phillips, Alphonso Pinkney, Lew Pringle, Morris Rosenberg, Dan Rossides, Maurice and Charles Saatchi, William Selkirk, Florence Skelly, Arthur White, Dale Wilson, and Dan Yankelovich; all of our colleagues at Yankelovich Clancy Shulman whose brilliance, creativity, and dedication are a continuing well-spring of inspiration; we are particularly grateful to Lisa Carter, Doug Haley, Peter Kreig, Tom Lix, and Steve Tipps for their contributions to the models and systems discussed in this book; and, of course, our clients whose intellectually stimulating discussions and marketing problems have fine-tuned our thinking and enriched our lives. We are especially grateful to Wallis ("Wally") Wood, a very talented writer and editor, who devoted a year of his life to help pull our ideas together; Elinor Clancy for the wonderful exhibits inserted throughout this book, which sometimes communicate better than our words, and Robin Shulman whose encouragement and support kept things moving along just when our task seemed overwhelming; and Virginia Smith at HarperCollins and Katherine Ives, whose comments on style and substance helped transform a good manuscript into what we hope is a great one.

THE MARKETING REVOLUTION

1

THE MARKETING REVOLUTION IS COMING

A marketing revolution will transform American business in the 1990s as top managements comprehend marketing's significance to their companies' future and drive this new thinking through their companies.

They will demand that marketing executives do new things in new ways. They will compel marketing departments to abandon myth and ignorance and consider hundreds—or hundreds of thousands—of alternatives to every marketing decision to find the optimal one. And they will hold marketing executives accountable for a measurable return on the marketing investment.

Philip Kotler, professor of marketing at Northwestern University and among the most influential figures in American business, describes the developments taking place today as a paradigm shift: "A paradigm shift, as used by Thomas Kuhn in *The Structure of Scientific Revolutions*, occurs when a field's practitioners are not satisfied with the field's explanatory variables or breadth."*

The marketing revolution is coming because failure is self-evident and everybody—stockholders, directors, CEOs, customers, the govern-

---

*Philip Kotler, "Philip Kotler Explores the New Marketing Paradigm," *Marketing Science Institute Review*, Spring 1991.

ment—is angry because marketing, which should be driving business and marketing, doesn't work.

We believe, based on our years of experience consulting to consumer and business-to-business marketers that sell both products and services, that

- Marketing needs a major shake-up;
- Most marketing professionals (including bosses) do not appreciate marketing's complexity;
- Many companies are currently engaged in *death-wish marketing;*
- Mountains of data and the tools to transform them into useful information currently exist;
- A company can use these tools to improve its marketing effectiveness dramatically. They require only top management's attention to see they are employed properly.

You, as top management, don't have to use these tools; you need only know they are being used. But you do need to know the questions to ask when faced with a marketing plan. *The Marketing Revolution* will give you both the questions to ask (or to be prepared to answer) as well as the information on which the questions are based.

≣ Shuffling Assets Doesn't Grow Businesses

The way to grow a business is through marketing. "Because its purpose is to create a customer," says management guru Peter F. Drucker, "the business enterprise has two—and only two—basic functions: marketing and innovation. Marketing and innovation produce results; all the rest are 'costs.'"*

Yet many American corporations spent the 1980s—in a frenzy of asset-shuffling—acquiring companies, fighting acquisition, or struggling to make themselves indigestible by going private or taking on debt or both.

In the 1990s all this must change. "The money has been moved around as much as it can be," says John O'Toole, president of the American Association of Advertising Agencies. "Now, somebody's going to have to make some more of it."†

We looked at the ten *Fortune* 500 companies that grew the most in

---

*Peter F. Drucker, *The Practice of Management* (New York: Harper & Row, 1982), p. 37.
†John O'Toole, telephone conversation with author, 17 July 1991.

annual sales between 1980 and 1990 (that is, those that placed on both lists). Ranked by compound growths that range from 34 percent to 13 percent, are

1)   ConAgra
2)   Philip Morris
3)   Digital Equipment
4)   Hewlett-Packard
5)   Unisys
6)   Sonoco
7)   Sequa
8)   Dow Jones
9)   Bristol-Myers
10) Anheuser-Busch

We estimate, however, that in some cases organic growth—the growth of the business with which they started in 1980—was less than 5 percent.

Take ConAgra, at the top of the list. ConAgra is one of the smartest, most successful companies in America. During the 1980s, it bought Banquet, Singleton Seafood, Sea-Alaska, Country Pride, Armour Food Co., Chun King, Morton, Patio, E. A. Miller boxed beef, Monfort, Swift Independent Packing, O'Donnell-Usen, Blue Star, and Cook Family Food ham.

Philip Morris, the tobacco giant, bought General Foods in 1985 and sales jumped 70 percent even though the company sold Seven-Up in 1986. It bought Kraft in 1988 and saw sales leap 51 percent the following year. But if Philip Morris's total compound growth between 1980 and 1990 was almost 19 percent, we estimate its organic growth during the period at closer to 8 percent—still respectable, but not quite as spectacular.

We suspect that hidden within many companies' consolidated financial reports is the shameful secret that they've been able to report growth *only* because they've acquired other companies. Strip away the mergers and the acquisitions, and you find a core business that is limping along because it has ignored the basic purpose of a business.

"The purpose of a business is to get and keep a customer," writes Theodore Levitt in *The Marketing Imagination*. "Without customers, no amount of engineering wizardry, clever financing, or operations expertise can keep the company going. To be the low-cost producer of vacuum tubes, to have the best salesmen of what's not wanted or wanted only by the few whose ability to pay won't even pay for the overhead—these can't save you from extinction. To do well what should not be done is to do badly."

The principle is simple: sell the company's products or services to more people or sell more to existing customers or do both. The idea may be simple, but executing it is not.

This book may not make the executing any easier. It *will* help top managers who want their companies to thrive in the 1990s to provoke their own marketing revolution. We describe both the issues and the new tools available to marketing management. We give you the questions to ask about any marketing program. Our experience with scores of American and foreign corporations tells us that this will be a time when sophisticated companies begin to use the marketing tools that quietly evolved during the last ten years or so. Marketing will become less of an art and more of a science. Companies will become more productive not by cutting costs but by adding value, and by becoming more productive they will become more profitable. If the 1980s were the decade of dealing, the 1990s will be the decade of marketing.

≡ The Current State of Marketing: Terrible

During the 1980s, speakers at numerous marketing conferences discussed their discipline in enthusiastic, upbeat, and sometimes even exhilarating terms. Many presented impressive case studies of their successes—sometimes a product no one in the audience had ever heard of before—or offered colorful anecdotes of marketing triumphs. Anyone attending marketing conferences, listening to the speeches, and chatting with the marketing professionals in the audience would have concluded that marketing's general health was robust and major companies' marketing efforts were reasonably successful.

Yet that was only the public face—the one marketers put on for conferences and for the press. The truth, we believe, is the opposite: marketing is deteriorating.

As we'll show in a moment, the general state of marketing is unhealthy, and reports of marketing successes in packaged goods, financial services, and other areas are widely and wildly exaggerated. Indeed, we argue that marketing efforts are in practice rarely successful—*if* you define success as demonstrating a reasonable return on investment.

The issue, after all, is not how much you sell, but how much you sell at a profit. And the evidence, which is neither circumstantial nor selective, shows that—even when they can measure the return on investment—most marketing programs do not provide an acceptable ROI. They do not achieve their sales and profit goals. They do not obtain a market share great enough to justify their existence.

This is a change for the worse. We recently did a survey for the American Marketing Association among marketers, marketing researchers, and presidents/CEOs of *Fortune* 1000 firms, and two-thirds said it is much more difficult to launch a new product today than it was a decade ago. They told us that fewer than one-quarter of their new products are successful today—an unexpected revelation in a survey that we thought would result in substantial overclaiming, the tendency for respondents to give us the answer that makes them look smart. Although we cannot project the results to all American business, the findings suggest that marketing's happy public face masks deep private malaise.

We asked these respondents to express their attitudes toward various marketing statements. Using a five-point scale ranging from "Disagree Strongly" to "Agree Strongly," two-thirds agreed with this statement: "New product failure rates have increased during the past two decades." Only slightly more than half, however, agreed with this statement: "Marketing in the late 80s is more effective than marketing in the 60s and 70s." And only about a third agreed with this: "Most marketing programs produce a reasonable return on investment."

These respondents are grizzled veterans of the marketing wars. Citing the impact of business-world experience, they have changed their early marketing beliefs. When we asked them, "What is the *main* principle of marketing that you believed when you first started your career that you no longer believe?" they told us that they no longer believe that

- Good marketing sells or could sell any product;
- Marketing is a science not an art, a step-by-step textbook process;
- The best product wins the biggest market share;
- Advertising is the most effective tool in the marketing mix;
- To be successful a product has to have mass appeal;
- The lowest price sells the most product;
- The results of marketing research could affect top management or that companies realize the importance of marketing research.

And although the majority agreed that "a line extension is easier to introduce than the same product under a new brand name," only about four out of ten agreed that "in the coming years, marketers will realize more profit from managing existing brand equities than from creating new brands."

One CEO admitted last year, "We would have made more money if we had taken all of the money we spent creating and introducing new products in the last ten years and put it into certificates of deposit." This comment is supported by widely reported analyses of brand share profitability data. The analyses show that in many product categories, brands ranked lower than number three in market share fail to produce a reasonable return on marketing investment or on sales or both.

One frequently hears that most new packaged goods fail. But most CEOs don't realize the seriousness of the problem. According to Bill Gorman's *New Product News*, a trade magazine, businesses are facing a 1990 new product failure rate of 80 percent. This rate is up from 70 percent during the 1960s, 1970s, and early 1980s. Yet despite the dismal chances for success, companies continue to introduce new products. According to *New Product News*, companies introduced 8,042 new products to American consumers in 1986; five years later they introduced 13,244, a 65 percent increase.

To call all these food items, health and beauty aids, household supplies, and paper, tobacco, and pet products "new" may be a misnomer, since they include line extensions—an existing brand in a new flavor, size, or color. Only 5 to 10 percent of each year's total are products that might truly be called "new." But even these are not doing well.

Alvin Achenbaum, as chairman of a New York–based consulting company specializing in marketing strategy, found using SAMI/Burke data that fewer than 200 products introduced in the past ten years had more than $15 million in annual sales, and a handful produced more than $100 million in sales. According to Achenbaum, now vice-chairman at Backer Spielvogel Bates Worldwide, this means that "less than 1 percent have even a modicum of success."*

Of course, packaged goods are not the only marketplace failures. We have been collecting statistics for more than a decade, and our numbers suggest a comparable failure rate for new financial products and services—credit cards, insurance plans, brokerage services. Our research also suggests that the new product failure rate among consumer durables—including cars, appliances, and consumer electronics—is not much different. The American automobile industry, for example, is one big marketing failure. *Car Catastrophes* would be an easy book to write.

A Wharton School of Business study highlighted reasons for marketing failures. Of the products studied, 32 percent failed because of inadequate research and development, 23 percent because they were bad ideas, 14 percent because of higher-than-anticipated costs, 13 percent because of weak marketing strategies, 10 percent because of timing, and 8 percent because of competitive activity. We argue that all new product failures can be avoided and that, after reading this book, you will have the tools to beat these grim percentages.

But new products are not the only problem. The average brand in the average category is dying a slow death; its sales erode by about three-tenths of a share point each year. Typically, management notes

---

*Alvin Achenbaum, "How to Succeed in New Products," *Advertising Age*, 26 June 1989, p. 62.

this decline without reacting for a couple years: after all, how serious is a 0.3 percent drop? It may be nothing more than a statistical anomaly. But when the slump becomes too apparent for business as usual and the company finally decides something must be done, what happens?

Top management pulls the marketing director on the carpet and says, "We've got to resuscitate this dying brand! We've got to breathe some life into it! We want you to get the agency to put together a new ad campaign. Put some extra dollars behind it; increase our share of voice; come up with a new copy claim. How about a product reformulation? Is there anything out of R&D? A new promotion plan? Jazz it all up, and make it as successful as it can be."

A year later, after another 0.3 share drop, the new campaign is launched, and marketing management sits back to wait for the results. In our experience—and we've been doing this research for almost two

Figure 1.1 *Ad Copy*

decades—nine out of ten times nothing happens. Attempts to relaunch or reposition dying products and services fail to reverse share declines. Even in our survey of marketers, marketing researchers, and presidents-CEOs (who had good reason to exaggerate their own company's performance) fewer than one in five (17 percent) agreed that most campaigns designed to increase sales of existing products or services are successful. Elvis is more likely to turn up alive than a turnaround attempt is to succeed.

Marketing plan failure is so common that our company ran an advertising campaign in 1990 using the headline "Every 7 Minutes Another Marketing Plan Dies" (Figure 1.1). The headline was based on our estimate that there are at least 150,000 major marketing programs running in the United States each year, including consumer, industrial, and not-for-profit campaigns. Even if only half of them are failures (e.g., they fail to produce a reasonable return on investment)—and we think that this figure is too low—a major program is failing every seven minutes.

≡ Choose the Best of 13,800,000,000 Combinations

Products fail because marketing is difficult. Whether the objective is to launch a new product or relaunch an existing product, most marketing plans break down because marketers do not consider enough alternatives and cannot choose the optimal strategy.

That reasoning may sound unlikely, but consider the process. To introduce a new consumer or industrial product or service, marketers

Table 1.1 *"Case of Escalating Sevens"*

---

1. Market target (7 choices)
2. Positioning (7 choices)
3. Advertising execution (7 choices)
4. Product/packaging configuration (7 choices)
5. Pricing (7 choices)
6. Distribution type/level (7 choices)
7. Media spending (7 choices)
8. Media mix (7 choices)
9. Media schedule (7 choices)
10. Promotion spending (7 choices)
11. Promotion mix (7 choices)
12. Promotion schedule (7 choices)

Note: Assume that in any marketing plan there are twelve decisions to be made and only seven choices.

make at least a dozen key marketing decisions. These include the market target, positioning, product design, pricing, distribution type and level, advertising message, media spending, media mix, media schedule, promotion spending, promotion mix, and promotion schedule.

Suppose for the sake of illustration the company has only seven alternatives for each of the dozen decisions (see Table 1.1). In the real world, of course, it may have fewer than seven for a given decision—but it also may have more. If there are only seven options for each of the marketing mix's twelve ingredients, how many different programs could a marketing manager develop? What do the escalating sevens total?

Not 7 times 12, or 84 different programs.

The answer is 7 to the twelfth power, or 13,841,287,201 different marketing programs. That's 13.8 *billion*—a number only God and CFOs can comprehend.

Among all these possible programs, of course, a few would be unmitigated disasters; many would be neither successful nor disastrous (but probably would not be successful enough to meet typical sales and profitability hurdles either), and a few would be successes. It's a standard bell curve, illustrated in Figure 1.2.

But the odds that a marketing manager will pick one of the resounding successes from the 13.8 billion choices—even if he or she works late—are slim, which is why most new product introductions and repositioning efforts fail. Fortunately, just as the world has been changing in ways that make traditional marketing more difficult and less effective, other changes are giving marketers new tools to improve the likelihood of success. Today two developmental streams run strong in marketing:

Figure 1.2 *Bell Curve*

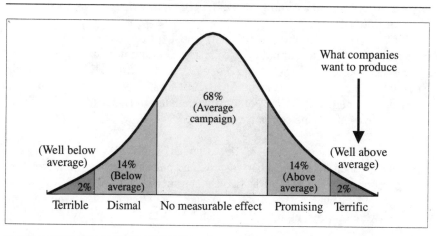

- Business's ability to generate information—to measure consumer behavior—has grown phenomenally. Marketers are capturing more information about more customers than ever before: what they watch, what they read, what they hear, and what they buy. This is the *descriptive* side of the equation, and it will continue to be a significant part of marketing for the foreseeable future.
- At the same time, researchers have improved a marketer's ability to make decisions based on that information—the *prescriptive* side of the equation.

Most large companies today use sophisticated financial tools when deciding whether, say, to build a new factory or dig a new oil well. They look at formulas for net present value, return on investment, and more. Before turning the first spadeful of earth, management knows what the new factory's investment should return or what "making a hole" will produce.

Few companies, large or small, use sophisticated financial tools when deciding whether to launch a product, revamp the advertising, change the advertising message, alter the product's positioning, or even redesign the product. Most advertising managers would be lost if asked the return on the advertising budget. They use experience, judgment, and intuition, all effective in themselves but inadequate to deal with today's complexities.

Advertising's unknown return on investment is a particularly troubling issue because companies spend so much money on it. We estimate that companies spent more than $130 billion on advertising in the United States in 1990 (*Advertising Age* reported $124 billion in 1989). Compare that spending to the $22 billion the federal government spent on education and the $5 billion on the environment. Seventeen of the nation's largest advertisers have ad budgets larger than entire companies in the *Fortune* 500 list.

Yet little is known about what most advertising accomplishes. Christopher Whittle, founder of Whittle Communications, eloquently addressed this topic as the keynote speaker at the Advertising Research Foundation's annual meeting in April 1991. Whittle said that about ten years ago he began to notice something unusual in the studies of various advertising vehicles his company conducted:

Most of our studies were of the pre/post, control/test variety. There would be long discussions between us and our clients about whether the movements in the test cells (which measured our new vehicles) were large enough, but nothing was ever said about the fact that the control cells (which represented all other spending) almost never moved.

At first, Whittle tentatively asked his clients what they thought about this. Did it bother them that the $20 million they spent in the control cell didn't show any change? "Any time we brought this up, there was an almost noticeable discomfort, and the subject would invariably be changed."

He began to see this pattern in study after study and became increasingly curious. One day, during a discussion of test cell response versus control cell's inactivity, he said, "Well, why don't you just pay us based on how we perform against the control cells. If we're better, pay us more, and if we're less, pay us less." No one, he reported, was interested.

I began to wonder why, in twenty years in this business, no one had ever shown me a piece of research that definitively demonstrated the effectiveness of their advertising in other vehicles—if for no other reason than it would have been good negotiation. Originally I had thought they must have this information. Why would they continue to spend all this money if they didn't. Then it struck me that perhaps it wasn't there.

Today after years of investigation Whittle is convinced that it isn't there.

Advertising, however, is not the only component in the marketing mix with an uncertain contribution to sales and profits. Today, two out of three marketing dollars spent by packaged goods companies goes into consumer and trade promotion. What do we know about the ROI of promotion? Unknown? Hardly. It is now known that it's negative: most promotion programs are unprofitable. We'll have more to say about this later.

Promotions basically accomplish two things: they lower the price of goods sold, and they increase brand disloyalty. And these ignominious effects go well beyond packaged goods. Is there an airline executive in America who wouldn't like to return to the days before frequent flyer programs (outside of those who work in the promotion department)?

Some products, of course, should fail. They are poorly designed, cheaply manufactured, overpriced, or a "me-too" product without a unique advantage. But more commonly, they fail because companies employ death-wish marketing.

≣ The Tell-Tale Signs of Death-Wish Marketing

Death-wish marketing is our name for those efforts that managers, unconsciously or unknowingly, undertake to kill a product, a brand, or, occasionally, an entire company. Fortunately, a chief executive does not have to be a professional marketer to spot death-wish thinking. Here are some of its symptoms:

1) Key marketing decisions are based on judgment alone (if marketing judgment were so good, why are so many programs so bad) or circuitous reasoning such as, "This is the way we made the decision last year." This is death-wish marketing.

2) The company has analyzed its competition as a guide to what opportunities to pursue. However, the competition may be making a mistake, or its situation may be very different. Watching the competition for guidance is death-wish marketing.

3) Top management demands short-term marketing results. But marketing is a process, one that when followed tends to increase the odds of success. Carefully following the process—not always, because sometimes you have to react quickly, but generally—takes time.

4) Because marketing is still a bit of an art (even though we argue it should be more science), corporate structures tend to create marketing programs that build consensus within the organization but don't address real customer needs with real solutions. Many times, what will sell internally ends up as the marketing program. This is death-wish marketing.

5) The marketing decision-making process considered five or fewer decision options for each of the twelve decisions we discussed earlier—that is, fewer than five targets, positionings, advertising executions, pricing levels, media spending, product/package configurations, etc. Death-wish marketing.

6) The analysis of these marketing decision options emphasized what buyers think, believe, want, or would buy with little or no emphasis on profitability. More death-wish marketing.

7) A large percentage of the marketing and middle managers are baby boomers. These are people who, until recently, have been more interested in being "different," "creative," "exciting," or "sexy" than in being right. Beware of young marketing managers in $2,000 Italian-made suits wearing Ralph Lauren glasses; they bring death-wish marketing.

8) The marketing plan rests heavily (or entirely) on death-wish research, including focus groups, or small, strange samples of atypical consumers (fewer than 300 people) roaming through shopping malls in a semicomatose state with time on their hands.

9) Because marketing directors do not know manufacturing costs,

they cannot calculate profitability and cannot therefore assess a marketing program's return on investment. Death-wish marketing.

10) Companies promote marketing managers before they've had to live with the brands or programs they've launched. More than once we've seen situations in which an executive launches a brand, but the plan is a mess when it reaches the market. Somebody else has to clean up, however, because the instigator has been promoted five times since the launch. Death-wish marketing is promoting managers before they've had to live with their brands and had to demonstrate a return on investment.

If you assign ten points to each symptom, and a given plan scores fifty or more, you are looking at death-wish marketing. Such faulty marketing planning is insidious because it gives the illusion of information. Which is worse—no planning or death-wish marketing? We believe that death-wish marketing is worse because it gives the illusion of information. Marketing executives think they are making sound decisions, unaware the basis is fatally flawed. If you know your boat's compass is broken, you'll steer by dead reckoning or by the stars or by compensating for the sun's position, and you may reach land safely. But if you don't know the compass is broken—and based on a study we conducted recently among CEOs that we'll describe in the next chapter, most don't know—you'll end up on the rocks. Your marketing plan will become a statistic.

≣ A Radical Manifesto for Dominating the Marketplace

"Today, demand for many consumer products is growing at only the same slow rate as the population," proclaimed *Business Week* at the beginning of 1990. "And technological advances have resulted in a slew of products of similar quality, which makes it tough for companies to stand out, while price competition has resulted in margin-killing battles for market share." No company can win these battles by cutting costs and by continuing to market the same way it has in the past.

However, even with all the changes in technology, in the business climate, and in American society, many company managers in their deepest hearts regard production or finance as the secret to success. Too many still regard marketing as an adjunct to sales. And even within companies serious about marketing, executives disagree over basic methodologies.

We believe—and we demonstrate throughout this book—that a company can stand out in this environment, that computer-aided marketing planning technology exists today to help companies make their marketing decisions. But even though marketers have far more data than in the past (so much, indeed, it's become a form of intellectual pollution), and even though computer programs can now manipulate that data faster and less expensively than ever, neither the data nor the computer is the solution.

The marketing revolution in the 1990s is management's recognition that, for every decision in the marketing mix, the company must evaluate hundreds, thousands, tens of thousands, even millions of alternatives. And it must evaluate all these alternatives in terms of forecasted profitability—not appeal, demand, share, sales, or warm "feelies."

We show you what's wrong with many marketing tools in wide use today—focus groups, gap analysis, perceptual maps, and more. And we describe the tools a manager can use to evaluate alternatives in order to generate profitable solutions to marketing problems.

The marketing revolution will come about, however, not because of new data or new technology (although they will help). Top management, boards of directors, stockholders, and employees will unite in their demands for a marketing revolution. They will no longer accept the myths of marketing. They will no longer tolerate death-wish marketing. They will no longer countenance routine marketing failure.

2

BEYOND MYTH
AND IGNORANCE
TO MARKETING
INTELLIGENCE

Perhaps the best way to illustrate the scope of marketing's current problems is to describe our actual experience with a marketing plan for an antiperspirant that was based entirely on marketing myths. The antiperspirant plan that follows, of course, did not incorporate every myth we've uncovered over the years. But it did reflect some of the more than two dozen we spell out in this chapter.

Seeing these marketing myths in action will make you wonder what CEOs really know about marketing. How can marketing executives continue to present marketing plans without answering the hard questions that might expose these plans' weaknesses? In the second half of this chapter, we report what we found in a recent study of CEOs and what they know about marketing.

≣An Antiperspirant Marketing Plan That Was All Wet

In early 1988 we sat through a meeting in which a major packaged goods firm (which as you'll see must remain anonymous) presented a $25 million plan to introduce a new antiperspirant. We were there because we were to do the simulated test market research that would provide the company with early returns on the product's sales and profitability.

The product manager flipped through a chart, presenting the product's background. Researchers in the company's laboratory had developed a formulation that was 37 percent more effective than the market-leading antiperspirant. It offered twenty-four-hour protection. "We found in a series of twelve focus groups that women remain concerned about perspiration and underarm odor," said the product manager. "They are not entirely satisfied with the products they currently use, and our new entry is designed to answer these concerns."

What would be the target market? "We're targeting eighteen- to forty-nine-year-old women, because that group accounts for 62 percent of all sales for this type of product."

The product positioning? "We're going to position it as an effective, convenient solution to perspiration. In all the concept tests, the product scored very high in terms of consumer appeal scores."

How did the new formulation do in product testing? "It performed measurably better than the leading products in blind product tests."

Pricing plans? "We plan to price it at twenty cents—at retail—below the market leader. We feel this will be the best way to penetrate the market quickly. During the introductory phase, we'll be dropping 50 million coupons in free-standing newspaper inserts."

Advertising? "As you can see from the planned advertising campaign, we've loaded both the television commercials and the print advertising with five key selling messages about the product, messages that will appeal to most people in the target market, and we're supporting them with an advertising budget comparable to the market leader."

Our role in such a meeting is not to challenge a plan's basic assumptions. We were invited because we were expected to include the plan's particulars in our simulated test market research.

Less than six months later we were back in the same conference room with our forecast that the product would be an unequivocal failure, a marketing and financial catastrophe. Hearing this, the product manager angrily attacked us: "This may not be the greatest answer to every American woman's perspiration problems, but my product—given this company's resources and experience—*is* going to be a success. I think you should seriously consider revisiting your sales and profitability estimates." (*Revisiting* is a marketing code word for revising the numbers upwards.) "They're wrong! This product will perform *much* better than you've projected!"

The manager then went on to question our research methodology, forecasting model, quality of the data, and anything else he could think of that might have intervened between the promise (his hopes for a great forecast) and the performance (our projections of how the product would actually perform).

As an aside, marketing executives routinely ask if there aren't circumstances that would lead us to adjust simulated test market forecasts upwards. We have *never* been asked to revise a sales forecast downwards.

We said as diplomatically as we could that we had carefully followed the marketing plan's assumptions, and while we would certainly review our work for mistakes, unless we found something unusual we could not adjust the forecast.

The product manager, growing more and more agitated, said in passing, "If this product is killed, I won't have a brand." Because this is an important client and because the product manager was so distressed, we offered to spend some time (at our expense) reviewing in detail the strategy and research on which the company had placed their bets.

We spent almost a day studying the company's research and the assumptions based on the research findings. We discovered that at every juncture, from original product concept to launch, the research had suggested mediocrity: most likely failure, at best marginal success. The product, however, had taken on a life of its own, gradually gathering momentum until nothing, not even our eleventh-hour prediction, could stop the introduction.

The company did launch the product in 1990, but all its resources and experience could not prevent a costly failure.

≡ Marketing Plans Based on Ignorance Compounded by Mythology

As you may have already realized, this corporation had developed a marketing plan based almost entirely on myth. This company is hardly alone, since many firms base their marketing plans on what the dictionary might call "an ill-founded belief held uncritically, especially by an interested group."

What specifically were the beliefs underlying this plan? We can clearly identify eight:

1) *Myth:* Since many marketers define marketing as "the discipline concerned with solving people's problems with products for a profit," marketers attempt to discover what problems buyers are having in their product categories. This company, like most marketers, *didn't* attempt to identify consumer problems in any scientific or reliable way.

2) *Myth:* Because most consumer packaged goods companies target their advertising to eighteen- to forty-nine-year-old women, they are a good target. (Indeed, this is marketing's all-time most popular target for a wide range of product categories.)

3) *Myth:* Heavy buyers (also known as "heavy users," "high rollers," "big spenders") are the best target for many marketing programs, including consumer and business-to-business products and services. (In fact, as we'll be showing in Chapter 4, heavy buyers, like "eighteen- to forty-nine-year-old women" and other popular targets, are usually terrible targets.)

4) *Myth:* Qualitative research techniques, particularly focus group interviews, are serious, helpful marketing research tools.

5) *Myth:* Most marketing research tools in widespread use, including concept testing, product testing, and advertising testing, have demonstrated reliability and validity.

6) *Myth:* Because pricing is such an important component in the marketing mix, most firms have a serious price strategy based on businesslike pricing research.

7) *Myth:* The more messages that you pack into a television or print ad, the more effective the advertising.

8) *Myth:* Advertising wears out quickly and must be continually refreshed.

The antiperspirant marketing plan, in other words, incorporated myths about targeting, marketing research tools, pricing, and advertising. These eight myths, however, are only some of those we regularly find among companies large and small, companies that sell to consumers and that market products or services to other businesses. We've found that marketers—and their bosses—believe the most remarkable things.

We are not, at this point, going to debunk these myths. We show you in the rest of the book why we say these are myths and indicate what we think is the reality—and why—so that you and your people can build plans based on marketing intelligence.

For example, when they discuss market targets, it turns out that many marketers believe that

1) *Myth:* The "middle market" for products and services is dying. Products and services need to be positioned at the "high end" or "low end" of the market to be successful today.

2) *Myth:* Industrial and consumer marketers believe that a company's best prospects for a company, product, or service are people who "look" very much like current customers.

3) *Myth:* Psychographics and consumer attitudes are useful bases for segmenting markets.

4) *Myth:* Needs-based segmentation strategies (that is, identifying different market segments on the basis of what buyers say is important) provide the most profitable way to segment and understand a product market.

When they discuss positioning, they say things like

1) *Myth:* Positioning strategies based on gap analysis (that is, gaps between buyer needs and product delivery)—perhaps the most commonly employed positioning tool of marketing, advertising, and public opinion researchers—will be successful.

2) *Myth:* Perceptual mapping and choice modeling, two high-tech research tools in widespread use, offer prescriptive insights that help marketers develop improved marketing strategies.

Product development is surrounded by its own beliefs:

1) *Myth:* The more appealing a new product is—that is, the more people who say they intend to buy it—the more likely the product will be a success.

2) *Myth:* Most firms base their pricing decisions on a clearly articulated strategy supported by pricing research.

3) *Myth:* Line extensions are the least risky way of introducing new products.

4) *Myth:* A company must offer "zero defect" quality products. The higher the level of quality, the greater the chances of marketing success.

Black magic, mystery, and much mythology surround the marketing research function:

1) *Myth:* Focus groups and other forms of research undertaken among small, nonprojectable samples of consumers and industrial buyers is a wise basis for marketing decision making.

2) *Myth:* A product that scores high in a concept test will be a sure winner in the marketplace.

3) *Myth:* Advertising testing, concept testing, package testing, product testing, and other tools in widespread practice in the marketing industry have proven track records of reliability (i.e., if you measured the same thing twice, you'd get the same score) and validity (the tool measures what it's supposed to measure).

4) *Myth:* You can generally find a good idea for a new product, ad name, corporate image, or whatever, by testing a few—say, three to five—alternatives and picking the winner.

5) *Myth:* When choosing between options for a new product, ad, product formulation, or whatever, researchers are using criteria related to profitability. That is, the "winning" option will be more profitable than the losing option.

Advertising has developed its own body of beliefs:

1) *Myth:* Lots of data exist that prove that advertising is a good investment. How else can you explain an annual expenditure of $130 billion?

2) *Myth:* It does not matter whether people like your advertising or not. What matters is how memorable and persuasive it is.

3) *Myth:* Advertising works best in markets where a brand is doing poorly. This is where you have the greatest opportunity to impact sales.

4) *Myth:* For at least thirty years, marketers have purchased media based on costs per thousands of people exposed, known in the industry as CPMs. This has been, and will continue to be, helpful.

5) *Myth:* The more people are involved in television programs, the less likely they are to pay attention to advertising. High-involvement programming, therefore, results in low-impact advertising.

6) *Myth:* Given enough cues and prompts, most people remember something about your television commercial the day after they watched it.

7) *Myth:* Front-loaded advertising campaigns (i.e., allocating a disproportionate amount of media dollars to the first quarter) is a useful strategy across a broad range of product categories.

Beliefs surround test marketing as well:

1) *Myth:* No $100,000 "laboratory" study in three months (a simulated test market) can provide the same value as a $3 million, eighteen-month in-market test.

2) *Myth:* Failure in test market is sufficient cause to scuttle a new product introduction.

3) *Myth:* Sales of a new product always increase in year 2, so if year 1 is successful, year 2 is assured.

4) *Myth:* Technology does not exist to use test market or simulated test market data in order to transform a dog into a star.

As far as general ideas about marketing, here are some of the more popular beliefs:

1) *Myth:* Most marketing programs work. Even when they don't generate a clear return on investment, they produce a significant effect on sales at the very least.

2) *Myth:* A company must offer the *highest* level of service. The higher the level of service, the more satisfied are the firm's customers, and the more profitable the marketing program.

3) *Myth:* A knowledge of consumer values may be helpful in describing what people do, but not in predicting how they will behave in the future.

4) *Myth:* Market share determines profitability across all industries.

5) *Myth:* Artificial intelligence shows little short-term promise in marketing and advertising. Certainly machines will not be built before the year 2000 that can replace marketing and advertising managers.

And finally:

1) *Myth:* CEOs know a great deal about marketing. They've studied it, practiced it, and become adept at it. (In fact, most CEOs know little about marketing, and much of what they've studied, practiced, or become adept at won't help them during the marketing revolution of the 1990s.)

≣ How We Measured the CEO's Marketing IQ

Most chief executive officers—with certain notable exceptions—do not understand marketing, partly for historical reasons. Years ago, virtually all manufacturers thought only about production. Business theory was simple: manufacture quality products, then find people to buy them.

But over time, the corporation's nature changed. The 1950s saw large single-product corporations, which, as they grew and made money, bought related and unrelated businesses, leading to the conglomerates of the 1960s. The late 1970s (again, oversimplifying shamelessly) saw managements struggle to manage their conglomerates, and the end of the 1980s saw divestitures as managers realized they couldn't manage these polyglot companies.

Given the financial backgrounds of so many CEOs, it was natural for them to look for financial solutions to their companies' challenges. If all you have is a hammer, every problem looks like a nail. Finance, perhaps because it seems to be more quantitative than other disciplines, may have appealed to many executives. Business school students during the 1970s and 1980s recognized that finance was the fastest track to the CEO's chair. According to the *Digest of Educational Statistics*, both the absolute number and the percentage of banking and finance graduates rose almost steadily during the 1980s (while 6 percent fewer students received a master's degree in marketing management and research in 1987 than in 1980).

If that's the situation at the career pyramid's base, what's happening at the top in the 1990s? According to *Business Week's* 1990 profiles of 1,000 chief executives, the largest group, 31 percent, reached their positions through finance-accounting. Another 27 percent came up via merchandising-marketing, while 22 percent came via engineering-technical (other routes included production, manufacturing, and legal).

To compete effectively in the 1990s, more CEOs will have to know more about marketing than they know today, and to find out what they do know, we surveyed 1,003 executives of U.S. companies with annual sales of $500,000 or more. For companies with sales under $50 million, we interviewed the CEO or owner. For companies with sales between $50 million and $100 million, we interviewed both CEOs and executive vice presidents with profit and loss responsibilities for the entire firm; at companies doing over $100 million we also interviewed some senior vice presidents with P&L responsibilities for the entire firm.

To keep the test simple, we developed fifty statements that could be answered "definitely true," "probably true," "don't know," "probably false," and "definitely false." Half the items were correct—the right answer was "definitely true"; the other half were incorrect—the right answer was "definitely false."

The statements covered marketing theory (widely accepted ideas), methodology (marketing research methods), facts (marketing knowledge), real-world practice (beliefs and approaches in common use), and people (the work of leading marketing academics and consultants). They encompassed seven functional areas: marketing strategy, advertising, market segmentation, pricing, distribution, new product and service development, and marketing research.

To score the answers (and come up with numbers that resemble standard intelligence quotient scores where 100 is average and 160 is genius), we gave a 160 to correct answers. That is, we gave a 160 to the CEO who answered "definitely true" when the statement was correct or answered "definitely false" when the statement was incorrect. We gave a 120 to partially correct answers (when the CEO answered "probably true" to a correct statement), an 80 to "don't-know" answers, a 40 to mostly incorrect answers, and a 0 to patently incorrect answers.

Once we averaged the scores for all fifty items on a questionnaire, we had the CEO's marketing IQ, which could range from 0 (a dummy who got everything precisely wrong) to 160 (someone who knows an impressive amount about marketing).

≡ What's the Marketing IQ of America's Top Management?

Before we tell you the results—results we find scary—we should say something comforting. Executives seemed to take this test seriously. They did not answer true or false indiscriminately, or check "don't know" promiscuously. Rather they seemed to take the time to think through the questions and answer as best they could. And when they didn't know an answer, they said they didn't.

For example, one statement read, "Professor Theodore ("Ted") Levitt is well known for his views on *marketing myopia*." Although the editor of the *Harvard Business Review* and Edward W. Carter Professor of Business Administration at the Harvard Business School is one of the most widely read and respected figures in marketing, 85 percent of these respondents checked off "don't know."

On the other hand, when they thought they knew the answer, they gave it. Take, for example, the item: "Most pricing decisions are undertaken without any serious, formal research." Here's the percentage for each answer:

Definitely true	Probably true	Don't know	Probably false	Definitely false
14.6%	31.2%	3.9%	40.6%	9.7%

In this case, the statement is correct, so about half of these executives (45.8 percent) were right, but as you can see, virtually everyone had an opinion.

For some statements, the respondents knew the right answer. Take this statement: "The percentages of all television homes tuned in to particular stations or programs at a given time are referred to as 'ratings.'" The answers:

Definitely true	Probably true	Don't know	Probably false	Definitely false
37.5%	42.6%	10.1%	4.3%	5.5%

Since the statement is true, the vast majority answered correctly.

They did not do quite as well with this statement: "Most people exposed to an ad in a television program can remember something about it—given enough cues and prompts—when contacted the next day by a research interviewer." The answers:

Definitely true	Probably true	Don't know	Probably false	Definitely false
7.1%	54.4%	15.0%	21.1%	2.4%

Since the statement is not true—most people exposed to commercials cannot recall anything about them the next day—the majority were wrong.

Some of the statements were forms of the myths we've just listed, and, confirming our point, certain respondents think they're true. For example, "In most product categories, heavy buyers (or heavy spenders) are a highly profitable market target." The answers:

Definitely true	Probably true	Don't know	Probably false	Definitely false
16.2%	50.3%	18.9%	13.4%	1.2%

That's a myth, as we demonstrate in Chapter 4, yet more than two-thirds of these respondents thought it was true.

Here's another example: "More often than not, the information produced by focus group research is as accurate and useful as the results of survey research at less than half the cost." The answers:

Definitely true	Probably true	Don't know	Probably false	Definitely false
4.9%	36.3%	40.1%	13.4%	5.3%

Focus group research (as we'll demonstrate in Chapter 5) is neither as accurate nor as useful as survey research, and cost therefore is meaningless. If you need blueprints for your new house, and correct plans are $300, what good is the $100 set, if it's wrong?

Yet companies like focus group research. We asked these executives their opinion of the statement, "Generally speaking, a firm *should not* allocate a high share of its research budget to focus group interviews." The responses:

Definitely true	Probably true	Don't know	Probably false	Definitely false
4.1%	27.0%	40.7%	26.0%	2.2%

Since this is almost a perfect random distribution of the answers, about as many were wrong—the statement is true—as right, with the largest percentage uncertain.

These top executives stumbled on the statement, "To identify which competitor to compete most vigorously against, a manager should conduct a market share assessment." The answers:

Definitely true	Probably true	Don't know	Probably false	Definitely false
16.2%	55.8%	13.6%	12.2%	2.2%

Since the statement is false, more than two-thirds of these executives got it wrong.

They did even worse with the statement, "The *best* prospects for an established product or service are people who are very *similar* to current customers." The responses:

Definitely true	Probably true	Don't know	Probably false	Definitely false
25.0%	63.7%	4.0%	5.9%	1.4%

Since, as we show in Chapter 12, the best prospects for an established product or service are often *not* people who are similar to current customers, the statement is false, yet only 1.4 percent of all executives gave this response, and only an additional 5.9 percent replied "probably false."

These are only eight items, however. How did management perform overall? If the average IQ in this country is 100, do American executives score better than 100 in marketing IQ? If they do score highly, then the future of marketing programs today must be blamed on someone other than top management. Maybe the fault lies with the designer suits in the marketing department or the advertising agency.

Not to worry. If the buck stops at the top, that's where the problem seems to be. CEOs and their staff seem to know little about marketing. The average marketing IQ is 79. This is a sobering figure when you realize that someone who answered "don't know" to every question could have obtained an 80.

What is somewhat comforting is that scores rise with the size of the company. People with higher marketing smarts are running bigger companies. *Yet not even one top executive of a major firm had a marketing IQ above 120.*

Perhaps this will change for the better as more and more marketing people assume top management positions. Korn/Ferry International, the executive search firm, reported in mid-1990 that some 60 percent of the CEO slots it has filled in the past five years have been with executives with marketing backgrounds. Gary Silverman, a managing director of the company's Chicago office, says, "Clients at leveraged companies are placing a premium on marketing expertise. Their businesses have been stripped down to the core, and now they need to build. Marketers are the ones best positioned to do it." We like the Korn/Ferry trend: it's a good sign, but only if these new marketing-trained CEOs are trained to avoid death-wish marketing.

≡ Marketing Is a Science, No Longer an Art

How do you raise your marketing IQ? It's not impossible, since one can become more knowledgeable about and sensitive to marketing and the available technology. "The ever-wider application of technology has sped up the rate of economic change, globalized markets, and brought unanticipated opportunity," says David L. Birch, founder and chief executive officer of Cognetics Inc., an economic research and consulting firm in Cambridge, Massachusetts. It's also brought unanticipated competition. "You have to be smarter because you're called on to spend your intellectual capital faster than ever before."

Intellectual capital is the fund of specialized insight or know-how people often use to start their businesses. But one of the CEOs' great challenges is to replenish their own intellectual capital while being consumed by administration, sales, and firefighting. "You have to be at the edge of something or somebody else will be there," said Birch. "You have got to keep producing new intellectual capital." In the 1990s, CEOs will have to start replenishing their intellectual capital by understanding and improving the marketing function.

New marketing technology means that companies have better tools to identify consumer problems, to design products to solve those problems, and to acquaint prospects of the solutions. Today it is possible for marketers to know so much about their markets that the mind overloads. Research companies have developed new data and new ways to massage the data.

Small examples: It is possible for a Folger's brand manager to sit at a computer on Monday morning and learn how coffee was sold throughout America the week before—by units, price, and market. The computer reports the markets in which Folger's did better than average, the markets where it did worse than average, and how the competition did, and indicates any special market activity—a price cut, coupon drop, or advertising campaign.

It is possible with nothing more than license plate numbers recorded in a store's parking lot to learn where customers live (that's easy) and also what kinds of people they are, the media they watch and read, their approximate incomes, and their lifestyles.

It is possible, knowing the characteristics of a sample of profitable consumers, to obtain—by name and address—all similar individuals from among 180 million Americans. In other words, it is possible to build a bridge from a relatively small group of customers to virtually every American adult who is a prospect for your product or service.

Note: We are not advocating research to cover your rear. We are not suggesting that people hide behind research and never make decisions. Research is really a complement to management judgment in the decision process. It's saying, "I want to bring my customer into the equation." In the absence of research, managers are not bringing customers into the process. Managers speak on behalf of the customer when they use their own judgment. If they are close enough to their customers to do so (sometimes in a small business), fine. Usually, however, managers cannot truly speak from the vantage point of the customer.

In the future, we're convinced, everyone will have smaller, more efficient competitors. They may be former divisions or subsidiaries of larger organizations. Management teams are buying highly leveraged businesses, and they are buying them after they see that spreading oneself too thin is hazardous. These executives are going to be extremely focused, almost narrow in their approach to business, and marketing will be the only way they can survive.

This means that CEOs must begin to ask hard questions about their marketing efforts. We believe you should adopt what we're calling *clean slate marketing*, our analogy to zero-base budgeting. Assume nothing

Figure 2.1 *A Revolutionary Model for Marketing Planning Based on Marketing Intelligence*

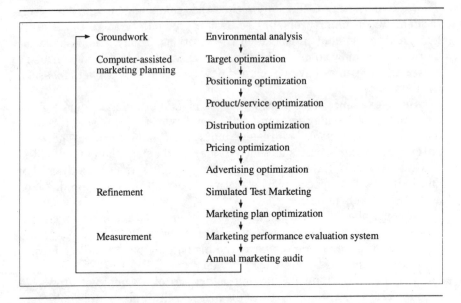

about the environment or the consumer. Be aware of the myths in your organization and challenge them. Incorporate the marketing planning loop illustrated on this page into your company's planning. Provoke your own marketing revolution, starting with an environmental analysis.

Figure 2.1 indicates that marketing planning is both a four-step process and an endless loop. Once you've done the groundwork and clearly understand the environment, there are six computer-assisted steps to optimize the marketing process. This leads to refinement during simulated and real world test marketing. Measurement evaluates the process, which leads back to the environment that the company's marketing activities have changed.

 **3**

IF THE DINOSAURS HAD DONE AN ENVIRONMENTAL ANALYSIS THEY WOULDN'T BE EXTINCT

To market anything successfully—consumer or business-to-business, product or service—we have to first go through a number of steps:

1) Evaluate the environment in which the company operates.
2) Track the changes in consumer values.
3) Understand how the changes in these values affect the company's products or services.

Based on our research, for example, we see profound changes in the way consumers buy and use products and services in the 1990s. The companies that thrive will understand these changes and respond to them.

What questions about the marketing environment must a CEO ask of any marketing proposal? Or, from the other side of the conference table, what questions must marketing management be prepared to answer? They are something like the following:

THE BOTTOM LINE: WHAT A CEO WANTS TO KNOW

1) Are we aware of the changes in our business environment?
2) How are we tracking those changes?
3) How are the values that our customers and prospects hold changing? How will these changes affect their decision making as consumers and as businesspeople buying business products and services?
4) What do these changes mean for the way we do business? What have we done in our marketing planning to take account of the changing trends?
5) How are these trends reflected in the marketing plans we are about to implement?
6) What should we be doing differently in the future to cope with these changes?

≣ An Environmental Analysis Means No Blind Decisions

When the environment changes—when, for example, consumers show more interest in fitness and style—they buy exercise shoes. In retrospect, this seems obvious. (Although in retrospect, everything seems obvious.) But it was Reebok Chairman Paul Fireman who, in 1981, spotted the aerobic exercise fad and designed the distinctive white leather exercise shoe.

It was the right product at the right time. Reebok's annual sales, $1.3 million in 1981, doubled, then tripled, then increased fivefold in each of the next two years before tripling again in 1986. By 1987 sales were $1.4 billion, and two years later $1.8 billion.

Of course, not even those in the business made the connection between exercise shoes and the consumer's growing concern with fitness and style. Nike, which should have seen the trend, stumbled when its executives insisted the firm continue producing the same style of jogging shoes consumers had accepted as the appropriate footwear to wear with blue jeans throughout the 1970s. As Nike spokesman Kevin Brown told *Financial World,* "We said aerobics were a fad, not a sport, but we learned. We let Paul Fireman become a big company." An environmental analysis would have helped Nike learn the true importance of aerobics sooner.

The latest evidence from the *Yankelovich Monitor* (about which we'll say more in a moment) suggests that the marketing environment is changing again. The fitness craze is waning. Fitness is not as important today as it was ten years ago, and it will be less important tomorrow. We wonder what will happen to the exercise shoe business.

To make sure we're all talking about the same thing, a marketing environmental analysis is research based in large part on secondary sources—as you'll see in a minute. It may also include some primary research, but the analysis helps the CEO understand the environment in which a company functions.

The social, political, and economic milieu in which companies operate changes more rapidly than ever as technology develops and the world shrinks. Not only *can* people know more—about the world and their economy, about products and the environment, and about everything else—they *do* know more. One can argue that the recent political changes in Eastern Europe occurred because enough people knew the difference between their situation and the West's, and they were no longer willing to tolerate the official, local version of reality.

Company management must be aware of changes and their implications or risk being like Darryl F. Zanuck who, in 1946, when head of 20th Century Fox Studios, said, "Video won't be able to hold onto any market it captures after the first six months. People will soon get tired of staring at a plywood box every night."

An environmental analysis looks at everything a chief executive needs to grasp about the market and the company's place in it. With such an analysis, a CEO will not be forced to make decisions blindly; the executive can see, as clearly as humanly possible, what will probably happen in the future.

Unfortunately, the future refuses to stand still. Not only do the company's decisions affect the future, so do everyone else's decisions—those of other CEOs, government officials, consumers, everyone—which means a company cannot turn out one analysis and use it for the next ten years. A company should do one every year or whenever it appears the environment in which the company operates seems to be changing.

This is not, we know, a radical or revolutionary idea. Most CEOs *do* think about the arena in which the organization competes. Some may not think about it in a structured or rigorous way, but they do look at what's going on in the world.

Richard DeVane, a Washington, D.C., consultant, tells us that in the past, the poorly managed companies focused just on their own business, and the better managed companies at least understood general industry conditions. Today, of course, that's not enough. "We think that with the horizon of investment decisions lengthening and with certain major strategic decisions, the CEO has to take one step further outside the company and look at all the trends affecting the business—general regulatory trends, technology trends, demographic, and general social and cultural trends," he says.

In DeVane's experience, although managements of well-run companies understand the need to consider the company's circumstances, they usually do not consider all relevant trends, nor do they often consider how trends affect each other. How, for example, does information technology growth impact the shrinking labor pool? A company will look at information technology and its labor pool, says DeVane, but seldom the effect of one on the other.

Many factors touch a corporation, and a comprehensive environmental analysis covers them all. Top management must understand each, focusing on trends taking place or developments under way and their implications for the company.

In the next few pages, we describe what such an environmental analysis looks at, focusing on changes in consumer lifestyles and values. We'll discuss how these values relate to marketing and what consumer issues we see affecting marketing in the 1990s and indicate how all this connects to the real world of making money.

≡ What a Marketing Environmental Analysis Covers

A company is affected by various factors:

• *Economic conditions,* both domestic and, if the company does any business overseas, international. Where is the economy going? What's happening to interest rates, employment figures, commodity prices, exchange rates? These figures are available from the general business press, government reports, and private forecasters. The *Wall Street Journal* and *Business Week* routinely watch the economy. The U.S. Department of Commerce's Office of Business Analysis and Economic Affairs offers its *Economic Bulletin Board* to anyone with a personal computer, and the department publishes the *United States Industrial Outlook* every December.

• *Consumer demographics.* How is the population changing in age, composition, birth rates, and education levels? If reading levels continue to decline, how will the company have to adjust its advertising, instructions, and labeling? As baby boomers move into middle age, how will their purchase habits change?

Demographic trends influence products or services to a greater or lesser degree. How? Twenty-five years ago coffee was a major U.S. industry. But today coffee consumption, like domestic car buying, is associated both with declining demographics—the down-scale, older segment of the population—and with declining social value characteristics. The fitness craze is over, but health concerns are increasing. And as consumer health concerns rise, coffee consumption declines. As a result, U.S. coffee consumption is dropping markedly.

Another demographic example: Fifteen years ago, American Express wanted a growth forecast. How many cards would they have in force in ten years? There are many different ways to forecast sales: regression analysis, plotting growth year by year and forecasting into the future, and more. But since the company had card data going back only about fifteen years, we felt that a ten-year forecast based on these figures would not be actionable.

Since American Express card ownership is closely related to demographics, we therefore created a table of thirty important demographic cells, dividing the population into young, middle-aged, older; college, high school, undereducated; income, etc. We asked demographers at the University of Pennsylvania to tell us the proportion of the U.S. population each of the thirty cells represented. Demographic models tend to be more accurate than economic models because population trends are not as volatile as fiscal trends. We therefore asked the demographers to predict the number of people who would be in each cell in 1980, in 1985, and in 1990.

We assumed that the proportion of American Express card holders in every one of the thirty cells in 1975 would be the same proportion in 1980, 1985, and 1990—that is, that penetration would remain constant. In other words, we assumed that card ownership growth would be a function of changing demographics alone. If the demographers forecast no population change in one of the thirty cells over the fifteen years, we forecast no change in card ownership. But with relatively simple arithmetic, we had the forecast. And when we looked at the actual data ten years later, we could see that almost all change in American Express card performance was connected to demographic change. Penetration numbers were relatively constant, and the groups containing the most card holders were growing bigger over time. One might call this type of marketing environmental analysis *demo-eco forecasting.*

If a company checks the marketing environment and learns that, in its industry, certain demographics or psychographics are linked to product usage, it must know whether it is riding a cresting wave or sliding toward oblivion. American cars, for example, are associated with declining and unappealing demographic and psychographic characteristics (see the box below).

To obtain this information, we analyzed statistically the *Monitor* data to identify those characteristics that best discriminate domestic from foreign automobile owners. Most owners, for example, of *both* domestic and foreign cars are middle class. Disproportionately more domestic car buyers, however, are lower middle class, while disproportionately more foreign car buyers are upper middle class. Since more and more are college graduates with white-collar jobs with a pragmatic link to their automobiles, the trends suggest foreign brands will be doing well in the future.

If a company knows it is sliding and wants to change, it must seek a different demographic-psychographic group, develop new products, or both. But the point remains: marketing environmental analysis gives management the information it needs to start the decision-making process.

CAR OWNER PROFILES

Key differentiating characteristics	Owners of domestic automobiles	Owners of foreign automobiles
Age	50 and older	Under 50
Marital status	Married	Single
Education	High school	College graduate
Occupation	Blue collar	White collar
Dominant region	South	West
Sociography	Lower middle class	Upper middle class
Psychography	"Buy American" attitude	"Buy quality" attitude
Link to cars	Emotional	Pragmatic

Source: *Yankelovich Monitor.*

Most companies sensitive to consumer demographic changes know that the U.S. Bureau of the Census—not to mention private vendors—can supply figures on these and virtually any other question about the American people. Various sources routinely suggest how these changes may influence the company or its markets; we like the monthly *American Demographics* magazine, but there are other channels as well. For consumer psychographic changes, the sources include the *Yankelovich Monitor*, SRI's VALS, and the National Opinion Research Center (University of Chicago) General Social Survey.

• *Consumer lifestyles.* How will changing consumer attitudes, beliefs, and values alter the company, its products, and its business practices? Several companies, including ours, produce an annual study that tracks these basic shifts in American life. Our *Yankelovich Monitor* tracks social values and lifestyles and their impact on marketing decisions. This annual survey of 2,500 American consumers over sixteen years of age measures changes in eighteen core and thirty-six peripheral social value trends. A different group is questioned every year, but the results are nationally projectable and can be compared from year to year.

Figure 3.1 *A Model of Consumer Behavior*

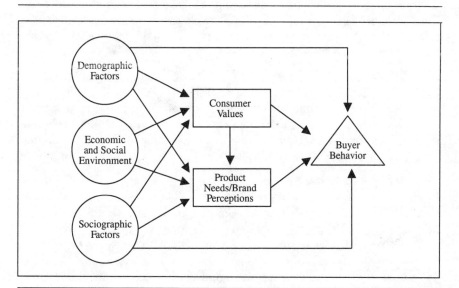

These social values exercise as much, if not more, influence on purchase behavior as income, education, life stage, or any of the other factors marketing strategists routinely consider (see Figure 3.1). These annual in-home interviews last two hours each, and because YCS been conducting *Monitor* surveys for over twenty years, we have been able to compare changing social values to actual marketplace activity. We'll show how these attitudes, beliefs, and values will influence marketers in the 1990s.

- *Industry trends.* These trends take in costs, production volumes, and entrance and exit barriers. What's happening among the company's competitors (not to mention supplier competitors) that will be a threat? That may be a benefit? Answers to these kinds of questions come from annual reports and 10-Ks (available instantly from on-line computer databases like Dialog), business publications, trade associations, and the like, but also from sales staffs, vendors, and suppliers.

- *Distribution channels.* What's happening among the company's distributors and retailers? Consolidation? New competitors? Are new channels opening?

- *New technology.* What new inventions, processes, or materials will be influencing the company's products? The company's suppliers? What about substitute products? These are questions for the folks down in research and development, and if the company does not have its own R&D staff (and more firms are farming out the research function), new product specialists should be able to answer to them. Have them check the National Technical Information Service, the central source for public sale of government-sponsored research, or the Federal Laboratory Consortium for Technology Transfer.

- *Employee relations and supply.* What's happening to the labor pool? What labor negotiations are coming up? How will any proposed changes affect union contracts? How will the staff react to the new product, the new advertising, the new production system? Human relations could fill an entire book: indeed, libraries' shelves are filled with volumes on the subject of employee relations.

- *Foreign markets.* Are they possible targets for expansion? Or will foreign companies become a threat at home? There's a wealth of information available, starting with the Commerce Department's *Catalog of Market Research Reports* and its *Overseas Business Report.* Have someone talk to the International Trade Administration's Export Counseling Center or even to one of the Administration's Country Desk Officers—experts on a particular country's economic and commercial situation.

• *Corporate image.* How do customers and noncustomers, employees, opinion leaders, government officials, and other stakeholders perceive our company compared to our competitors? What do they know about us? What do they like about us? What do they dislike? Would they buy our products or services, recommend us to prospective employees, invest in our stock, or support us in a proxy fight? Information of this sort is usually available on a custom basis through major research companies.

• *Political and regulatory changes.* Has new legislation been passed and new regulations enforced? Have government policies changed? The best source for this information is the company's trade associations, but management can also call state and federal representatives for word on pending legislative changes.

• *Key players in the category.* Who are they? What are their strengths, weaknesses, and apparent goals? What are their share of market and share of voice, and how have these been changing?

To investigate these topics and how they may impact the firm and the industry, a company can consult a variety of sources, some of which we've indicated. For the most part, this is all secondary research—material that someone, somewhere has already published. The challenge in the 1990s will seldom be to find information. The challenge will be to distinguish the truly useful from the merely interesting. Because most corporations have people on staff able to investigate various topics in depth, we do not believe it necessary to employ an outside company to do this investigation, but such independent research firms exist. If hiring one is the only way the chief executive can get a marketing environmental analysis when he or she needs it, the fee is well spent.

Because some of these issues change rapidly (the economy, for example), and because some subjects are specific to an industry or to an individual company (new technology, employee relations), we cannot discuss them in detail in this book.

However, because lifestyle changes *do* apply to virtually all marketers—business-to-business and consumer companies marketing products and services—we discuss them in some detail. These consumer value shifts are, we believe, the most significant that will affect American companies in the 1990s. One might, therefore, consider the following a limited—and very general—marketing environmental analysis in print. With these insights into American society and how it is changing, however, a CEO may see ways to sharpen the company's marketing efforts.

≣ Social Seismology: The Changes in Consumer Values

If one looks at many different marketing plans (as, in the course of our work, we do), one becomes aware of what they typically do—and don't—include. Here's a rough idea of what one would find in 100 typical plans:

WHAT'S IN/WHAT'S OUT OF THE TYPICAL MARKETING PLAN

Factors	Prevalence in marketing plans	In-depth coverage if included	Critical for success if missing
Demographics	90%	50%	40%
Market share assessment	90	80	10
Competitive analysis	90	90	50
Consumer needs and wants	80	40	80
Consumer lifestyles and values	20	10	70
Political and economic	10	20	25

The figures (which do not add to 100 percent because each line and column is independent) mean that virtually all the marketing plans we see include demographics, market share assessment, and competitive analysis. Almost as many include consumer needs and wants. Very few, however, consider consumer lifestyles and values or political and economic factors.

Among plans that *do* include demographics, about half give the topic in-depth coverage (the second column), but it would not be a serious omission if it were missing (the third column). On the other hand, we believe an analysis of consumer lifestyles and values *is* critical for the success of a marketing plan, although, of the plans we see that consider lifestyles and values at all, only about 10 percent cover them in depth.

The last column reflects our judgment about how serious the omission can be. Factors vary in seriousness. If a car is missing a back seat, that's a problem, but it's not critical for running the car. If a car is missing a steering wheel, that's a problem and a critical one. Similarly, if the marketing plan is missing the political factors, that's a problem, but it's probably not critical in many industries. If the plan does not contain consideration of consumer lifestyles and values, that's also a problem and, for most companies, a critical one.

So what has been happening to consumer values? Americans have lived through substantial changes since the end of World War II.* We have twice changed our ideas of how to live and how to organize society. The first, obvious shift took place in the 1960s, the second in the early 1980s, and although the latter shift was quieter, it has had an equally significant effect on our lives and on the decisions we make in life and in the marketplace.

One can look at these massive shifts as conforming to Hegel's dialectic process. Hegel first proposed that, in history, a thesis is opposed by its antithesis, which is followed by synthesis of the two, which then becomes a new thesis.

In our terms, the thesis is the aggregation of traditional values that most people held from roughly 1945 to 1960. In the next five years or so, a revolution in values occurred, and by 1965 there was the antithesis—new values that lasted until roughly 1979. In the mid-1960s, the baby boomers were beginning their college years. They believed that America's economic success could be taken for granted, and they began to challenge what they viewed as an overemphasis on materialism. At the same time, they began to want to have it all. They elevated the importance of experiencing, and the experiences included everything from gourmet food to hang gliding to travel.

≣ The Baby Boomers Changed Virtually All Values

By 1970 just about everything Americans had held sacred in the 1950s had been discarded by a whopping 80 percent of the population. The have-it-all baby boomer cohort had moved into the "me" decade. The group that changed the most was women who entered the work force, went back to school, and got out of the home. Food marketers, as one example of the impact of these changes, learned to cater to every whim, the American fascination with newness and quick preparation. There were family sizes, single serve, and flavors of the month. Jello offered six different chocolate puddings, from plain old chocolate to Bavarian double dutch—plus ten other flavors.

If the traditional values had held that the route to success lay in following the "rules" of the Protestant ethic—hard work, discipline and self-denial, obligation to and responsibility for the well-being of the group, conformity to the expectations of others, and a focus on the future at the

*The following discussion is based heavily on the work of Susan Hayward, senior vice president, Yankelovich Clancy Shulman, which the authors acknowledge with thanks.

expense of the present—the new values in the 1960s emphasized the self—self-fulfillment, self-examination, personal choice, and individual freedom. As these values spread, Americans viewed everything from clothing to politics and from toothpaste to war from a personal perspective.

By the late 1970s, however, even the most optimistic consumer had begun to sense that not everything was going well. The economy, the social environment, even the consumer's personal situation was showing signs of deterioration. Economic ills—inflation and international competition—began to jar the consumer's everyday life and expectations; worse, they were beyond the individual's control. The social safety nets of the 1960s turned out to be full of holes. Although society had spent enormous amounts of money and energy, the war on poverty had not been won, the environment had not been cleaned, and sexual and racial discrimination remained. Finally, lifestyle choices, thought to be desirable in earlier years, turned out to have disadvantages. Resistance to marriage left many men and women isolated and without family support systems. Women's "right to work" and "need to work" created a growing number of latchkey children.

Consumer response to this new world depended to some extent on age and early experiences. Older consumers, breathing a sigh of relief, returned substantially to the old ways and the traditional approach of dealing with difficult times.

Younger consumers, who had never experienced hard times, found themselves in something of a dilemma. They recognized they had to adapt their behavior and expectations to current realities, but they had no skills to do so. They dropped the hedonistic "anything-goes" habits of recent experience and began learning new skills with which to cope with the new reality, beginning with the marketplace. Led by the affluent and the well educated, the American population gradually acquired a very pragmatic focus on the criteria for good decision making. For several years in the late 1970s and early 1980s, the consumer's primary measure of self-worth was the ability to "win," in the sense of getting the best possible deal in every situation. A strategic shopper was a good person.

≡ As Baby Boomers Grow Older, Their Values Change

By 1985, however, consumers had learned the skills and used them habitually. About this time, it began to occur to many people that there ought to be something more to life than being a super consumer. Something was missing. This transition period, from roughly 1980 to

1985, marked the end of the new values antithesis and the beginning of the synthesis, which we call *neotraditional values.*

These neotraditional values are neither a continuation of 1970s values, nor are they a return to the 1950s. They are not entirely novel or revolutionary, but contain elements of both previous approaches to living. Each neotraditional value represents a new solution to one of the basic questions human beings confront. While some questions remain as consumers continue to change, these six values appear to be fairly completely formed, and each stands on its own as a blueprint for life in the 1990s. Below are the six, together with the comparable traditional value of the 1950s and the new values of the 1960s.

We describe these six neotraditional values in detail and indicate some implications for marketers, but, for now, it's important to note that most adult Americans support each value in one way or another. These are new approaches to some of the eternal issues that are part of the human condition—issues like work, change, family, relationships with others, self-expression, and the organization and management of time. Of course, not every consumer has sorted out all the questions, but our research indicates that the general approach to these six is becoming clear.

≣ Neotraditional Values: A Framework for the 1990s

While the descriptions of these six neotraditional values may sometimes sound almost as fuzzy as a horoscope, we cannot at this point be

CHANGES IN AMERICAN VALUES		
Traditional *(Late 1940s–late 1960s)*	*Transitional* *(Late 1960s–late 1980s)*	*Neotraditional* *(Late 1980s–?)*
Permanence	*Transience*	*Substance*
Simplicity	*Complexity*	*Streamlining*
Security	*Freedom*	*Risk management*
Discipline	*Self-indulgence*	*Self-control*
Obligation	*Entitlement*	*Accountablity*
Conformity	*Individuality*	*Personal style*

any more specific without stretching our research further than we think it can go. And, while the descriptions may seem general, we can indicate how they apply in specific situations.

1) *Substance* stresses relevance and meaning. It implies reliability, simplicity, and clarity. Substance does not connote stuffiness or ponderousness, but rather a sense of wanting things to be what they seem to be and to have a real purpose, whether serious or frivolous. Irony is out, sincerity is in.

Substance combines the 1950s' traditional values of permanence and durability with the 1960s' new values of transience and trendiness. The synthesis produces the consumer's interest in long-term goals and attraction to relationships, products, and companies that are trustworthy and that offer quality, durability, authenticity, and worth—characteristics that can be both tangible and intangible. Nevertheless, personal choice and whim also play a role.

2) *Streamlining* reflects the consumer's need to allocate scarce resources within an increasingly complex environment. It suggests setting priorities and disengaging from things that may be appealing but are less necessary. Streamlining also implies having the confidence in one's ability to improvise when unforeseen needs or events occur. *Streamlining* does not correspond to *tradeoff*, with its negative sense of giving up one thing to get another, but rather this value suggests a sense of being content with what is possible.

Streamlining combines the simplicity and order of traditional values with the complexity and randomness of the new values. It highlights a continuing need for convenience, simplification, delegation of responsibility, and the willingness to accept things that are "good enough"—not cheap or ineffective but also not necessarily the top-of-the-line. Streamlining is one reason we see growth in the "middle market" in the 1990s, a development we discuss in more detail later.

3) *Risk management* describes a willingness to accept risk while, at the same time, minimizing the risk's negative consequences. This value suggests the consumer needs information with which to evaluate risk and to control, or minimize, negative effects. This value also includes the need for protection from involuntary risk in areas where the individual cannot exercise personal control, particularly in technological or marketing environmental issues. A company that even inadvertently puts consumers or their children at risk either through shoddy engineering—like the Dalkon Shield IUD—or by harming the environment—like the Exxon *Valdez* oil spill—will suffer.

Risk management synthesizes the security and risk avoidance that characterized earlier traditional values with the insistence on freedom and the tendency to ignore risk that new values of the 1960s and 1970s reflected. It suggests a continuing interest in strategic consuming, in product guarantees, in "safe adventure," and a reliance on things that have been proven to be effective—choices that work.

4) *Accountability* is the neotraditional view of responsibility; that is, who owes what to whom. Its message is that all parties should be held accountable for their actions, receiving credit or blame for their activities. It carries a strong sense that those whose deeds cause harm to others should be required to clean up the mess. Accountability is a balance between the 1950s view that society's institutions (business, government, schools, the church) were all-important and deserved the individual's consideration and cooperation, with the 1960s and 1970s reversal of that position which put the onus of obligation on society at large and awarded the right of entitlement to the individual.

Accountability has far-reaching implications for the relationship between marketer and consumer. After several years in the early 1980s, when consumers seemed to prefer a partnership with business, today consumers feel the marketer has a greater obligation than the consumer. Although consumers understand they have some responsibility, marketers who want to thrive must be consistently responsive, truthful, competent, and reliable—more so than ever in the past. Bad news spreads fast, and with modern communications, it spreads ever faster. Consumers who knew nothing else about Audi knew—or thought they knew—that the car could accelerate without warning, and Audi's sales plunged. (It is interesting to note that Audi's problems were a media-created event. "Unintended acceleration," like the nineteenth century concept of ether, about which we say more later, did not exist.)

5) *Self-control* represents an equilibrium between the extremes of discipline and indulgence. The neotraditional consumer recognizes that some discipline is necessary to avoid chaos and believes that indulgence and fun are a legitimate and desirable part of being human and so combines the two. Exercising some discipline (as in a diet, a schedule, or a budget) minimizes the potential risk in relaxing the rules and enjoying oneself; the discipline is not a rigid end in itself but rather provides a safety net. This discipline is self-imposed; it cannot be dictated from outside. The self-indulgence is largely guilt-free.

For marketers, this seemingly contradictory mix of "good" and "bad" impulses offers broad opportunities to support both simultaneously. The neotraditional consumer will not be confused by the promise of control and indulgence at the same time: foods that claim to be "good for you" and "taste great"; financial institutions that promise to help you save while offering to make possible a fabulous vacation; automobiles that promote both safety and high performance.

6) *Personal style* addresses the issue of self-expression—of individuality versus conformity. The neotraditional consumer wants to make a personal statement of style and difference but to make it while referring to the understanding and acceptance of those whose opinion and good will he or she values. The goal is to be "me" in a way the group approves and admires. This affects how the consumer calculates self-image in all its forms, from lifestyle to dress to speech habits.

A sense of personal style is the outward expression of confidence in one's own choices and of respect for the opinions of others. It suggests some resistance to change for the sake of change, either to conform to some notion of what's right or to keep up with the latest trendy developments. Personal style expresses a secure self-image: "I am what I am, and what I am is OK."

This value suggests marketers avoid rapid unconnected changes in either the style or the substance of the products and services they offer the neotraditional consumer. Consistency and a sense of what is appropriate will strongly influence consumer choices. The consumer will create variety and individuality using basic familiar elements in new combinations to create a personalized, customized style.

≡ How the 1990s Will Be Different

Through three decades, U.S. consumers went from buying whatever they were told to buy, to proving they'd buy whatever they felt like buying, to becoming the world's most competent shoppers. Americans are reevaluating their priorities and revising their ideas about what is really important and worth having, particularly in view of the emerging economic realities. For the first time in many years, Americans are getting back to basics. Families are important, as are good steady jobs, and friendships, and enjoying life. There is a new spirit of realism. Americans are discovering what kind of goals are possible and desirable, and marketers will have to understand this revised approach to life to be successful.

Our research suggests that consumer spending will slow in the 1990s, not only because of temporary economic conditions but from a basic shift in consumer attitudes.

Americans are moving away from the excesses and obsessions of the

1980s. People are paying less attention to the process of consuming than in the past, and they have less and less interest in new options, new products, new messages. Status will not motivate purchase the way it did once. As a result of environmental concerns, more and more people will be reusing more and more items; they will recycle paper, glass, aluminum cans, and when possible they will use products longer.

We do not see evidence that these changes are motivated by economic fears; there is no indication of strict economizing, and consumers have no increased interest in savings. Economic conditions may, of course, exaggerate trends to less spending.

We find that women are apparently nearing a breaking point as the stress of multiple roles—wife, mother, career woman, cook, nurse, chauffeur—has intensified with no relief in sight. We find more women shifting their attention and involvement away from work (many fewer bringing work home from the office) and toward family and personal life (many more spending more time with children) with emphasis on personal time rather than time management. This focus on the family and personal life has two grounds, a desire for emotional enhancement and guilt about shortchanging the kids.

Nevertheless, we find no suggestion that most women will leave the work force, if only because money, not fulfillment, is the major reason they work, and the money is essential. The continued presence of women in the work force will, we believe, create pressure for change similar to that of the early 1970s.

Men in the 1990s feel similar stresses, and this manifests itself in more involvement with children than in the past and more participation in household chores. Men are apprehensive about women's roles, and they are concerned about carrying the entire responsibility for the family's income. This concern makes them anxious about downward mobility and the quality of their lives.

We're finding a new priority in our research, an interest in emotional enhancement. Consumers will play down work and control goals in favor of real pleasures and emotions. In so doing, they will be concerned with the quality of their lives, not "lifestyle." They will be seeking substance, satisfaction, comfort, and simple pleasures. More than in the recent past, they will be making connections—with family, kids, friends, and groups. They see leisure as a counterbalance to work and to the sense of being controlled. As we mentioned above, they are looking for responsible self-indulgence, reward without guilt. They want fantasy, romance, humor, and fun.

There has been a shift in the definition of personal success and of status. Consumers in the 1990s will not emphasize externals or achievement or "what I have" but will put more emphasis on internal values, happiness, and on "what I am." They will have less interest in maximizing and perfecting their skills as consumers, and more interest in contentment and satisfaction. Both men and women indicate a greater interest than ever in restoring romance, mystery, and adventure to their lives.

When we look at consumer attitudes toward health and physical fitness, we find that these concerns continue to become routine. Individual diet issues are giving way to a holistic view, and consumers are bringing exercise into perspective. They are shifting their attention from the short to the long term with less interest in a "quick fix" and more emphasis on the future big picture. Similarly, consumer attitudes toward physical appearance are also changing. The focus is on looking good and being well-groomed over the long term with minimum effort. We see signs that Americans are turning away from fashion perfectionism; there is less attention to "latest fashions," less competitiveness, and more interest in physical and emotional comfort.

A recent Spiegel catalog illustrates these changes. The copy says,

The question used to be, "Is it good for you?" Now the question is, "Is it good to you?" You could take a hike and not count the miles. Go for a swim and not count the laps. You could stop counting reps, calories, minutes, milligrams. You could stop counting all together. And start enjoying yourself. Biking with a friend. Walking the dog. A long, hot bath. We're talking about an approach to fitness that includes as much pleasure as pain. With a goal of not just building a body, but building a life.

≡ The Green Movement Is a Trend, Not a Fad

But if consumers are less concerned about their own condition, they are much more concerned about the environment's. Concern about the environment in public opinion surveys has doubled in the last three years. Americans see a deteriorating environment as a threat to the personal, social, and global quality of life, a concern reinforced by a growing positive interest in nature. But not only are consumers concerned, they are willing to take action and to make sacrifices, believing that individuals can make a difference. Further, they expect marketers and government agencies to take action, although at this point they are more interested in voluntary action than in regulatory pressure.

Americans now see the environmental problems and their solutions changing with improved information. They give priority to involuntary risks—those environmental hazards over which the individual has little or no control—and we find a general consensus across all regions of the country. We see consumers moving away from "quick fixes" to more basic solutions—recycling, reusing, and consuming less rather than buying "biodegradable" or "environmentally safe" products. Almost two-thirds of all consumers said they would be willing to pay as much as 10 to 15 percent more for products, if they could be sure they would not harm the environment.

Manufacturers, aware of the concern, are reacting. Just one example: ICD Products has introduced "environmentally friendly" Today's Choice sanitary napkins, which declares on its 100 percent recycled paperboard carton, "Most women aren't aware that the absorbent materials in many feminine hygiene products are bleached with chlorine gas. This process has been linked to dioxins, which have proven hazardous in our oceans and rivers. Today we're offering [a pad] whose absorbent material is not bleached with this chlorine." We can multiply examples endlessly. Consumer goods manufacturers that have a package of any kind had better think about its environmental impact. We have a client that has been thinking about introducing a whole line of "environmentally correct" automobiles.

Nevertheless, few top executives appreciate how important environmental responsibility has become, although the signs are everywhere. The taxpayers of Martha's Vineyard paid scientists from Wood's Hole to monitor Edgartown harbor water quality; there is a strictly enforced ban on pumping sewage into the harbor; and sailors who moor at Edgartown Marine must separate their trash into six different bins.

People are concerned about the environment and are trying to do something to improve it. Groups attacked McDonald's restaurants because, while the company says it is in the forefront of the environmental movement, it was revealed that McDonald's cups—which claimed on the side to be biodegradable—were not. Last fall, the company gave up its plastic foam hamburger boxes because they were seen to be environmentally harmful.

Not long ago, the *Economist* suggested that not more than 200 companies in the whole world regard the environment as being one of the main determinants facing their businesses. As Richard DeVane suggests, "Most managements just have not come to terms with environmental trends. They don't believe they are relevant, important, or measurable." Environmental trends are, of course, all three, and they will profoundly affect many, many more than the 200 companies now actively addressing the issues.

One implication of this serious and growing consumer attention to the environment is that environmental "lip service" claims by marketers could boomerang.

≡ Consumer Distrust of Business Continues to Grow

Our research finds that in the 1990s, consumer distrust of business has continued to grow. Service and responsiveness are still key issues, while product quality is becoming an issue. Americans suspect the motives, integrity, and responsibility of marketers. Companies are too big, they feel. It's difficult to know where to go with a complaint or a request, and even if you do know where to go, it's usually a waste of time to complain to a big company about dissatisfaction with a product or service.

More and more consumers reject company exaggeration, regard hype and omission as lies, and want to see "full disclosure." For what small comfort it may be, consumers blame this sorry state on both labor and management, while another source of dissatisfaction is the recent takeover-merger spree. People mostly believe that stockholders and management benefited from LBOs while consumers, workers, and taxpayers were the losers.

The consumer is in a "solution agenda," and being open to a solution means not limiting one's options. Our work has picked up a growing antibusiness sentiment. It's already bigger than in the 1970s and still growing. Why?

Because, in the 1980s, consumers had to learn new economic rules to survive, and they did. They learned them from marketers, and they've concluded that marketers don't pay attention. Marketers don't really listen. So consumers are making decisions while the marketers are in a vacuum.

Item: Women are not satisfied with their experiences in car dealerships.

Item: Few, if any, hotel and motel chains or resorts know what percentage of the time a family on vacation wants to spend together and what percentage they want to be alone.

Item: How pleased are food shoppers to learn a packaged dinner really contains MSG? Manufacturers aren't required to warn on the label that MSG is included in the ingredients of a packaged dinner, but that's not what consumers want to hear. And they're *not* pleased.

≡ The Middle Market: I Don't Need the Best

One of the results of these changing consumer trends is that the middle market will grow more significant.

Like the generals of cliché, marketers often fight a new war with the weapons and tactics of the last one. So we all understand how the battlefield has shifted, let's review a little history. In the 1970s it was appropriate for a company to introduce an endless stream of new products and brands. At that time, consumers were demanding personalization, novelty, and change for change's sake. But sometime in the late 1970s or so, America changed.

This consumer shift evolved in part because of two major consumer trends that emerged during the 1980s: strategic consuming and the rise of the yuppie workaholic. Strategic consuming was the consumer's response to a perception of limits. After a decade of credit card–supported instant gratification, consumers began to realize they had only finite amounts of time, money, and energy. They recognized the need for and began to develop the skills to make better buying decisions—skills like gathering and using information, comparing prices, reading labels and guarantees, waiting for sales, and clipping coupons.

Affluent consumers first demonstrated this behavior, thereby dissolving class barriers in the marketplace. Wealthy people could—and did—boast about finding a bargain as loudly as anyone else. The consumer's preoccupation with bargains and deals provoked a variety of responses from marketers, including generic products, private label goods, discount "warehouse" stores, off-price branded merchandise outlets, continuous sales and promotions, and so on and on and on.

The other important trend in consumer purchasing patterns we saw was the stereotypical yuppie workaholic, although sometimes this was only the strategic consumer wearing a different personality. These consumers in the 1980s, besides needing to gain control of their spending and to avoid wasting resources, confronted the realization that the world is a competitive rather than a supportive place. To become a winner requires effort and planning.

For consumers to demonstrate to themselves and to others that they actually *were* winners, they needed a way to keep score—and that was money. As the bumper sticker said, "The one who dies with the most toys wins." The winners in the Reagan 1980s were those who could, through hard work or clever manipulation (or both), earn large amounts of money and spend it ostentatiously. The marketplace response was also highly visible: luxury sports cars, exotic travel destinations, expensive imported cheeses and wines, electronic appointment books, gourmet take-out dinners complete with candles and flowers, and single malt scotches and vodkas with silver labels.

Although the need for control and success continues into the 1990s, consumer interest is shifting away from process (learning and demonstrating the ability to live well) toward substance (the meaning and the experience of living well). Consumers today are more interested in improving the quality of their lives than in showing off their skills as consumers or demonstrating themselves winners through their choices in the marketplace.

≡ What the Changes Mean to Marketing in the 1990s

The rules have changed. The companies that thrive in the 1990s will be the firms that enthusiastically embrace the marketing revolution. They won't follow yesterday's strategies or yesterday's tactics. The following marketing issues are key for the 1990s:

- Retain customer loyalty and maintain market share.
- Overcome continuing resistance to new products and brands.
- Emphasize brand or company name and image rather than gimmicks or promotions.
- Look for opportunities in the middle market.
- Combine mass market products and niche marketing tactics.
- Emphasize service, defined as practical efficiency.
- Look to packaging as a route to differentiation.
- Address environmental concerns quickly and clearly.

The American consumer in the 1990s will be less interested in conspicuous consumption, compulsive spending, pursuit of new products, and paying attention to the marketing game, which means less interest in coupons, rebates, sweepstakes, one-day sales, and other short-term promotional gimmicks.

Consumers will put more—or new—emphasis on the quality of life, on connections and relationships, on substance and reality. Concurrently, they will be seeking enjoyment, pleasure, fun, fantasy, romance. We will see more measured consuming in the 1990s rather than sudden splurges followed by severe budgeting. Consumers will be aware of high-tech drawbacks and be environmentally active, if only to vote with their dollars to support products that promise to be environmentally benign. At the same time consumers will continue to rely on the familiar.

Consumers will maintain their ongoing concerns about balance, streamlining and simplicity, self control and self-reliance, risk management, and personal style—the values we described above. We see these values becoming only stronger during this last decade of the century.

Established companies can take advantage of the consumer's continued interest in trusted brands. The familiar choice is safe, easy, quick, and carries no hidden problems. On the other hand, this consumer brand loyalty is practical rather than emotional, and a company can lose it through poor performance or the appearance of a superior alternative. Second-tier brands also have an opportunity in this environment; they are sufficiently familiar, and there is less need for "the gold standard," which means consumers will be satisfied with good enough quality if the product satisfies their needs.

In the 1990s, successful companies will return to a focus on a brand's substance, its core benefits. Consumers seek results and will not accept tradeoffs. These basic benefits can be concrete—such as the product's function, quality, durability, taste—or they can be emotional—such as a product that provides fun, prestige, or sensory gratification—or they can be both.

Companies should avoid the single-issue marketing bandwagon because buzzwords don't differentiate brands. The following have become virtually meaningless: *oat bran, high tech, recyclable, luxury, all natural, on sale.* The challenge in the 1990s will be to create a differentiating brand profile unique to the brand, not the category, and sustainable in the face of competitive maneuvers (and we suggest ways you can do exactly this).

Service businesses will continue to thrive in the 1990s as time-stressed consumers pay to delegate chores. But for all companies, service will be key as consumers look for efficiency and simplification in their lives and in the products they use. More than ever consumers want information. They are looking for products and services that either prevent problems or solve them (or both). Successful marketing organizations will deliver real and discernible service to attract and retain customers.

We see some price sensitivity giving way to a demand for quality, which the consumer defines as performance, function, and core benefits—not necessarily high-priced luxury. Because consumers are more knowledgeable than ever, the relationship between quality and price determines value. Further, the consumer's perception of value is subject to reevaluation. Consumers establish a personal price ceiling; they will not buy certain items "even if I can afford them" because the price is too high relative to the perceived value. Similarly, they set a quality floor; people will not buy some items "no matter how low-priced" because the quality is too poor.

Marketers in the 1990s must be honest and accountable, consistent and reliable, and environmentally responsible. This may sound like preaching to the choir. Few CEOs knowingly permit their organizations to be dishonest or irresponsible, inconsistent or unreliable. But one reason to commission a marketing environmental analysis is to uncover areas in which the company either is—or appears to be—irresponsible, inconsistent, or unreliable and to do something about it.

Successful marketers will develop a "scorecard" to evaluate new ideas, products, and campaigns against what we see as ten key continuing, new, and forecasted trends:

DEVELOP A SCORECARD BASED ON TEN KEY TRENDS

Continuing trends:

- Emphasis on streamlining all aspects of one's life.
- Growing need for control over one's destiny personally and at work.

Relatively new trends:

- Environmental activism.
- Growing distrust of business.
- Declining interest in science and technology in everyday life.
- Growing need to fill an emotional void in one's life.

Forecasted trends:

- Growing opportunities in the middle market.
- Emphasis on service in the 1990s.
- Brand loyalty reemerges with some catches.
- Renewed focus on the family with careerism on the wane.

The corporation also has key goals for the 1990s:

- Retain the existing customer base.
- Leverage the vitality of the middle market.
- Keep economic and demographic realities in focus.
- Head off regulatory pressure by earning consumer trust.
- Support existing brands.
- Retain and attract employee talent with meaningful support systems.
- Design communications to overcome consumer inattention.

While at least one of these, employee retention and attraction, is beyond this book's scope, the rest are not, and in the chapters ahead we suggest ways that management can deal with these challenges.

Before a CEO makes a decision committing hundreds of thousands (or millions) of dollars to a new marketing program, a new product, a new advertising or promotion campaign, he or she should understand as clearly as humanly possible the decision's consequences. The place to start with that understanding is, we believe, a marketing environmental analysis.

With such a report, the CEO can see possible problems before they become crises or develop into full-blown disasters. An environmental analysis places the organization clearly in the world; it delineates its relationship to competitors, suppliers, and the government. But perhaps most significantly, the analysis describes the buyer on whom everything depends.

But once one understands the buyer and the changing environment, how does one pick a target market?

A MARKETING CLIMATE REVIEW

To market anything successfully—consumer or industrial products or services—you must understand the marketing climate. An environmental analysis can help you.

- Become knowledgeable about changes in your business environment: economic, social, political, and governmental.
- Understand your competitors and their strategies and tactics.
- Analyze changing demographics and their impact on your business.
- Know what is happening in global markets and its implications for your products and services.

You must pay particular attention to shifting social values because these are often neglected in marketing planning.

- Develop a "scorecard" to evaluate new ideas, products, and campaigns in terms of social trends such as streamlining, the need for control, environmental activism, the growing distrust of business, the declining interest in science and technology, and the need to fill emotional voids in everyday life.
- Evaluate for your firm opportunities in the middle market, emphasis on service, the resurgence of brand loyalty, and the decline of careerism.

With such a report, CEOs can see problems before they arise: environmental analysis helps you adjust your sights before you fire at the target market.

4

HEAVY USERS ARE NOT YOUR BEST PROSPECTS, NO MATTER WHAT THE AGENCY SAYS

Assume the company has analyzed its environment and is now ready to find a target market.

As we've pointed out, marketers and their bosses subscribe to many myths about targeting. Perhaps the two most deeply entrenched are the beliefs that eighteen- to forty-nine-year-old women or heavy users are the best targets. We'll show why they're not, but we should start with some premises:

1) Buyers are individuals with diverse needs and wants.
2) The same product can no longer appeal to everyone.
3) If we think we know our target, we're probably wrong because we're assuming we know intuitively who has the needs and wants our product answers.
4) The only target that makes sense to go after is one on which the company can make money.

5) To develop a profitable targeting program, we have to make an exhaustive study of the market.

A company must segment the market in many, many ways, including demographics, psychographics, needs, and other criteria.

Once we've identified all relevant segments, we have to survey a nationally projectable sample of prospects to learn which mode of segmentation is best for the particular product or service since we cannot know in advance which is best.

Finally, based on the survey, we must compute the profitability of each potential target to identify the most profitable segment.

When CEOs work on the basis of clean-slate marketing, what questions about the market target must they ask? Marketing management must be prepared to answer questions like these:

THE BOTTOM LINE: WHAT A CEO WANTS TO KNOW

1) Has our target changed in the last few years? Are we going after the same target we've always gone after?
2) What was our rationale for selecting this target? What logic did we use?
3) What distinguished this target? What process did we use to find it?
4) Can we prove that the target we're going after is profitable? Can we show that this target has made money for us in the past or will make money in the future?
5) Is there some other target or targets out there that might be even more profitable?

The right answers, as you probably know, are yes, no, "Let me explain the logic," "Let me explain the process," yes, yes, and no.

Our explanation may get a little hard to follow in spots, but we think it's worth the effort.

≣ How Companies Miss Their Target Markets

Companies miss their targets in as many ways as there are companies and markets. Here are just three examples.

1) In the beginning, Federal Express ran trade magazine advertising aimed at shipping executives, trying to persuade businesses to buy a ser-

vice they had never considered. Federal Express soon discovered it was hitting that target, but missing the market. It switched to television commercials to reach everyone from secretaries to CEOs—every person involved in the shipping process, from the person who fills out the label to the person who approves the budget. "When it absolutely, positively, has to be there overnight" became a success because it focused on the real target's greatest need—a need shipping executives did not even know existed.

2) Although teens and preteens are by far the heaviest consumers of cola drinks, Pepsi Cola discovered that twenty-one- to forty-nine-year-old women were a more profitable target market. Why? Because women bought a disproportionate share of soft drinks for consumption in the home. They made the brand decision between Coke and Pepsi in the supermarket; children had little influence on this Coke or Pepsi buying decision; and it cost less to reach mothers through advertising and promotion than to reach their children anyway. The heaviest users—teens and preteens—were not the optimal target.

3) Colgate-Palmolive's research showed that while more than half of all American women had returned to work, 70 percent were still responsible for the family wash, and 80 percent were using three different laundry products, a detergent, a bleach, and a fabric softener. "These women are looking for convenience," said a Colgate spokesman. To answer that need among large families (those who buy a great deal of detergent), the company launched Fab 1 Shot. These washer-to-dryer packets contained both detergent and fabric softener. Because the packets cost about 25 cents a load, however, the product was not cost-effective for families. Also, because consumers could not control how much detergent they used, many did not like the premeasured packets. Colgate never targeted those segments that wanted convenience the most—college students, singles, and people living in small apartments. After the introductory activity, says *Adweek's Marketing Week*, Fab 1 Shot's sales plummeted.

Most companies are unaware of their targeting blunders. The few that are aware quietly bury them, so no one really knows how many other examples there may be. We suspect—based on the ways companies traditionally pick target markets—blunders are common. But in the 1990s, marketers will have to do better than they've done in the past in defining those people to whom the company should direct its marketing campaign. The tools exist to help them do better, and no company is so rich that it can continue to blindly chase the wrong market. After the marketing revolution, companies will routinely evaluate hundreds—or, more likely, thousands—of targets to find the most profitable one.

But how do companies make the mistakes in the first place? What's so wrong with what they're doing? And what should they be doing instead?

≡ Companies Evaluate Too Few Market Targets

Every marketing plan we've ever seen opens with a statement of the plan's objectives and goals, then immediately moves to the first strategic issue: the market target. In Chapter 1, where we talked about the escalating sevens, we assumed only seven possible targets. But this is hardly realistic.

Every product and every service has at least 10,000 possible target markets and perhaps 100,000 or more. (One might plausibly maintain that the United States offers 275 million target markets—the U.S. population. Most of the time—although not always—a company will want a larger target than one individual.) Like most marketing issues we talk about throughout this book, some of these targets are excellent, some are atrocious, and most fall somewhere between—the standard bell curve we illustrated in Figure 1.2.

And, like most other marketing issues, it is feasible to evaluate each one of 100,000 targets to identify the extraordinary few; indeed, we spend much of this chapter showing how such an evaluation works.

Yet how many marketing executives formally evaluate as many as seven possible targets? Very, very few. We regularly see marketing plans in which the company lists three or four target markets in rank order. When we ask how the targets were selected and ranked, usually the answer has to do with sales volume. The company ranks as its best target the market that buys the most, or, if a new product, the group that would buy the most if these prospects were aware of and could find the item in a store. If the marketer works for a packaged goods company, the odds are very high that he or she will pick only one target: eighteen- to forty-nine-year-old women.

Why? Companies inevitably answer that they use more product than anyone else. But suppose someone uses ten boxes of detergent a year and the average is five. Is that person a great target for our detergent? Not if they're buying the cheapest box on the shelf and ours is expensive. Not if they care only about whitening and our product features disinfecting. Not if they're intensely loyal to the brand they've been using for the last nine years and would switch stores before they switch brands.

If a company has 10,000 possible targets (forget the 100,000, which is actually a more realistic number), and it picks one at random, and the target is the same that every other packaged goods company is picking, what are the odds it has selected a target in the splendid-profitable-successful area of the bell curve? The odds, as everyone knows, are very low.

Nevertheless, American corporations typically take two common approaches to their targeting decisions; we call them the "knee jerk approach" and the "acerebral approach."

≣ The Knee Jerk Approach to Targeting

Everyone who's had a knee tapped by a doctor's rubber hammer and watched that leg twitch involuntarily understands reflexive behavior. The autonomic nervous system automatically controls the response rather than the brain. Many companies select target groups with a kind of reflexive, uncontrollable behavior. We need a target! Thump! Jerk! Here's one—eighteen- to forty-nine-year-old women!

Or hopping onto a recent bandwagon—baby boomers!

Or an even more recent fad—grey foxes, the upscale, intelligent, college-educated retirees, the parents of yuppies!

Or heavy users, the 10 to 20 percent of the population who account for the lion's share of sales volume in the product category!

One can trace the unthinking emphasis on heavy users to Dik Warren Twedt, a researcher who, in a 1964 *Journal of Marketing* article, coined the term "heavy-half" to describe the market segment accounting for a large proportion of an item's sales relative to the total. A small proportion of the population accounts for the most sales in many product categories—the ubiquitous 80/20 law applied to marketing.

More often than not, however, the heavy users—like eighteen- to forty-nine-year-old women—are as heterogeneous as all users in terms of product needs, media exposure patterns, or any other marketing measure we choose. In other words, the only thing that distinguishes women who buy, say, a lot of prepared spaghetti sauce from women who don't buy so much is only that they buy a lot of spaghetti sauce—not income, education, age, television shows they watch, magazines they read, their attitudes toward cooking, or anything else.

Paradoxically, for reasons we'll demonstrate in a moment, heavy users are virtually always less attractive than moderate users.

Another knee jerk approach is the current user theory, an axiom that drives much of direct marketing prospecting. This assumes that a company's best prospects must be people who look like its current customers. (Remember the myth from Chapter 2? A company's best prospects for a company, product, or service are people who "look" very much like current customers?) All the firm has to do is learn as much as possible about current customers and then find more people like them, and the technology exists to do both.

And while this *may* be appropriate, it may also be wrong-headed, depending on the situation. Take American Express. Its customers are high-income people who travel a great deal for business or pleasure, so it is no surprise to learn that its target market is high-income travelers.

However, people who look like American Express card members who do not currently have an American Express card are, for that reason alone, fairly unusual people. They have been the target of heavy advertising and promotion for years; they know what "Membership has its privileges" means; and they are regularly in restaurants or at airline ticket counters where they are reaching for a credit card. It may be that American Express alienated them at some point or that they are satisfied with an alternative, such as Visa Gold, MasterCard, Diner's Club, or Discover.

Or take BMW. If people look like BMW prospects—they have an income of $50,000 a year or more, they're over thirty-five, they live on one of the two coasts, and have all the other characteristics of current BMW owners—does that really mean they are hot prospects? We would argue that if we find those people and they don't currently have a BMW, it's because they have a "Buy American" attitude, or because they're very satisfied with some other import—a Mercedes or a Lexus or an Infiniti—and therefore are unlikely to buy a BMW.

We say that if a company really wants to know who its best prospects are, it has to study its target audience in great depth. The marketer cannot assume the best prospects are eighteen- to forty-nine-year-old women, heavy users, or people who look like current customers. That's a knee jerk approach. It's a step toward another marketing disaster.

≣ The Acerebral Approach to Targeting

Many marketing executives do know better than to take the knee jerk approach to picking a target market; they prefer what we call the acerebral approach. (If cerebral is "devoted to or engaged in the creative use of the intellect," acerebral is the opposite, although you won't find it in a dictionary.)

Rather than generate a target *group* by unthinking reflex, these executives compulsively choose a particular *mode* of segmenting for describing the marketplace. The mode could be personality characteristics, values, demographics, attributes or benefits, multiple tradeoff utility values, any number of possibilities. After choosing this mode (and for no apparent reason some firms consistently select one mode all the time), they do an analysis to reveal how many people "fall into" each segment (for example, 35 percent are neurotic; 12 percent psychotic; 17 percent manic-depressive, etc.). Finally they use judgment to help select one segment, based on that one mode, for the product or service. The project comes to an end when the brand manager begins to talk about "the neurotics" as the preferred market target for the, say, over-the-counter analgesic.

Note that in the knee jerk approach, companies select the target (such as eighteen- to forty-nine-year-old women) a priori. In contrast, the acerebral approach is operating when the mode of segmentation (such as personality characteristics) is selected a priori, but *the company selects the target based on what the research numbers seem to suggest and judgment.*

One finds this approach instituted when someone in an organization, perhaps after a divorce, has the notion that the best way to segment a market is in terms of, say, personality traits. "If we had only known each other's personalities better, this wouldn't have happened." Accordingly, a psychologist develops a long list of personality measures. Marketing researchers administer this list to a nationally projectable cross-section of 1,000 people; and the statisticians run various statistical analyses, often a cluster analysis, to group these people by various personality types.

We should take a short digression here to describe *cluster analysis,* an analytical tool to which we'll be referring again and again. Marketing researchers commonly employ cluster analysis to recognize patterns. Cluster analysis groups together people who are similar in terms of whatever criteria the researcher wants. The criteria might be buyer needs, brand attitudes and perceptions, psychographic or sociographic characteristics, consumer values or lifestyles, or even purchasing behavior.

Most commonly, marketing researchers employ cluster analysis to group people in terms of personality characteristics or by the attributes and benefits they seek in a particular product category. The more factors, the more difficult the analysis, but today the computer makes such analysis relatively easy.

The number of segments a study produces is partially a function of what the computer finds (the people who answer a questionnaire may be a very diverse bunch), but it is also partially a function of constraints that the researchers set. As a practical matter, it's just about impossible to deal with more than ten segments or so. So researchers usually tell the computer, "I want you to force people into no fewer than two and no more than eight segments," and the computer finds the best solution within that range. By grouping people through cluster analysis, the marketer can see patterns in what otherwise appears to be a homogeneous population.

Clustering people by personality type is usually fascinating. People are always interesting. Unfortunately, the results have questionable real world value, if only because personality by itself has little or nothing to do with market behavior. More than twenty years ago, three academics—William F. Massy (Stanford University), Ronald E. Frank (University of Pennsylvania), and Thomas Lodahl (Cornell University)—established in their book *Purchasing Behavior and Personal Attributes* that personality does not explain what people buy. As they concluded, "If we have rolled out a cannon to shoot a mouse [purchasing behavior] in this research, we can take some comfort in the discovery that the mouse turned out to be more elusive than was thought.... The best available cannon of modern multivariate statistics only hit seven percent of the mouse." That is, the most purchasing behavior that personality traits could explain was a mere 7 percent. This finding has been confirmed over and over again in the academic and applied marketing literature for two decades, but it hasn't seemed to have reached many marketing executives.

≣ Segmenting Buyers by Their Psychographics

One example of a psychographic segmentation is a study undertaken twenty years ago to learn whether psychographic classifications could apply to over-the-counter drugs. The Benton & Bowles advertising agency had 1,600 housewives respond to 214 attitude statements and report their product usage for sixty-nine different products and brand usage for thirty-eight products.* The attitude statements included items like, "If there's a flu bug going around, I'm sure to catch it," and, "Once you've got a cold, there is very little you can do about it."

Out of this, the researchers, using cluster analysis, classified six groups:

Outgoing optimists, representing 32 percent of the sample, were defined as "outgoing, innovative, community-oriented, positive toward grooming, not bothered by delicate health or digestive problems or especially concerned about germs or cleanliness."

Conscientious vigilantes, representing 28 percent, are "conscientious, rigid, meticulous, germ-fighting with a high cleanliness orientation and sensible attitudes about food. They have high cooking pride, a careful shopping orientation, tend not to be convenience-oriented."

The other groups were the *apathetic indifferents*, 14 percent; *self-indulgents*, 13 percent; *contented cows*, 8 percent; and *worriers*, 5 per-

*This research was reported in the April 1971 issue of the *Journal of Advertising Research.*

cent. These last are "irritable, concerned about health, germs and cleanliness, negative about grooming and breakfast, but self-indulgent with a low economy and high convenience orientation."

This is interesting stuff, but when the agency looked at product usage among these six segments, there wasn't a large difference between them. For example, 32 percent of the contented cows used upset stomach remedies, 65 percent of the worriers used them, with the others falling between these extremes. Those numbers may seem large, but by the time we take 32 percent of 8 percent, the number of contented cows, and 65 percent of 5 percent, the number of worriers, the difference in actual product usage between the groups melts to almost nothing.

Also, where 91 percent of the self-indulgents used pain reliever tablets, 81 percent of the contented cows used them, with the other four groups somewhere between. In other words, while it is possible to divide the American public into different segments psychographically, it's often of no practical use.

Another acerebral approach to segmenting the market in terms of psychology has been SRI International's Values and Lifestyles (VALS) Program, introduced in 1978. The original VALS procedure divided the American population into four personality groups and further divided the four into nine lifestyles. Survivors, for example, were old, extremely poor, fearful misfits, while Belongers were aging, traditional, intensely patriotic, and sentimental. SRI was (and is) selling this to companies to "enhance and increase the effectiveness of your product positioning efforts, new product introductions, sales and promotion activities, advertising campaigns, and respondent screening."

Many marketers, however, found problems when they tried to use the segments. "You can never find a way of classifying consumers so one group accounts for all the purchasing," said one General Mills research director. Even more harsh was Gerald Schoenfeld, president of Schoenfeld, Chapman, Alm & Pearl, a new-product development consultancy, who told *Adweek's Marketing Week*, "I don't use VALS and I don't know of anyone who ever got any use out of it. It doesn't matter if someone who drives a certain kind of car had a nasty mother or not. It's really arrogant to think that you could get a fix on someone's psyche and then manipulate it to get them to buy a certain kind of product."

SRI introduced a new VALS segmentation scheme in 1989. This version divides consumers into three major groups (people who are "principle-oriented," "status-oriented," or "action-oriented") and subdivides these into eight segments. Principle-oriented consumers, for example, "seek to make their behavior consistent with their views of how the world is or should be"; status-oriented consumers "have or seek a secure place in a valued social setting"; and action-oriented consumers "like to affect their environment in tangible ways."

Status-oriented consumers at the abundant resources end of the scale—that is, those with money—are the achiever segment, "successful career and work-oriented people who like to, and generally do, feel in control of their lives. They value structure, predictability, and stability over risk, intimacy, and self discovery.... As consumers, they favor established products and services that demonstrate their success to their peers."

We argue that an off-the-shelf segmentation scheme cannot possibly be as good as a customized segmentation done with a specific product or service in mind. VALS will help break the world into pieces, but the pieces may or may not have any relevance for any one brand.

It is true that some advertising agencies have been able to use psychographic definitions to aid their creative work. It may help a copywriter or art director to know that the advertising is supposed to reach, say, actualizers, who are "successful, sophisticated, active, 'take charge' people with high self-esteem and abundant resources." But such definitions are little or no help in finding an appropriate, *profitable* target market.

≡ Segmenting Buyers by Their Needs and Desires

A major advance in market segmentation occurred in the late 1960s when Dr. Russell Haley (one-time research director of Grey Advertising, later a founder of AHF Research, and currently professor of marketing at the University of New Hampshire) began to demonstrate that segmenting markets in terms of consumer needs was superior to segmenting markets in terms of psychographic characteristics. In his seminal 1968 paper in the *Journal of Marketing*, Haley laid a foundation for what has come to be known as *benefit segmentation*.

Different people, Haley argued, want different things from a product. In a toothpaste, for example, some people are interested in decay prevention, others are concerned about the brightness of their teeth, still others want sweet breath, and some are concerned only about price.

Haley's procedure was to ask a large cross-section of buyers to rate fifty to 100 different benefits (e.g., stops tooth decay) and attributes (e.g., tastes great) of a toothpaste in terms of importance (extremely important to not important at all). He then employed cluster analysis to group people into "benefit segments" (i.e., segments looking for different things in a product). The beauty of his procedure was that it was so logical—find out what different segments want—and could be applied to every type of business: consumer and industrial, product and service.

In retrospect, it was no surprise that this methodology reigned supreme as the preferred segmentation methodology for almost two decades. Benefit segments have been researched and revealed in product categories as diverse as airline travel, beverage alcohol, credit cards, computer software, frozen microwave entrees, heavy industrial equipment, lawn mowers, office equipment, small sailboats, soft drinks, telecommunications, and tractors.

≣ What's Wrong with These Approaches

We contend that all knee jerk and acerebral approaches—like picking heavy users or using an attitude and benefit profile—have at least four problems.

1) *The homogeneity issue* or, more correctly, the lack of homogeneity is a major flaw. Most target groups—whether eighteen- to forty-nine-year-old women, heavy users, baby boomers, grey foxes, belongers, achievers, or people who want a great-tasting toothpaste—are far more heterogeneous than homogeneous. Significant differences hide behind a superficial veil of similarity.

When a company looks at such a target, it is asking in effect, "Are these groups—whether heavy users or light, taste-conscious people or price-conscious, or any other defining variable—different in terms of anything other than the variable that defined the group in the first place?" And the answer is, often, no. Heavy users, for example, are rarely very similar in terms of anything other than their usage patterns and, perhaps, family size.

2) *The discrimination challenge.* The question a company should be asking here is, "Are these groups—heavy users or light, or taste-conscious or price-conscious, or whatever—different in terms of how they act in the supermarket?" It's asking about behavior rather than about demographic, psychological, or geographic characteristics. A company can learn that heavy users of spaghetti sauce buy more spaghetti sauce than light and nonusers. But that information hardly advances the company much. Its managers want to know, "Which light users can I induce to buy *more* of my prepared spaghetti sauce?"

Unfortunately, when the company examines demographic, psychographic, or geographic groups to see whether they differ in terms of brand preferences or, better yet, in buyer behavior, the results are uniformly discouraging. Rarely does a mode of segmentation explain more than about 10 percent of the variance in anything of interest. That is, consumer demographic characteristics *might* account for 10 percent of the prepared spaghetti sauce sales (although it's probably less). If someone could explain as much as 15 percent of the variance, market researchers would carry him or her on their shoulders into the Marketing Research Hall of Fame.

3) *The profitability question.* Most marketing executives and market researchers would agree—at least in theory—that in choosing a target market we ought to consider how profitable the prospects will be. In practice they almost always ignore profitability. More often than is good for their companies, they select a target group on the basis of "face validity"—that is, the target seems to make sense (if not to the marketer, at least to his or her boss).

That's a strong statement, but we actually surveyed consulting firms that had recently undertaken segmentation studies not long ago and found researchers selecting one group over another for reasons such as these:

- The best target had the heaviest users.
- These people are looking for product benefits our client's brand can deliver.
- More women eighteen to thirty-four, the group the client has always gone after, were in this target segment than in any other.

Managers reflexively choosing eighteen- to thirty-four-year-old women or acerebrally selecting achievers are not thinking about profitability at all.

Marketers and researchers generally ignore profitability when defining a target market because, we believe, few know how to take the large cross-sectional surveys most major advertisers conduct for market segmentation purposes and run them through the computer to answer the question, "Which target group is best?"

This is an especially serious problem with "benefit segmentation" because (1) the method is so popular and (2) so much about it makes sense. Assume for a moment that we are airline executives at United who have just done such a study. One segment interests us particularly, "the time conscious"—people most concerned about on-time arrival. They represent 37 percent of all business travelers and 51 percent of all airline dollars. They sound exciting, don't they?

What our benefit segmentation doesn't tell us, however (unless we really begin to analyze the data), is that these travelers have two favorite airlines, American and Northwest, and they are very satisfied with both in terms of on-time delivery. A United pitch to these travelers is not likely to move many of them in its direction. Worse, United likes to spend its money on television commercials, and on-time travelers are very upscale and watch little TV. A frontal attack on this superficially appealing segment is likely to fail because both the message and the media strategies will be wrong.

4) *The performance problem.* Companies sometimes act as if they don't want to know what happened when their marketing plans were taken into the marketplace. Surprising as it might seem, managements do not hold marketers accountable if only because they have no way to measure consequences. We know that current approaches often yield disappointing, if not depressing, sales results. Companies choose their targets without too much brain power, and their programs reflect it. We've seen heavy user campaigns that move light users more than heavy users, and we've seen attribute and benefit campaigns that had more effect on people out of the target group than those in it. The efforts might have had some results, but they didn't have the results they expected—and in those terms, the campaigns were failures.

We can understand why a brand manager or an advertising agency does not announce such fiascoes to top management. Because top management cares only about results—not what may or may not have produced the results—it is possible to pass off such campaign shortcomings as something else, if not success. But by refusing to learn from these flops, companies continue to do business as usual—which means they continue to waste money.

Clearly something is wrong. Marketers should be asking,

- What is the most appropriate way to segment my market?
- After I segment it, how should I select the best target?
- Which will be the most efficient, most profitable target?

≣ How to Find the Optimal Target Market

To answer these questions, let's invent a new product and describe the process by which a company can find the financially optimal target market for this—or any—product. This case is based on a carefully masked real-world situation. We have disguised it to protect a client, now reformed, who had the bad habit of continually making knee jerk (read: wrong) targeting decisions.

Our hypothetical credit card, the Open Sesame Vacation Card, designed for travelers, offers the following features and benefits: a high credit limit so the consumer can charge an expensive European or Asian vacation; discounts on cruises, hotels, and car rentals; the option to repay in low monthly installments or in one lump sum; low interest percentage; free traveler's checks; free trip cancellation insurance; and international medical assistance.

Assume for the sake of this discussion that the Open Sesame Vacation Card is a viable product. What's the market for it?

PROSPECTS VERSUS CUSTOMERS

Because this is a new product, let's make clear the distinction between *prospects* and *customers*. Prospects are people who have never bought a company's product; customers are those who have. This issue is particularly critical in product categories where people use only two or three different competitors and where loyalty is paramount. For example, a computer company's corporate customers have, at most, only three different computer systems. They may have many different copier or fax brands, but they're not using twenty different computer systems. Even with certain consumer products—cigarettes, laxatives, cold remedies, 35 mm film, and toothpaste—many people tend to be loyal to their brands.

This is in stark contrast to paper towels, crackers, scouring powder, plastic trash bags, or facial tissues, where the consumer has virtually no loyalty and may buy a different brand on every trip to the supermarket.

In the categories where people buy only one, two, or at the most three different brands, product loyalty is a central issue, and in this situation, our best prospect is our current customer. Also, in many categories—such as credit cards, insurance, and magazine subscriptions—it is much less expensive to hold onto a customer the company already has than to find a new one.

But for the sake of this Open Sesame Vacation Card exercise, we are assuming a new product, so the company is looking for prospects, not customers. The first step is to create a list of characteristics that might help segment different groups in terms of the Open Sesame Vacation Card. To find these characteristics, the company conducts brainstorming sessions, holds focus groups, and tries by any means possible to establish all the card's dimensions. It creates a questionnaire based on these dimensions and researchers conduct interviews in the home among a nationally projectable sample of prospects. The interviewer gives each respondent a list of statements that tap into attitudes toward travel, interests, hobbies, and the like. The respondents rank each statement on a scale of how well it describes his or her reaction—"completely," "very much," "somewhat," "slightly," or "not at all." The statements will be things like these:

- I'm the kind of person who likes to have a really good time.

- I'm the kind of person who would rather go to a party than stay home and read a book.
- I'm the kind of person who can't sit still for more than five minutes.
- When I come to a new city, I go to a museum right away.
- I usually watch foreign films rather than domestic.

But after collecting all of this interesting data, the autonomic nervous system takes over and the product manager finds herself drawn inexorably to make an a priori targeting decision. She concludes—and we must admit there is some logic here—that the two key variables (*drivers of revenues*, as management consultants say) are income and attitudes toward credit. The higher a person's score on *both* variables, the more attractive they will be as prospects.

To demonstrate the point, our product manager asked the researchers to break out the data from the study into the nine cells shown below.

REVENUE POTENTIAL PER RESPONDENT BY CELL			
		Income	
Attitudes toward credit	*Low*	*Moderate*	*High*
Unfavorable	$ 16	$ 50	$ 75
Indifferent	$ 41	$ 90	$ 205
Favorable	$ 110	$ 225	$ 290

The table indicates just about what we would expect: low-income people who have a unfavorable attitude toward credit are not terrific prospects for an Open Sesame Vacation Card; they yield just $16 in potential annual revenue each. High-income people who have a favorable attitude toward credit, on the other hand, look profitable; they represent $290 per person per year.

We condense the nine cells into three "target group" categories— "hot," "warm," and "cold." In this case, the prime target, the "hot" group, are those people in the lower right three boxes—the moderate/favorable group (yielding $225 in potential annual revenue), the high/indifferent group ($205), and the high/favorable group ($290). These three account for 45 percent of the revenue potential while they represent only 20 percent of the people.

The secondary target, the "warm" group, are those three groups running on the diagonal from low/favorable through moderate/indifferent to high/unfavorable. They represent 45 percent of the population, but only 35 percent of the revenue potential.

The last, the "cold" group, the people in the top left three boxes, account for 35 percent of the population, but only 20 percent of the potential revenue. See the following table:

LABELS SELECTED BY PRODUCT MANAGER			
	Hot prospects	*Warm prospects*	*Cold prospects*
Percent of population	*20%*	*45%*	*35%*
Percent of spending	*45%*	*35%*	*20%*

Excited by this "discovery," the product manager then announces, "The search for a new target is over. We have found the best prospects." Another marketing general is about to lead the corporate cavalry into oblivion. Unfortunately, this goes on all the time.

Another company might acerbrally segment the market on the basis of what people like to do on vacation—camp, cruise, or climb mountains. They automatically pick a target on the basis of the way people behave.

But having gone through this exercise to segment the market, who should the company go after? The biggest group? The group that accounts for the biggest market share? The small, but high-consuming group? Unfortunately, at this point too many marketing executives say, "We'll take the group that accounts for the most volume." The "hots" win almost every time.

≡ Volume Is Not the Same as Profit

Although taking that group may seem reasonable on the surface, it ignores the question of profitability. Or perhaps the marketer assumes that if we have the sales, profitability will take care of itself. Or, more likely, the company evaluates the marketer's performance by sales, not by profit.

But to be truly effective, the marketer must consider many different ways to segment the market while simultaneously estimating profitability, everything from simple demographics to sophisticated psychographic and attitude clusters. They include such possibilities as personality traits, social values, category involvement, usage patterns, and the attributes or benefits the prospects seek.

A company must consider all these possibilities because, as Daniel Yankelovich argued more than thirty years ago:

We don't know before we do the research which mode of segmentation is best for a particular product or service. We shouldn't begin to narrow our focus until we explore the alternatives.

Few marketing executives would debate the assumption that we can segment the market many different ways. Some might even agree that we do not know a priori which is the best way to segment. Nonetheless, a great many behave as if they *do* know without any investigation or research which segment is best for a given product or service. They preface their opinions with things like, "I've been in this business for ten/twenty-five/forty years, and I *know* who'll buy ..." Or, "I spent ten years in the field/in a branch/in retail, and our customers ..."

Such marketing executives are mistaken. They may be accurately reporting their experience (even that, however, is doubtful), but they cannot generalize from their experience to the new situation. The moment they do so, they are taking a knee jerk or acerebral approach to targeting. Remember, if a company is to choose the most profitable target market, it must evaluate thousands of options. Yet marketing executives mindlessly choose a target or a mode (or, at most, three or five targets) every day, inadvertently sabotaging their efforts and their companies. By contrast, the sophisticated marketing executive creates many different ways to segment the market—some simple, some complex, based on theory and past research. The marketer then screens and evaluates each segment using intelligent, rational, *profit minded* criteria. Were all marketers to do so, it would be a marketing revolution.

≣ Where to Begin a Target Market Search

If, for an example, a company were looking for the Open Sesame Vacation Card's target, how many factors would it consider? Twenty? Fifty? Actually, when we helped a financial services company find its target for a similar product using an optimization approach, we found many more.*

Segmentation is a five-step process.

1) *In the first, or "hypotheses development" phase, we reviewed research undertaken by the company in the past.* We investigated sec-

*The authors would like to thank Professors Mary Lou Roberts (University of Massachusetts at Boston) and Melanie Lenard (School of Management, Boston University) for their contributions to this discussion.

ondary sources—syndicated research, published articles, papers, and the like—to find what other companies had learned about the credit card market. We ran in-depth idea generation sessions among different levels of the firm's marketing, financial, and operations management and held a dozen focus group sessions with people who currently used and who did not use the company's payment vehicles.

Out of all this effort, we obtained a long list of factors and variables we (and our client) believed influenced credit card and other payment vehicle ownership and usage. Of course, income and attitudes toward credit were on the list. Some factors, like religion, might seem strange, but even in the 1980s when we conducted this study, religion and religiosity had a lot to do with how people use credit. Relative income—a respondent's household income compared to his or her neighbor's—also turned out to be significant. If a family earns $100,000 and its neighbors all earn $200,000, the family is *relatively* poor, and relative income has as much to do with how the family behaves as its absolute income.

2) *Once we identified all these factors, we developed and pretested a set of survey questions.* We did this to obtain reliable and valid measures. That is, if we repeated the questions with the same people at another point in time, we would obtain the same answers within a narrow range—say ± 3 percent— so the questions are *reliable*. Also, by carefully constructing the questions and the way in which the answers are derived, the data actually reveals the subject in which we were interested, so they are *valid*.

This is a key point. We cannot ask a person, "How important is culture to you?" because virtually everyone will say, "Extremely." Rather, researchers ask something like, "How frequently do you visit museums?" Or they use a "describes-me"/"doesn't-describe-me-at-all" scale with statements like, "I like to visit museums in foreign countries," "I am very interested in theater," "I visit galleries two or three times a year." To measure a factor reliably and validly, the careful researcher employs various items that tap into the same dimension, then calculates an average score for all the items. The more items that tap into the same factor, the better the measure.

3) *Once we developed and tested the questions, our company interviewed a nationally projectable sample* of 2,800 Americans with incomes of at least $10,000. We interviewed them in their homes for an average of an hour and twenty minutes. Note that we didn't try to segment the market based on twelve focus groups, 150 people cruising shopping centers, or the first 300 people we could get to answer questions on the telephone.

4) *From these surveys we created fifty-six different modes (or variables) for segmentation.* We derived these modes in different ways.

Some were quite simple, based on a direct question ("What is your approximate age?"); others represented information we knew about respondents before the survey (such as where they lived). Many measures, however, turned out to be complex, based on:

- *Multivariate statistical analyses of responses.* For example, in cluster analysis of lifestyles the computer examined all the answers to group similar people together.
- *Arithmetic manipulation of simple variables.* To calculate the company's share of credit sales, for example, we took each individual respondent's total credit charges and divided them by the company's credit card charges. If an individual's total annual credit card charges were $3,000 and $1,000 of those were on the company's card, the company's share was 33.3 percent.
- *Mixed analysis levels.* We calculated relative income, for example, by taking reported income as a percentage of the average reported income of respondents in the same geographic area (defined by zip code).
- *Composite measures.* These measures were developed by combining data from different questions to create new variables. For example, we defined socioeconomic status as a composite of household income, respondent education, and the head of the household's occupation.

The full list of all fifty-six variables follows. Since many of these headings are comprised of more than one mode of segmentation, there were actually 130 altogether. For example, we calculated a number of these for each of the six major credit and charge cards separately.

Although we developed these variables specifically for a credit card client, the *process* is the same whatever the product or service. The important point is that neither marketing executives nor researchers can know before performing the research which potential segmentation variables will be important to a given product.

5. *Once we had obtained data on all of these 130 variables, we analyzed them, plus all two-way combinations of them.* For example, age and sex are two variables; sex and age together, as in eighteen- to forty-nine-year-old women, represent yet another variable. Since eighteen- to forty-nine-year-old women are the most common target group in American marketing, and because they are the target with which most researchers, marketing executives, and their bosses are the most familiar, we use two-way combinations to be consistent with what marketers are doing right now. But nowhere is it carved in stone that this analysis has to be limited to two-way combinations. The analysis could use three-

way combinations (or more), although as the combinations increase, the numbers grow very big, very quickly.

But back to the Open Sesame Vacation Card. With the 130 variables we identified, plus all two-way combinations, we have 8,515 different ways to segment the market (130 + [130 x 129 ÷ 2]). If we had looked at all three-way combinations, we would have had too many to even think about.

And each one of these variables has a number of different categories. For income and attitudes toward credit, there were, as we saw earlier, three categories (low, average, high). But for region of the country, there are nine census regions, and for several cluster analyses we examined seven different groups. On average, looking at all 8,515 different ways to segment the market, there were five groups per possible mode of segmentation (or variable). With 8,515 different ways to segment the market and five groups each way, that's 42,575 possible target groups. A total of 42,575 possible targets is a long way from saying we should focus on the heavy users, eighteen- to forty-nine-year-old women, or even high-income, favorable credit types.

We now look at each one of the 42,575 targets using a set of quantitative, profit-related criteria (see box). Marketers often neglect these criteria when they evaluate alternative target markets.

CRITERIA FOR AN OPTIMAL MARKET TARGET

1. Responsiveness	The more responsive a target group appears to be to a firm's marketing efforts, the greater its value.
2. Sales potential	The more a target group buys or uses, the greater its value.
3. Growth potential	The more a target group is growing in size, the greater its value.
4. Decision-making power	The more responsibility a target has for making sales decisions, the greater its value.
5. Media exposure	The less expensive a target is to reach with media, the greater its value.

POTENTIAL SEGMENTATION VARIABLES

Demographic Variables

*Age
*Occupation (respondent and head
  of household)
Occupational Status (respondent
  and head of household)
Census Region
Current Residence (urban, subur-
  ban, rural)
Current Residence (population
  size)
Political Orientation
Property Ownership

*Religion and Religiosity
*Education
Geographic Mobility
*Sex (i.e., gender)
*Income (personal and household)
Income (relative)
Similarity to Card Members[a]
Social Mobility
*Life Cycle[b]
*Socioeconomic Status[c]
*Socioeconomic Status II[d]
Marital Status

Credit Card Variables

Actual Charge Volume on Credit
  Card
Age Acquiring Credit Cards
Air Travel Insurance Ownership
Bank Services Used or Owned
Club Membership
*Credit Card Acquired First
*Credit Card Ownership

Domestic or International Travel
*Lifestyle Activities[e]
*Media Exposure Patterns
Percentage Credit Usage[f]
Usage of Client and Competitive
  Cards in and out of Town
*Usage by Sales Executive Type
  for Personal/Business Reasons

Note: We used more than one mode of segmentation to create several of these headings. Under Attitudinal Variables, for example, we calculated Benefits of Payment Vehicle Services for each of six major credit and charge cards separately.

Also, we've marked the twenty-five factors most strongly related to whether a consumer will adopt and use Open Sesame Vacation Card with an asterisk. They are, as researchers say, variables with high power to discriminate.

a. We calculated and averaged standardized scores for age, personal income, and travel frequency; we then compared each prospect with the average of all card members.

b. Young single, young married, no children; married with young children (under thirteen); married with older children (thirteen to seventeen); married with grown children (eighteen-plus); older, widowed, divorced, no children; divorced, young children; divorced, older children.

c. We used a composite of household income and occupation of head of household and education of respondent to measure socioeconomic status.

d. A scoring of personal income, occupation, and education.

Other Behavioral Variables

Media Exposure Patterns
*Relationships to Client Company[e]
Share of Charge[h]
*Share of Charge/Share of Pocket
*Share of Pocket[i]
Share of Uses/Share of Pocket

Share of Uses/Transactions
*Travel Frequency
Type of Place Grew Up
Usage of Client Financial Services
*Vacation Travel

Attitudinal Variables

*Attitudes toward Client

Familiarity with Credit Cards[e]
*Attitudes toward Credit[e]
Familiarity with Major Cards
Attitudes toward Travel[e]
Perception of Family Income

*Beliefs/Attitudes toward Payment
  Vehicles
Perception of Personal Financial Situation[e]
*Benefits of Payment Vehical Services[e]
*Travel and Dining Concerns[e]
*Credit Card First-to-Mind
Preferences for Credit Card (i.e., Best Card)

e. Derived from cluster analyses. For each mode of segmentation indicated, we created and examined multiple cluster analytic groups (i.e., "solutions"). For example, we included three different segmentations (three, four, and five solutions) for the Benefits of Payment Vehicle mode.
f. Of all transactions in the past year, the percent made on credit or charge vehicle.
g. A simple measure based on whether the respondent is a current client card member, former card member, or never a card member.
h. Of all dollars (reported) charged on cards, percent of dollars charged on client products.
i. Of all cards owned, percent client ownership.

Notwithstanding the complexity in calculating their effect on each of the targets, these factors can make the difference between a profitable and a middling target. They include

- *Responsiveness.* The more a target group responds to a company's marketing efforts, the greater its value to the company.
- *Sales potential.* Similarly, a target group that buys or uses more of the company's product is more valuable than one that buys less.
- *Growth potential.* A growing target group is more desirable than a static group or one that is shrinking.
- *Decision-making power.* The more responsibility the target prospects have for making a buying decision, the more significant they are to the company.
- *Media exposure patterns and media costs.* We have to look at these since it usually makes little or no sense in the real world to define a target a marketer cannot reach through media.

To show how these profit-related criteria are used, let's return to the Open Sesame case. For purposes of simplicity we walk through this example with only three of these criteria: responsiveness, sales potential, and media exposure patterns and media cost.

• How many people in each group have an acceptance problem? That is, their current credit card is not accepted in many places where our Open Sesame Vacation Card would be accepted. The bigger the acceptance problem a person has, the more likely it is that he or she would be responsive to Open Sesame's marketing efforts.
• How many people have positive attitudes toward the company marketing the Open Sesame Vacation Card and would therefore be responsive to an Open Sesame Vacation Card marketing program?
• How many people, because of their expected greater responsiveness (because they have an acceptance problem and a positive attitude) could we expect to buy the card, and therefore what percentage of total potential revenues do they represent?
• What would it cost to reach each group? We express this cost as cost per thousand (CPM) and in gross rating points (GRPs). In the real world, the figures come from the company's advertising agency. In this hypothetical (though realistic) case it is much more expensive to reach the hot prospects group—with a $78 CPM—than the cold prospects.

Running the data through the computer would give the following figures:

PROSPECT CONSIDERATION TABLE

Target group labeled by product manager	Size	Potential revenue	Acceptance problem	Positive attitudes	Potential shift	Cost per 1,000
Hot prospects	20%	45%	50%	50%	11.25%	$78.00
Warm prospects	45	35	70	80	19.60	35.00
Cold prospects	35	20	50	60	6.00	26.40

In other words, while the hot prospects represent only 20 percent of the market's total number; they represent 45 percent of the potential revenue. About half of this group have an acceptance problem, however, and half have a positive attitude toward Open Sesame, so they suggest a potential shift of 11.25 percent, the dollar revenue percentage that our new card can obtain. To obtain the potential shift figure, take the total potential revenue (45 percent), multiply that by the people who have an acceptance problem (50 percent), and multiply that answer by those who have positive attitudes (50 percent—e.g., 45% x 50% = 22.5% x 50% = 11.25%).*

The so-called hot prospects are not as positive toward the company as the warm prospects, *and* they are significantly more expensive to reach. Now which is the prime prospect group? Which is *really* hot?

To find out, we evaluate the expected profitability of these three potential targets. In this case, we use the figures from the previous table and estimates of what a complete advertising schedule would cost using a base of 10 million prospects and $800 million in potential revenue (these would be figures based on the company's research).

We use these figures to estimate each group's forecasted dollar revenue and maximum potential profit (the dollar revenue less the advertising expense).

ADVERTISING EVALUATION

Target group labeled by product manager	Size	Number of prospects	CPM	Cost of 10,000 GRPs[a]
Hot prospects	20%	2,000,000	$78.00	$15,600,000
Warm prospects	45	4,500,000	35.00	15,750,000
Cold prospects	35	3,500,000	26.40	9,240,000
	100%	10,000,000		

a. To obtain the gross rating point figure, multiply the cost per thousand by the number of thousand prospects; in the first case, $78 x 2,000. Multiply this figure by 100 to buy 10,000 gross rating points.

We now find that while the hot prospects account for $360 million in total dollar revenue, they represent only $90 million in forecasted revenue (11.25 percent of $800 million). This is less than the warm prospects because, while their total dollar revenue potential is smaller than the hot prospect total, the potential shift is much greater.

The maximum potential profit (forecasted dollar revenue less advertising) is now larger for the warm prospects than for the hot prospects— $141 million for the warm prospects versus $74.4 million for the hot prospects. The point here is that while the total market may be $800 million, no company can hope to take all of it, and it costs more to reach and persuade some targets than others.

*In this simple illustration, we are performing these calculations on the aggregate level, for the group as a whole. In practice we recommend that the calculations be made for each individual survey respondent. And for purposes of simplicity we have left the factors of growth potential and decision-making power out of the equation.

POTENTIAL PROFIT EVALUATION

Target group labeled by product manager	Percent potential revenue	Total dollar revenue	Potential shift	Forecasted dollar revenue	Maximum potential profit
Hot prospects	45%	$360,000,000	11.25%	$90,000,000	$74,400,000
Warm prospects	35	280,000,000	19.60	156,800,000	141,050,000
Cold prospects	20	160,000,000	6.00	48,000,000	$38,760,000
	100%	$800,000,000			

Once a company sees figures like these, *the warm prospects, not the hot prospects, appear to be the prime market target for our Open Sesame Vacation Card.* This, of course, is only one analysis; we still have about 42,572 to go. Fortunately the computer does this for us, and, in fact, we examine and evaluate all the variables and combinations of variables to produce a single recommendation for our clients.

Even with the computer, however, the process is long and tedious. From data cleaning through presentation, a project such as this takes three months and costs more than $100,000 in analysis time and computer charges. And although the company has been remarkably successful with its product, there is a faster, less expensive way to accomplish the same end.

This faster way has been slow to win approval, however, because people understand the approach we've just described, it's familiar, and people continue to use it. The notion of having an optimization model to search through millions of possibilities to find an answer is so frightening to many executives that they don't want to do it. Most companies reject new approaches. The technology makes most marketing and advertising executives uneasy.

More than a decade ago, for example, one major New York advertising agency introduced a computer model to the media department. If you set the media program's objectives, the model would search through millions of combinations to tell you what media to buy. The first time the agency tested the model against the media planners, the model's recommendations were 22 percent more efficient than the planners'. The model routinely beat the planners by 10 percent or more, but it was never adopted. The agency does not use it today because people feel it's too unorthodox, too scary, too threatening—because they feel marketing is an art, not a science.

☰ A Better Approach to Targeting

The process we described with the Open Sesame Vacation Card, while comprehensive, is time-consuming and expensive and not the only way to target. There is another approach. The goal here is to answer the targeting questions in hours rather than months at a fraction of the cost.

Consider the following table, which shows the relationship between a company's ability to specify target group characteristics and the group's size.

THE MASS/DIRECT MARKETING MATRIX		
	Size of target group	
	Large	*Small*
Ability to specify *Low*	Mass	—
target group		
characteristics *High*	—	Direct

If a company's ability to specify a target group's characteristics is low—if there's virtually nothing characteristic about these prospects—and if the target group's size is large—if everyone in the country is a prospect—then the company can use mass marketing techniques efficiently. Conversely, if a company can clearly specify the target group's characteristics, and if the group is relatively small, then the company can use direct marketing techniques efficiently.

The more focused and smaller the target market and the more clearly a company can identify individual prospects, the cheaper direct marketing—mail, telephone, personal selling—becomes. As the number of prospects grows, however, direct marketing becomes less and less efficient because the cost of marketing each item rises.

As a general rule, the more clearly a company can identify its target markets, the more efficient its marketing effort can become. Everything else being equal, the less money a company wastes reaching people who will never be prospects, the more it can spend reaching and selling to its genuine prospects.

To do so, the company starts at the level of the individual respondent and estimates his or her profitability using the same criteria previously discussed. The marketer researchers feed these estimates into a nonlinear math programming model designed to solve simultaneously for volume potential, decision making, responsiveness to a particular product and positioning, media exposure, and media cost.

To do all of this, the programming model is linked to a large data base, which might be custom designed or drawn from data already available to the company or the entire industry. We have worked on an application of the model using Simmons Market Research Bureau (SMRB) data, but you could also use Mediamark Research or other suppliers.

To use this approach, however, marketing managers must provide the researchers with detailed background information such as the size of the product category in units and dollars. They must answer such questions as, "What is the maximum ad budget feasible?" and "What is the minimum target group size or media reach you would find acceptable?" See the following box.

TARGET GROUP OPTIMIZATION

Management Constraints

Size of vacation credit market	*Any size (in this example, $800 million)*
Size of advertising budget	*Any size from $1 million to $200 million*
Business area	*Across all types of service establishments or any one or combination of businesses (e.g., hotels and restaurants)*
Business source	*Across all three profit streams (acquisition, retention, portfolio expansion) or any one or combination of sources*
Minimum reach of schedule	*Minimum percent of target group exposed to advertising at least once (e.g., 80%)*
Minimum optimal target group size	*Minimum percent of target group acceptable as an optimal target (e.g., 10%)*

The manager must also provide marketing research input from a consumer or industrial product or service study—the same kind of data we discussed earlier in our Open Sesame Credit Vacation Card case. This data base enables the model to calculate the economic value of each buyer (dollar volume accounted for multiplied by decision-making power multiplied by a growth factor index—if this type of buyer is increasing or decreasing in size in the population). In addition, the model requires the following (from the survey data base):

- Knowledge of how responsive the buyer is to the company's product (or new product concept in the case of Open Sesame), the logic being "if they hate you, it's probably not worth the effort to go after them."
- Information concerning the buyers' responsiveness to as many as ten different positioning strategies for the product.
- Media exposure information for each buyer (i.e., magazine and newspaper readership, television viewing, and radio listening).
- The costs of exposure in each medium and some estimate of the differential impact of each media vehicle.

MODEL INPUTS FOR MARKETING RESEARCH INFORMATION

Individual respondents

Type	Source
Economic value	
Responsiveness to product concept	
Responsiveness to 10 alternative positionings	Market segmentation study
Media exposure (37 types)	

Media Costs

Cost of a single exposure in each of 37 media vehicles	Client and advertising agency

Media Impact

Estimates of the differential effectiveness of 37 media vehicles	Agency or consulting firm norms

---

The computer provides a description of the "optimal" target by searching through literally billions of possible choices. When we have compared forecasted profitability of management's favorite target—usually the "hot" prospects, those heavy users that seem on the surface to be so attractive—with the forecasted profitability of an optimal target, the differences have been striking. Optimization wins every time—and more to the point, the success carries into the real world where the computer-designed target does what the machine forecast.

In the case of Open Sesame, the model identified a group of people who represented 34 percent of all prospects, the positioning strategy that turned them on, and the most efficient media buy—all simultaneously. No other target group could produce a better return on investment than this one. The model can then go on to describe this "optimal" target in a conventional manner with psychographic, sociographic, and demographic profiles. For example:

VACATION CARD OPTIMAL SOLUTION

Positioning	An inexpensive European vacation
Target size	34% of all prospects
Reach	88%
Gross rating points	6,197
Budget	$21,870 mm

MEDIA SCHEDULE

Vehicle	%Budget	GRPs
Late news television	33%	1,285
Prime time television	21	862
Major daily newspapers	15	632
Drive time radio	13	1,808
News weeklies	10	400
Business weeklies	8	1,210

The computer's ability to sift through all possible alternatives to identify the one most profitable is only a single example of how computing technology will continue to change tomorrow's marketing. Marketers can—and should—begin with a clean slate and segment any consumer or industrial market in thousands of ways, and they have thousands, if not hundreds of thousands, of targets from which to choose.

Many marketers unfortunately make the mistake of evaluating—if they do any evaluation at all—a relatively small number of targets, and they do so without considering profitability. As a result, over and over again they select target groups that in fact are not desirable and a marketing plan built on a foundation of sand.

Although the computer means that marketers can perform the kinds of analyses we've been describing faster and cheaper than ever before, the computer itself is not the key to profitable targeting. The revolutionary idea we're proposing is that we don't pick a target—such as heavy users or women eighteen to thirty-four—because it consumes product. We don't decide a priori how to segment the market, but we do evaluate thousands of targets and consider each on the basis of its profitability.

When we've taken the steps we've described, we have a target that is sizeable, profitable, and defensible. There's also a certain appeal in being able to explain what we're doing rather than retreating into hunch, tradition, or experience: "I'm pretty sure this'll work," "That's the way we've always done it," or "That's how I've always done it."

But once we've identified a profitable target, how do we position our product or service to appeal to those prospects?

HOW TO IDENTIFY THE OPTIMAL TARGET

1) Begin by rejecting outright "knee jerk" and "acerebral" approaches. They don't work.

2) Carefully consider hundreds, thousands, hundreds of thousands of alternative targets based on variables hypothesized to drive profitability in a particular product category.

3) Evaluate each target in terms of criteria related to profitability:

- *Category expenditures:* The more a target group buys or uses, the greater its value.
- *Decision-making power:* The more responsibility a target has for making sales decisions, the greater its value.
- *Responsiveness to our brand:* The more responsive a target group appears to be to a firm's communications, the greater its value.
- *Growth potential:* The more a target group is growing, the greater its value.
- *Reachability:* The easier or more cost-efficient it is to communicate with a target, the greater its value.

4) Pick a winning target and build a successful marketing program around it.

 # 5

THE BATTLE FOR
THE MIND IS OFTEN
LOST BEFORE THE
FIRST STRIKE

Positioning starts with a product, a service, a company, an institution, a person, a country, or almost anything, but it is not something we do to the product. As Al Ries and Jack Trout say in their book *Positioning: The Battle for Your Mind*, "Positioning is what you do to the mind of the prospect. That is, you position the product in the mind of the prospect."

The whole notion of positioning is giving a product a meaning that distinguishes it from other products and induces people to want to buy it. We want our positioning to be in harmony with the larger social context—the lifestyles and values we've discussed. We don't want to introduce a product that talks about multifunctionality and requires an inch-thick instruction book in a culture that is streamlining and simplifying. And we have to know *which* minds we want to affect, so we have to know the target.

Therefore, to be effective,

- Positioning has to be done with a target in mind.
- We have to understand what motivates people to buy in the category—what explains their behavior.
- We have to understand the degree to which our product satisfies the target's needs.
- We have to understand how our competition performs against those needs.

Ideally what we want to find is a need that the consumer says is important, that our product satisfies, and that the competition does not meet as well as we do. For example (because virtually everything we've been talking about is as true for business-to-business marketers as for consumers), suppose clarity is important to long distance telephone customers. Suppose our system is brilliantly clear. This is a positioning only if we are perceptively more clear than other long-distance carriers. If there's virtually no difference between our signal and everyone else's, we shouldn't base our positioning on it.

Unfortunately, positioning cannot be developed from what people say they want (because either they don't know or can't or don't want to articulate). Fortunately, there are ways to learn what people do want.

If CEOs were working on the basis of clean-slate marketing, what questions about positioning must they ask? What questions must marketing management be prepared to answer?

THE BOTTOM LINE: WHAT A CEO WANTS TO KNOW

1) Have we given serious thought to a clear positioning strategy for our company and its products?

2) Did we develop and formally evaluate (i.e., test among a random cross-section of buyers—not focus groups) a broad spectrum of possible positionings?

3) Does our positioning address what we have determined to be the key motivators in the business?

4) Is this positioning based on something that our company or brand can deliver?

5) Does our positioning truly distinguish us from the competition?

≡ How One Successful Positioning Worked

The car rental business has always been very competitive. Although it's still dominated by Hertz and Avis, numerous smaller companies have been making significant inroads on the basis of lower rental prices. Many of these companies have matched their low prices with improved services and operations. As a result, the car rental business and car rental advertising have become increasingly commodity-oriented with price determining the purchase decision much of the time.

Avis was maintaining its number two position behind Hertz, but in 1987 lagged by approximately six market share points. Hertz consistently outspent Avis in advertising by 20 percent or more. Consumer perceptions of Avis and Hertz were similar; they offered good service but at a premium price.

Since the car rental business is a service industry, Avis could command superior pricing only by promising (and delivering) superior service. Experience had shown, however, that service innovations that resulted in a competitive advantage were invariably short-lived because competitors could copy them easily. Such innovations were therefore unsuitable as the basis for a long-term positioning effort. Although consumers could and did recall the "We Try Harder" advertising of years past, they did not feel it was relevant to the company today. The challenge was to build a positioning that would strengthen Avis's image of quality, improve its price image, differentiate it from Hertz and others, and be effective in national image advertising as well as locally, in internal employee communications, and within the travel industry.

Shortly after Avis assigned Backer Spielvogel Bates its advertising, the Avis employees bought the company through an employee stock ownership plan in October 1987. When the agency conducted strategic research on the importance of employee ownership, it found that employee ownership was a powerful "reason" for Avis employees to really try harder, be more competitive, and provide greater value than other companies. In fact, the rationale was so strong that BSB was able to extend the original claim to, "Now we're trying harder than ever."

After two years of in-market use, the campaign strategy helped Avis achieve its highest share of market in history (28.5 percent in 1990), closing the gap with market leader Hertz (31.2 percent). Positive personality characteristics associated with the company have also improved, and employee motivation is up significantly. Positioning works.

≣ Positioning Is in the Consumer's Mind

One can think of positioning as the hub of a wheel, with targeting, product design, message strategy, media selection, and pricing as the spokes. Each spoke should reinforce and express the basic positioning.

Everyone agrees that positioning is important, but there's a lot of argument about exactly what it is in practice. Advertising theorists are behaving like the judge who said, "I can't define pornography, but I know it when I see it." We know when, because of the styling, one automobile is positioned as a luxury sports sedan, another is an economical family car, and a third is a high-performance sports car. They are all automobiles, but all with distinctly different positionings. The challenge is to find a positioning that is powerful, credible, tenable, and appropriate.

Because, as Theodore Levitt points out, people do not buy products, they buy solutions, one way to position a product is to find a consumer *problem* that your product or service solves.

One multibillion dollar package goods company tells its people, "Marketing is the discipline of solving people's problems with a product at a profit."

Sounds impressive—until one asks, as we have, "How do you identify people's problems?"

Sudden mumblings and subject changing. It turns out that this marketing giant, a leading American corporation, *has* no formal method to identify consumer problems. They develop new products the way just about everyone does; the R&D people come up with a new formula that beats the current product's cleaning power by 13 percent, or marketing management suggests focus groups or other research to inspire a new approach.

We think that marketing management's first task is to identify buyer problems. Once a company has identified a problem, it can ask R&D to develop a new formula, instruct product designers to devise a new package, request the advertising agency to create new advertising, or do whatever is necessary to market profitably.

Three tools are available to detect people's problems. We like to call them the preposterous, the problematic, and the preferred: the preposterous include focus groups, importance ratings, and perceptual maps; the problematic include problem detection, gap analysis, choice modeling, and quadrant analysis; the preferred is strategic cube analysis, about which we have much more to say later. Marketers misuse some of these tools, asking them to do things for which they were never intended, or they use an old tool when a new one will do much better. We believe that in the marketing revolution, companies will junk these outdated tools and will begin to make positioning decisions that truly distinguish a product in the market, helping move buyers from enemy brands to their own.

≡ Focus Groups Give Fuzzy Data

The most popular form of preposterous research is the ubiquitous focus group interview.

In a focus group, a handful of people under a moderator's direction focus their discussion on a certain topic, product, or product category.

They describe how they use a product, what caused them to buy it, and what they think about it. Focus groups spread like a contagious disease from package goods companies into financial services, hard goods, and industrial applications. They became the most widely used type of market research in the 1980s, says Thomas L. Greenbaum, an executive vice president of Clarion Marketing Communications and author of a handbook on groups.

Focus groups appeal to marketers because they are easy, cheap, and sometimes conducted in interesting places. They can represent a junket for the marketers and researchers—a surprising number are held on the outskirts of Las Vegas and near Disney World.

Companies use focus groups to answer too many marketing questions. Remember the myth? "Qualitative research techniques, particularly focus group interviews, are serious, helpful marketing research tools." And the item from the CEO questionnaire? "More often than not, the information produced by focus group research is as accurate and useful as the results of survey research at less than half the cost."

Unfortunately, focus groups cannot replace other, generally more expensive, more reliable, research techniques. Although people use them for this purpose, focus groups cannot tell a marketer how prospects will really react to a new product, a new positioning, or a new advertising campaign.

To put the issue into another context, consider presidential election surveys. Why don't research companies use focus groups to forecast election results? Both political parties choose candidates who try to appeal to more than 50 percent of the electorate because a candidate has to have a majority to win. To obtain a level of sampling precision, researchers typically poll 600 to 1,200 people nationwide, so they can say that the study shows Candidate Wintergreen preferred by 55 percent of the voters, plus or minus three or four percentage points. So why can't we obtain the same results with focus groups?

1) *Volatile results.* A typical focus group has eight to ten respondents. A typical client does about four focus groups on a given topic to answer a question, so the total sample is thirty-two to forty people. The sample is too small to give stable results; do the research again, and the results may be entirely different.

If a research company conducted four focus group sessions and everything else were held constant, it might conclude that product X, or positioning Y, or promotion Z is the most appealing. If another research company replicated the research—did it exactly the same way—it is just as likely to conclude that product A, positioning B, or promotion C is the most appealing. This volatility can lead to disaster.

2) *Not only are the results unstable, they are not representative of any segment of the population.* When a reputable research company does a poll, it makes sure that the sample includes people in proportion to their incidence in the population. So if 20.7 percent of the U.S. adult population lives in the Northeast, approximately 20.7 percent of those sampled live in the Northeast; if 60 percent of the people are registered Democrats, 60 percent of the sample are registered Democrats. Political researchers make sure a study is weighted geographically, by urban area, by gender, and sometimes by religion because all these can affect the study's outcome.

No one has any idea how representative a focus group may be. Even if a company holds 100 focus groups so that it includes 1,000 people (an admittedly crazy idea), focus group organizers do not choose representative samples. After all, many researchers today conduct focus groups in suburban malls, among people who have the time to participate in the research. We've said, half-seriously, most focus groups are made up of semicomatose people with time on their hands who are roaming through shopping malls searching for some excitement, which comes when an attractively dressed woman offers them $15 to participate in a group. These are not representative samples.

3) *Dominant voices affect the group.* Even if a company conducted many focus groups and designed the groups so they were representative of the population, the groups are so dominated by a few voices—sometimes just one—that what the research picks up is not many voices but a relatively few because a small number of voices in each group colors the expressed beliefs of the other group members.

Also, what people say in a group setting with strangers is not necessarily what they might say to an individual interviewer, whether the conversation is at home or in a mall or on the telephone. Many people do not contribute their opinions and views, on topics they've never thought about before, or on topics they're embarrassed to talk about, or on topics they regard as confidential, in a group with one or several dominant voices. So some people say too much, others too little.

4) *The moderator's abilities, interests, predilections, and predispositions color or temper the group's response.* Different moderators definitely elicit different things from groups.

We recently observed some groups for a client that used three different moderators. They came to three different conclusions. Perhaps the variety came about because the sample was small or was not representative or because one voice dominated the groups, but in fact one moderator was psychoanalytically oriented, one was consumer-behavior oriented, and the third was simply dumb. Each came to conclusions based on her orientation, training, and background.

5) *Different observers often interpret the same group differently.* A number of years ago, a major packaged goods company (our client) with excess capacity in its potato chip division decided to develop and test fruit flavored potato chips—cherry flavored chips, lime chips, lemon chips, etc. The research director commissioned a large number of focus groups in which people first talked about the concept and then tried samples. He attended some of the sessions and had to watch only two or three to conclude that the concept was an unequivocal flop. Talking about the concept, people tended to grow green, and they became greener after they tried the product.

The research director was dumbfounded about three weeks later when the associate research director's memo summarizing the focus groups suggested that in fact a fruit-flavored potato chip was a wonderful concept that showed great promise. People not only liked the concept, but, after tasting the product, said they would buy it.

He called his associate into his office and said, in effect,

> This is just nutty. I went to some of those focus groups, and people hated the concept. I don't know how you came to this conclusion, but I want you to transcribe all of the comments. Then go through those transcripts yourself with a red and a green felt-tip marker, and any time anyone said anything negative about the concept or the product, underline it in red, and when you find something positive, underline it in green. Then add up the number of comments, and I will demonstrate that that concept isn't worth the time we're giving it.

A week or so later, the associate research director returned with the interesting news that the number of red and green comments were just about equal across the groups.

We suspect that the research director and his associate observed what they wanted to observe, heard what they wanted to hear, and, through a process of selective perception and forgetting, took away from the groups what they brought to them. This is a trap everyone—not just researchers—should avoid.

In twenty years of observing focus groups, we have *learned* something significant from them probably fewer than a dozen times. Usually the focus group reveals what has already been turned up by analyzing copy claims, generating ideas from copywriters, or discussing the situation with corporate management. We cannot think of a single thing a focus group "discovered" that a client eventually adopted.

Focus groups can be helpful when a company wants to explore a topic, obtain some suggestions (or wild ideas), or provoke opinions. They can be an interesting vehicle for picking up the language of consumer behavior—for knowing how people talk about different things. But a company cannot use them to reach any conclusions, to draw any real inferences, or to make any decisions. And we find it frightening that so many companies today are doing just that.

≣ Importance Ratings Establish the Obvious

Attribute benefit research, an attempt to develop positioning and advertising message strategies, has a fifty-year history. Back in the 1940s, the standard approach was to ask people, "What's important?" Consumers would rate a long list of product characteristics on how important these characteristics were to them on a five-point scale, and the items they said were the most important wound up in the positioning statement and in the advertising.

So every beer, cigarette, and soft drink in the country was advertised as having "great taste" since, when asked, people would say that "great taste" was very important. Every headache remedy was "fast acting," every toothpaste would "whiten teeth," and every laxative was "gentle." As everyone who has spent any time in front of a television set recently can attest, this approach to positioning and advertising has continued up to the present.

Importance ratings came out of asking people to rate product features and benefits on whether each is important or not. Interview automobile buyers, for example, asking what's important, and 96 percent will say a car has to have a steering wheel (the other 4 percent don't know George Bush is president), 94 percent say it must have four tires, and 90 percent say it must have a seat, typically one in the front and one in the back.

This may sound silly, but many smaller, less sophisticated marketers make decisions this way. They say, "Let's go out and find out what people think is important." The approach however suffers from several problems.

1) *There are two parts to the equation in predicting consumer behavior: What do consumers want, and what are they getting?* The situation in which consumers want a feature and are getting it is very different from the one in which they want it and are not getting it.

2) *Asking people what's important almost begs for a rational, tangible answer.* Very few people will say, "I bought my Mercedes to impress my neighbors" or "I bought a red sports car because it makes me feel like a sexy young stud again." People say something like, "I bought a Mercedes because its performance is unparalleled in the automobile industry" or "I bought a Miata because Mazdas are so reliable."

Yet as we know, people do buy products for emotional, intangible reasons. If a company bases its positioning or its advertising only on importance ratings, it is liable to miss its mark entirely.

≣ Lost on a Perceptual Map

Here is one way to think of perceptual maps. Imagine we had only the distances between major American cities. We knew that New York is 2,794 miles from Los Angeles, 2,913 miles from Seattle, and 475 miles from Cleveland; that Miami is 2,780 miles from Los Angeles, 3,393 miles from Seattle, 1,266 miles from Cleveland, etc. If we entered all intercity distances into a perceptual mapping program, the computer would draw an approximate map of the United States.

What is the brand counterpart to intercity road distances? Without getting into the technicalities, it's the difference consumers perceive between brands. If they see one brand as expensive and another as cheap, there's a large distance between the two; if they see them both as expensive, there's little distance. In a perceptual mapping exercise, consumers provide ratings data which indicate where, on a grid, they think brands belong. A clever way to map the car industry is to have people park miniature cars in an imaginary parking lot, a board with the axis labeled such as the recently published one on the next page.

To create the map illustrated, the advertising agency asked respondents to rate automobile manufacturers on fifteen image attributes (quality, sporty, technologically advanced, and the like) and to place the cars on the map. According to the executive reporting the research, people *do* see cars in these dimensions—from "affordable younger person's car" to "luxurious, comfortable older person's car" and from "technologically advanced" to "family car." But they might well have chosen other dimensions, from "cheap" to "expensive," and from "dated" to "contemporary," for example.

Where does a Honda Civic go on such a grid? Mercedes? Chevrolet Beretta? We were intrigued by one study we saw in which Saab was positioned relatively alone in the parking lot because people did not

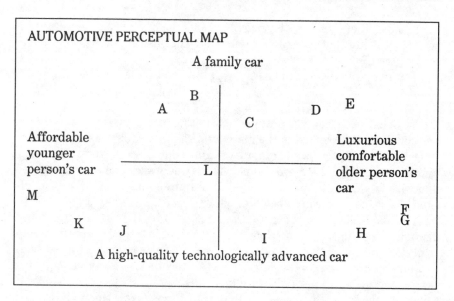

AUTOMOTIVE PERCEPTUAL MAP

A family car

Affordable younger person's car

Luxurious comfortable older person's car

A high-quality technologically advanced car

know where to put it—an imported car, but not upscale like a midsize BMW or Mercedes, not exactly a sports car like Porsche and Miata and Nissan 300ZX. If the company computed the distance between Saab and all other cars, it was farther away from any other automobile.

Researchers like to show marketing managers perceptual maps. They're easy to understand—just two axes with all the competing products assigned to one of the four quadrants. What could be more sexy? But we question the value of perceptual mapping, especially when a company uses it to prescribe a positioning strategy.

The first problem with this method is that the end points on this map are not polar opposites. An affordable younger person's car is not the opposite of the luxurious, comfortable older person's car; a family car is not the opposite of a high-quality technologically advanced car. Therefore anything in between cannot be interpreted.

The second problem is a working assumption that different people walk around with pretty much the same perceptions of brands and products. It assumes that if a research company has fifty people produce fifty perceptual maps and puts them on top of one another, they will all be about the same. That's the technical assumption.

But there is no reason to believe it's true. It contradicts all other forms of marketing research, which assume that people are different. Indeed, if it were true, researchers wouldn't need to do perceptual maps on large groups of people. And so, many perceptual mappers, working as if the assumption were true, then justify doing small-scale research—fifteen, twenty, or thirty people—because they argue they don't need bigger groups. It creates a vicious circle: "I believe it's true, ... therefore I'll act on my belief that it's true, ... and when the results come back, I'll say they're true."

But perceptual maps have other problems, such as the following:

Q. Why are there only two dimensions?

A. Because to communicate to marketing management, people who are generally not trained in the mathematics of mapping, researchers are forced to explain the brands in a two-dimensional framework. The mapping exercise becomes more complicated if the brands are shown in three dimensions, and if the perceptual space requires four, five, or six dimensions, most managers are absolutely bewildered.

Yet, when we do a perceptual mapping study, the researchers often discover "back in the kitchen," as they're concocting the report, that they really require four, five, six or more dimensions to explain differences in consumer perceptions between products. Recognizing they cannot present these incomprehensible results to management, they transform—some would say distort—the data to force everything into two dimensions. It's easy to show two dimensions on a flat piece of paper or screen during a presentation.

Q. Can the two forced dimensions really be interpreted?

A. Perhaps in some cases, yes; in others, no. Sometimes the researchers don't know how to interpret them. We once did a study among heavy beer drinkers for a major brewer who requested a perceptual map. When we finished the study and had the map, we did not know what it meant. We hired a top academic consultant—a perceptual mapping expert—and he didn't know what it meant. In desperation, we built a Tinker Toy model of the beer category and held four focus groups (one each night for four nights straight) among heavy beer drinkers. All week we sat around after work eating sandwiches, drinking beer, looking at the model, and having the beer drinkers talk about it. All we accomplished for the week was making about forty beer drinkers tipsy. We knew less about what the map meant after the sessions than before.

Q. Is there any evidence that a positioning change based on a perceptual mapping study improved sales?

A. None, despite a twenty-five-year history of application.

A company can use perceptual mapping to obtain some insight into where consumers place a product or brand and to see how it relates to other products. This is interesting *descriptive* information. Even if the perceptual map study cannot generalize the characteristics because of all the problems—lack of representative sample, sample sizes, and all the rest—as a simple description of how competing products are perceived, the map, as primitive as it may be, can serve a purpose. But maps are nothing a sensible management would use to make a marketing decision. *Description* is one thing; *prescription* is something else.

When a company uses perceptual mapping for *prescriptive* purposes—when management begins to draw inferences concerning the future based on the procedure—the results could be catastrophic. Knowing where a brand is right now cannot tell you where it ought to be.

≣ Problem Detection Doesn't Detect Some Problems

To overcome problems endemic to focus groups, importance ratings, and perceptual mapping, marketers have attempted to develop new technologies to learn what is really important to the consumer.

The Batton, Barton, Durstin & Osborne advertising agency (now BBDO International and part of Omnicom) has a very simple but powerful credo developed in the mid-1960s: Know your prospect; know your prospect's problems; know your product and how it can relate to the problems; and break the boredom barrier.

But until around 1970, BBDO, like every other agency, had no way to actually learn how to know the prospect's problems and how to overcome them. The credo, like so many advertising platitudes, was a nice, interesting wish, but not anything the agency could easily act on.

In the early 1970s, BBDO developed a methodology called "Problem Detection" to identify the consumer's problems. The agency believed—and still does—that a positioning based on importance ratings runs several risks.

Attributes and benefits nearly always return to the product's essential function, to those attributes and benefits that give the product category a right to exist and that represent the standards to which every product in the category must, in the consumer's eyes, comply. So an analgesic must relieve pain; a refrigerator must preserve food; a television set must show a picture; and a toothpaste must whiten teeth. Claims like these are unlikely to encourage the consumer to switch brands, since the positioning offers no attribute or benefit not already present in the brand the consumer uses currently.

Also, when a company asks consumers to name product attributes and benefits they consider to be important, they usually parrot what they have learned from advertising they have heard or seen. Ask enough consumers about toothpaste, for example, and the company will record all other advertising claims as respondents merely repeat what other advertisers have been telling them to say. Just as consumers in focus groups do not produce original insights, consumers can rarely think up important product attributes about what marketing and advertising specialists do not already know.

Consumers *can* tell the specialists, however, about their problems—problems they have had with the product or a brand or both.

In 1970 BBDO, New York, developed a research method to identify a consumer's problems with a particular product, and within a few years, the technique was adopted by researchers around the globe. The agency defined *problem* as a frequently occurring, bothersome source of dissatisfaction. Ideally the agency identifies a solution to the problem that preempts competitive brands. That is, the agency identifies a solution the brand's competitors do not offer, or which, at the very least, is a solution the consumer does not feel the brand's competitors are claiming to offer.

Problem detection begins with an extensive list of possible problems. This first phase is critical, since it is necessary to develop as long a list as possible. The longer the list, the better the study. While a company can obtain problems from retailers, wholesalers, the advertising agency, researchers, and company employees, it will often conduct focus groups or individual in-depth interviews during which consumers, in their own words, express the full range (or rage) of dissatisfaction with the product or service. This phase ends with a list of at least sixty to eighty problems but often as many as 150 to 200 or more.

The next phase determines which of the problems are really important to the prime prospects and offer real opportunities for the company. To obtain this information, researchers ask 200 or more prospects about each problem:

- How often does it occur? (Frequency)
- How much does it irritate you when it occurs? (Bothersomeness)
- In your opinion, which of these items are already being used as advertising claims by other brands or products? (Preemptibility)

Researchers calculate each problem's value by combining the three measures into a single score. The bigger the score, the bigger the opportunity.

Here's an abbreviated example provided by BBDO from the dog food category. The agency employed two different procedures to ask about attributes and problems. We've summarized the most important results from the questionnaires, arranged in the sequence by which consumers ranked the attributes and problems:

DOG FOOD CHARACTERISTICS RANKED BY ATTRIBUTES

Most important attributes	Ranking based on importance ratings	Ranking based on problem-detection
Well-balanced diet	1	18
Nutritive value	2	20
Must contain vitamins	3	23
Dog must like the taste	4	14
Easy to prepare	5	26

These five attributes are all claims dog food advertisements generally stress and they are generic to all dog foods (or they were when the research was conducted). Although consumers think a dog food must offer a well-balanced diet, diet does not appear to be perceived as a very important problem. An advertiser who promotes these five important attributes will not differentiate his brand from another. Furthermore, the high-scoring importance attributes are all good from the dog's point of view. But dogs don't buy dog food.

When the agency used problem detection to identify the problems with dog food, it obtained a list of the dog owner's problems rather than a list of the dog's problems. Here's what was found:

DOG FOOD CHARACTERISTICS RANKED BY PROBLEMS

Most important attributes	Ranking based on importance ratings	Ranking based on problem-detection
Too expensive	19	1
Smells nasty	16	2
No suitable quantities	34	3
The dog's teeth are dirty	17	4
Dog has nothing to chew on	40	5

These problems can help to differentiate one brand from its competitors. (They may also suggest new products or line extensions.) By positioning the brand with one or more of these attributes, such as low price or pleasant aroma, the advertiser gives the consumer a reason to prefer the brand.

Whenever a marketer has completed a problem-detection study, he or she knows which problems are really critical to the company's target market. The marketer evaluates the problem with the highest score and the ten or twenty top problems, and then studies the company's product to learn whether it can solve (or be modified to solve) a high-scoring problem.

Although problem-detection methodology can help a marketer identify problems associated with a product's tangible characteristics, it has two major weaknesses. First, it seriously underestimates the power of intangible, emotional attributes and benefits. Firms using this technique realized this failure when they began to apply it to product categories driven by intangible, emotional copy stories—soft drinks, perfume, cigarettes, alcoholic beverages, and others. These are all product categories in which problem detection fails to reveal the true power of emotional positioning strategies.

The second problem is that it totally misses positioning strategies that are "prices of entry" into the product category, things a brand must do before it can be taken seriously. A new dog food, for example, must be reasonably well-balanced and good tasting to be purchased at all. If it can do more than this, that's terrific. But problem detection focuses on "the things it would be nice for a product to have" and ignores "the things it must have."

≣ Choice Modeling: A Regression to the Past

The latest fad in marketing research is choice modeling. Like most fads in the industry, it will die when marketers discover that it doesn't work. Such a choice modeling effort begins when a new Ph.D. in marketing science waxes poetic about a new statistical model that can predict brand choice.

Encouraged by this news, marketing or agency researchers then interview a cross-section of consumers (or industrial buyers) and have them rate each of the competing brands in the category on a set of eight to twenty different attributes and benefits. Consumers then rate each of these brands in terms of purchase probability. The model (which goes by the name of *multinomial logit analysis*) then finds which attributes and benefits are most predictive of brand choice. The winning attributes and benefits, of course, are touted as likely candidates for a positioning strategy.

This approach, as it turns out, can lead marketers in the "death wish" direction for a number of reasons.

The first problem with this approach, like problem detection, is that it assumes rational decision making. Suppose the consumer can shop at one of three supermarkets. The A&P is a mile from the house, has the widest selection of products and brands, and generally the highest prices. Kroger's is five miles from the house, has the best quality meats and produce, and moderate prices. The Pathmark is ten miles from the house, has an average selection and average quality, but the lowest prices. Where will the consumer shop?

Obviously that's unanswerable (or the answer is, "It depends"), but ask the question in a research project and people will try to answer it. But asking the question assumes that the consumer, before setting out to shop, will weigh distance, prices, selection, quality, and every other factor to come up with a rational decision.

Choice modeling assumes high-involvement consumer behavior. It assumes, to change the context slightly, that people standing at the checkout line are making tradeoffs between Life Savers and Chiclets. And yet we know that most people make most decisions almost impulsively. Some people shop at the A&P (or wherever) because that's where their mothers shopped. Or they shop at the Grand Union because it's on the way to the bank.

The difficulty here is that the very process of giving the consumers choices forces them to think about the different alternatives, to be rational. This is not what happens most of the time. People do not think through the various alternatives (indeed, few people are aware of all the alternatives), and they make their decisions without weighing the pros and cons of each possibility. Because consumers don't choose rationally, any research that forces rational answers has to be flawed.

A second problem is that choice modeling assumes that the set of attributes and benefits employed to rate each of the brands represents the full range of reasons—tangible and emotional—that might explain brand preference, and that buyers can and will rate the less rational, emotional characteristics with the same reliability and validity that they rate the tangible ones.

The third and most damaging problem is that this aggregate level approach assumes that a correlation between attribute-benefit ratings and brand choice is *causally* rather than *casually* related to buyer behavior (an assumption most researchers rejected more than a decade ago). The tool begins to smell of radical empiricism when such correlations are assumed to offer *prescriptive* insight—that they can be used to forecast the future.

At best, choice modeling is 1960s postdictive regression (backcasting the past) masquerading as a breakthrough technology that can be employed to forecast the future. That's why we call it a "regression to the past."

≣ Gap Analysis Has a Large Hole in It

Recently we visited a major metropolitan newspaper that was undergoing extensive editorial changes—layout, design, story length, coverage, organization. The company's research director told us these were the most comprehensive changes in the paper's hundred-year history.

"Interesting," we said. "What are you basing the changes on?"

"We've taken more than a year and spent over $100,000 on an exhaustive gap analysis among readers and nonreaders. We know exactly what gaps exist in this market," said the director proudly.

We did not have the heart to tell him that if the $100,000 had found any gaps, it was only by accident and that the editorial changes might well alienate more readers than they attract. Here's how gap analysis works, and why managers draw correct conclusions from it only by accident.*

Gap analysis starts with a list of determinant attributes—a product's or brand's characteristics that lead the consumer to buy that item rather than another. For an attribute to be determinant, the buyer must consider it important *and* it must be available. Until automobile manufacturers began installing air bags, for example, it made no difference that some consumers said that air bags were an important safety feature. Car buyers correctly saw their alternatives as undifferentiated, at least in terms of air bags. This important attribute could not determine the consumer's choice.

Once car makers began introducing models with air bags, those prospects who considered them an important safety attribute now had a differentiated product that might influence their automobile choice. If this feature did affect a decision, an air bag became a "determinant" attribute for these buyers.

Gap analysis research asks:

- What attributes and benefits do people say they want or need in a product or service?
- How well does the product or service they currently use fill these needs?
- Are there any gaps between what people want and their satisfaction with the product they currently use? Such a gap, says the theory, may be an opportunity to reposition an established product or to create a new product that fills these needs more closely.

To determine the gaps, researchers first list a product or service's

---

*The authors want to thank Dr. Kathryn Britney for her contribution to this discussion of gap and critical attribute analysis.

characteristics that might be important to existing customers or potential customers or both. One commonly used scheme identifies characteristics that relate to tangible and intangible attributes and benefits. Here's an example of the kinds of characteristics that might be included in a study of a sporty new car:

SPORTY NEW CAR ATTRIBUTES AND BENEFITS

	Attributes	*Benefits*
Tangible	Removable hard top	Like two cars in one
	Short-throw, five-speed transmission	Better engine efficiency
	Two seats	More fun to drive
	Tonneau cover	Protects interior from weather
	Rear spoiler	Gives aerodynamic performance
	Headrest speakers	Improved stereo sound
Intangible	Manufacturer known for quality	Believe car won't break down
	Selected as Motor Trend "Car of the Year"	Makes you feel smart for buying it
	Distinctive design	Everyone will look at it and envy you
	Pace car at Indianapolis 500	Feel like a race car driver
	Sporty, youthful design	Recapture your youth
	Looks more expensive than it is	Reward yourself without going broke

Depending on the product or service being examined, researchers will generate a list of 20 to 200 tangible and intangible attributes and benefits. To be successful, the list must include all attributes and benefits that consumers believe are important. To identify all the attributes and benefits the gap analysis should test, therefore, researchers often conduct individual in-depth and focus group interviews with existing or potential users.

Out of all this comes a questionnaire listing all possible attributes and benefits, items such as,

- A good value for the money
- Sporty-looking
- Driver's side air bag
- A five-speed manual transmission

- A 36-month, 50,000-mile warranty

And on and on and on.

Respondents indicate how important each attribute and benefit is (whether currently available or not) and then indicate how well the product they currently use performs in terms of the attributes.

Typically, gap analysis employs either the mean or the percentage of respondents who had ratings in the "top two boxes" for each attribute and benefit; that is, they gave a 4 or a 5 on a five-point scale where 5 was "most important."* Here is a typical, if drastically truncated, example of the tables to which a CEO is likely to be exposed. (We are making up the attributes and the figures here, but the process is genuine.)

MEAN IMPORTANCE AND EVALUATION SCORES FOR A SPORTY CAR

Attributes	Importance rating	Evaluation rating	Gap
Steering wheel	4.8	4.7	0.1
Headrest speakers	4.5	4.0	0.5
Removable hard top	4.3	2.0	2.3
Antilock braking system	2.5	2.5	0.0
Tonneau cover	2.0	1.0	1.0

This table indicates that people say a steering wheel is very important to them (on a five-point scale, the mean score was 4.7), but it also indicates that, for the most part, their current car has a steering wheel that gives them what they want (the mean evaluation score was also 4.7).

To find the gaps, one simply subtracts the evaluation score from the importance score. The larger the gap, the larger the opportunity.

At the risk of redundancy, here's another version of the same information:

TOP TWO BOX IMPORTANCE AND EVALUATION RATINGS FOR A SPORTY CAR

Attributes	Importance rating	Evaluation rating	Gap
Steering wheel	96%	95%	1%
Headrest speakers	82	75.	7
Removable hard top	80	60	20
Antilock braking system	50	50	0
Tonneau cover	30	15	15

*When "means" (i.e., averages) are used, the technique is often called "grid analysis," following a paper by Martilla and James in the *Journal of Marketing*.

In this example, the importance ratings represent the percentage of the respondents who rated the attributes as "extremely" or "very" important—that is, the top two boxes on a five-point scale. The evaluation ratings are the proportion of respondents who rated the current brand's performance to be "excellent" or "very good."

In traditional gap analysis, the third column indicates what "gaps" exist in the market. In these two tables, the greatest gap exists for a removable hard top (2.3 or 20 percent), followed by a tonneau cover (1.0 or 15 percent), then headrest speakers (0.5 or 7 percent). *There is no gap for antilock braking.*

Typically at this point, the researchers would schedule a meeting to present the findings to marketing management, concluding that a removable hard top presents the best new product or positioning opportunity. A tonneau cover or headrest speakers might offer some possibility, and attributes such as a steering wheel or antilock braking system seem to present no opportunity for either a new product or repositioning an old.

Unfortunately, these conclusions will be correct only some of the time. Worse, there's no way to know which time they are correct.

The mistake underlying the analytical technique in traditional gap analysis (a not uncommon fallacy in market research) is that it takes data on *individuals*, converts it to *aggregate* numbers—that is, it adds them together, and then uses these aggregates (the mean figures or percentages) to draw conclusions about *individuals*. Aggregate means and percentages, however, do not necessarily reflect individual behavior; they *may* but they don't necessarily.

In the example we've just shown, let's see how this fallacy can work. Assume the following is the "truth" for the fourth attribute, a car with an antilock braking system:

- Everyone who *wants* antilock brakes in a sporty car knows their current car does not provide it.
- Everyone who knows their current car brand does provide antilock braking does not consider the feature to be important. (Although we are rigging the numbers to make a point, the example is not unrealistic.)

The table on the next page represents this situation.

The table shows that while exactly half the people sampled consider antilock braking in a sporty car to be important, none feel their current car model provides it adequately; these are the people in quadrant 1. (The marginals, which we add across and down, show we've accounted for everybody.)

INDIVIDUALS WITH DIFFERENT IMPORTANCE-PERFORMANCE RATINGS FOR ANTILOCK BRAKING

Evaluation of current product and service ratings	Importance ratings		
	Extremely or very	Neutral to not at all	Marginals
Good, fair, or poor	50% (Quadrant 1)	0% (Quadrant 2)	50%
Excellent or very good	0% (Quadrant 3)	50% (Quadrant 4)	50%
Marginals	50%	50%	100%

Also, of the 50 percent who indicated antilock braking in a sporty car is *not* important to them, all feel their current car provides it adequately; these are the people in quadrant 4.

This table shows a significant safety "gap" exists for half the market. The company is not currently delivering a safety-related product or service attribute (specifically antilock-brakes) that half of the market considers important—obviously is a potential market opportunity. But traditional gap analysis masks this opportunity by concluding there is no "gap" in the attribute of a sporty car with antilock brakes. In this case, and it is not as far-fetched as one might imagine, the opportunities the researchers reported to marketing management using traditional gap analysis—go for the removable hardtop, then the tonneau cover, then the headrest speakers—would have been totally misleading.

But that's not the only way the analysis can go wrong. Traditional gap analysis would indicate that a tonneau cover leaves little opportunity for improvement since only 30 percent of the sample respondents said it is important to them and 15 percent say they obtain it from their current car. The truth might look like this:

INDIVIDUALS WITH DIFFERENT IMPORTANCE AND PERFORMANCE RATINGS FOR A TONNEAU COVER

Evaluation of current product and service ratings	Importance ratings		
	Extremely or very	Neutral to not at all	Marginals
Good, fair, or poor	30% (Quadrant 1)	55% (Quadrant 2)	85%
Excellent or very good	0% (Quadrant 3)	15% (Quadrant 4)	15%
Marginals	30%	70%	100%

This table indicates a potential marketing opportunity far greater than the aggregate analysis indicated. The 30 percent of the respondents who consider a tonneau cover to be important are all currently buying a car they say does not provide one; again, these are the people in quadrant 1.

The 15 percent of the respondents who feel their current car satisfactorily provides a tonneau cover, those in quadrant 4, do not consider this characteristic to be important, and their responses reduce the gap to 15 percent.

As we saw earlier, traditional gap analysis suggested a smaller market opportunity for a removable hardtop than is in fact the case. Depending on management's cutoff point—"We don't want to look into any gap smaller than 17.5 percent"—this might well have meant a misguided decision to halt any further investigation into tonneau covers. But most managements, learning that 30 percent of the company's prospects consider a feature important and are not getting it, would do something about the situation.

Managements usually presume that if a gap is exceptionally small, it just doesn't represent much business. This judgment or cutoff point varies by industry. A tobacco company interested in a new cigarette that found a 17.5 percent gap would be delighted because in that category a 1 percent share is a very successful cigarette brand.

But for Coca-Cola, with a 28 percent market share, finding a 17.5 percent gap would be like the Democratic Party, with two out of three registered voters, finding a gap smaller than the 50 percent they need to win an election, going with it, and losing the election.

(As an aside, that's a problem for the Democrats. Every four years they jump on gaps smaller than the number they need to win the presidential election, and so they've been losing.)

Researchers who analyze aggregate data in traditional gap analysis will reach correct conclusions only by accident. Sometimes they're right, sometimes they're wrong, but all of the time there is no way to tell the difference.

When dealing with percentages—rather than mean scores—as the aggregate importance ratings move from the extremes (that is, from 1 percent or 100 percent toward 50 percent), the potential for traditional gap analysis to mislead increases. The biggest problem a company could have is finding exactly half the prospects want the feature and half are already getting it—a zero gap. But if half the company's prospects want a feature they're not getting, this is a huge opportunity for the firm—or a competitor.

≣ Quadrant Analysis: Better, But Still Inadequate

To overcome the problems of problem detection and gap analysis, we invented an approach in the mid-1970s we labeled *quadrant analysis* to help identify powerful positioning statements.

Quadrant analysis investigates the relationship between what people say is important and how they rate the product or service they prefer or use most regularly. The analysis isolates each respondent simultaneously on the two dimensions of importance and performance, the same thing we've talked about in gap analysis. Researchers typically examine 20 to 100 different attributes and benefits, and divide the sample into high versus low importance scores, and high versus low performance ratings.

These produce 2 x 2 tables or four quadrants for each attribute or benefit and the percentage of people falling into each. In the earlier sporty car example there would be five cross-tabulations, one for each of the attribute factors, steering wheel through removable hardtop. Such a table for the removable hardtop looks like this:

QUADRANT ANALYSIS FOR A REMOVABLE HARDTOP

Evaluation of current product and service ratings	Importance ratings	
	Extremely or very	*Somewhat to to not at all*
Good, fair, or poor	Major problem (Quadrant 1)	Small problem (Quadrant 2)
Excellent or very good	Modest problem (Quadrant 3)	No problem (Quadrant 4)

This table indicates that the people in quadrant 1 rate this removable hardtop as "extremely" or "very" important and feel that their current car on this attribute is only "good," "fair," or "poor." The people in quadrant 4 rate the attribute as "somewhat" or "not at all" important and, moreover, feel their current car's performance is "excellent" or "very good."

Based on tabulations for each attribute (and remember, a real study may be looking at 200 or more), the next step is to identify whether or not there are any "gaps" that suggest market opportunities for new products or services, or weaknesses in current product and service positioning. One approach is to rank order the attributes in terms of the quadrant 1 percentage of respondents. That is, rank the attributes by the percentage of people who feel the attribute is important *but is not* being delivered by the brand they currently use.

One could think of the people in this quadrant as indicating the problem they experience. In this respect, quadrant analysis and problem detection—two methodologically different procedures—produce similar results. If a dog food study reveals that terrible-smelling food is a big problem, then quadrant analysis among the same people will show that a large percentage of people who want decent-smelling dog food aren't getting it. Indeed, in our experience, the correlation between tangible problems measured using these two technologies is often 0.9 or higher—in other words virtually the same.

The next step in quadrant analysis is to test potential market response to products or services with those attributes heading the list. A company typically does this using concept testing techniques, which corroborate whether the "gaps" between what some people want and what they perceive they're getting truly indicates alternative new product or new positioning options. Concept testing also suggests how great the possible consumer response might be if the firm were to solve the consumer's problem by offering a new product or by repositioning a current product with this attribute or benefit.

To perform such a test, we show a concept statement to the original study's respondents or to new respondents who answer the original study's questions in the same way so they can be classified in the appropriate quadrant (they want the attribute but they're not getting it). The concept statement describes the product or service and contains the attribute being tested.

Using an 11-point "intention-to-buy" scale (discussed in detail in Chapter 6) to indicate their market response, one would expect the quadrant 1 respondents to have the highest proportion of respondents who exhibit a positive intention-to-buy a new product that promises this attribute. These, after all, are the people who said the attribute was important and said they were not satisfied with it.

At the other extreme, one would expect the quadrant 4 respondents would have the smallest proportion of respondents who would react positively to the new product and service concept. These are the people who said the attribute was unimportant and reported they were satisfied with the attribute.

This is exactly what we see in Figure 5.1.

The line indicates that as the magnitude of the problem grows in the consumer's mind, the consumer's intention to buy increases dramatically. This is exactly what one would expect. In our experience, the market response for the four quadrants is monotone, though not linear—that is, the line goes up, but it's not straight. The empirical evidence comes from twenty-four experimental studies in which we compared people's location in the four quadrants to their self-reported purchase probability for a new or repositioned product. Not surprisingly, the bigger the problem, the greater the market response.

What is surprising in this figure, however, and something we see in similar analyses across a broad range of product categories, is the mod-

Figure 5.1 *Expected Market Response Curve for a New Product Concept*

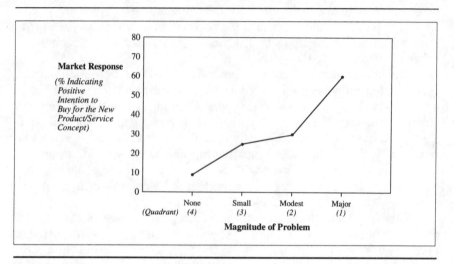

est difference in market response between people in the small (quadrant 3) and the moderate (quadrant 4) categories.

Basically we find that if consumers are "very" or "extremely" interested in a particular product attribute and perceive that attribute as being delivered very well or extremely well by a product they currently use, then they are still more interested in a new product that promises to solve the problem better than are consumers who are dissatisfied but do not particularly care about that product benefit.

In other words, if people have a big problem and it's not being solved, the product that promises to solve it will win their business. If people have a big need and a product they currently use *is* solving it, a product that promises to solve it more effectively *may* win their business. (Of course, this may simply mean positioning an existing product differently to highlight a benefit the product already has.)

If people are buying products to solve their problems, then the bigger the problem a company can solve, the more likely it is to earn someone's business. The better the technology the company has for uncovering people's problems, the more likely the company should be to predict future consumer behavior if it can solve the problem.

Despite the simple appeal of quadrant analysis and its widespread use in the industry, however, it shares a major problem with problem detection: It fails to reveal the power of critical intangible attributes and benefits.

Earlier we discussed the problems of importance ratings. The problems do not go away when we couple them to performance ratings in quadrant analysis. That is, people simply will not rate emotional attributes and benefits as important as they really are. Ask people how important a 50,000-mile, five-year warranty is for a car, and they'll tell you it is very important. Ask them how important it is that they impress their neighbors when they drive the new car home, and relatively few will admit that it is important at all.

Because the importance ratings component of quadrant analysis underestimates the true motivating power of intangible, emotional attributes and benefits, it is unlikely that the technique will reveal their true value. And without them, we are liable to miss entirely a powerful positioning opportunity.

Since quadrant analysis does not answer all the questions we want answered, there has to be yet a better way to determine a product's positioning.

≣ The Strategic Cube Identifies the Intangibles

Cube analysis is, we believe, the answer for clean-slate marketers. The cube is even more helpful than quadrant analysis in identifying tangible product characteristics and is less inclined to underestimate the power of intangible attributes.

A strategic cube analysis begins with the same audit of tangible and intangible attributes and benefits illustrated on page 101. The more the better; the company wants an exhaustive list that goes far beyond the me-too strategies that generally fill the marketplace. Ideally, the list includes creative, thought-provoking, innovative attributes and benefits—things like "a motor tuned to a throaty growl," "short-throw manual shift," "four-wheel double-wishbone suspension," "razor-sharp handling," and "no-deductible, 'bumper-to-bumper' warranty."

If the company obtains such a list, its problem becomes a good one to have: there may be too many ideas, and the strategic cube helps reduce the number of attributes and benefits to a more manageable set. Strategic cube analysis estimates the motivating power of each of approximately 75 to 100 rational and emotional attributes and benefits.

The methodology identifies those that are highly motivating, that are credible, and that are preemptible versus the competition.

One benefit of this research is that it overcomes the problems associated with the traditional approaches we've been describing. Unlike importance ratings, for example, the strategic cube doesn't overstate the importance of generic and rational features.

Strategic cube research illustrates each attribute and benefit with a visual stimulus—typically a photograph—and asks people how desirable each attribute or benefit is to them. Psychologists call this an *affective measure*. The research then supplements these self-reports by two other analyses—a *cognitive measure* (based on each individual's gap between attribute and benefit desirability and the performance of their current brand) and a *behavioral measure* (based on correlations for each respondent attribute ratings with product preference)—to construct a new measure of motivating power. The goal is to learn what the consumer thinks is desirable, whether what is desirable is addressed by their current product, and whether that attribute or benefit is linked with product preference behavior.

The research examines the three dimensions of motivation—affective, cognitive, and behavioral, perceptions of product performance, and perceptions of competitor performance—simultaneously, and it does so for every individual respondent. A strategic cube positioning study asks approximately 200 or more prospects in a particular product category to rate each of approximately 50 to 100 visual and verbal stimuli on a nine-point desirability scale like this:

```
DESIRABILITY SCALE

    9)  Extremely desirable
    8)  Very desirable
    7)  Somewhat desirable
    6)  Slightly desirable
    5)  Neither desirable nor undesirable
    4)  Slightly undesirable
    3)  Somewhat undesirable
    2)  Very undesirable
    1)  Extremely undesirable
```

We have talked about five-point scales, the most common scale in gap analysis, and suddenly here's a nine-point scale (not to be confused with the eleven-point purchase probability scale). In fact, the nine-point *is* the five-point scale (points 5 to 9) with the negative possibilities added (points 1 to 4). We do this because we want to measure attributes or benefits that may be negatively motivating.

Market researchers rarely do this. They seldom use a scale with negative choices, and as a result the traditional five-point scale often underestimates what is happening. Some consumers, for example, may feel turned off by the small size of the Miata two-seat sports car. If Mazda, therefore, had done a traditional study with the five-point scale, they might have learned that Miata's two-seat size was not particularly motivating, since the worst anyone could have rated the feature was as "Not desirable." By using the nine-point scale, they might have found some consumers rating the feature "Extremely undesirable." (We have no idea whether Mazda did any research of this type or not; we are simply using the Miata as an illustration.)

If we do a study for a company that tells us all the characteristics to be measured represent shades of positive affect for everybody, then we use the simpler scale. But if the company tells us this is a product category in which the attributes some people want may turn other people off, we want a measuring instrument that taps into both. A car, for example, that can accelerate from zero to 60 M.P.H. in under eight seconds is very appealing to some people but very disconcerting to others. The research should be able to measure both reactions.

Why use a desirability scale rather than an importance measure?

People tend to report intangible attributes and benefits as being more appealing when they answer on a desirability scale than when they answer on an importance measure. If you ask, "How important is it that the next automobile you buy impress your brother-in-law?" people tend to say it's not very important. If you ask, "How desirable is it that the next automobile you buy impress your brother-in-law?" some people will say it's "somewhat desirable." Couple this phrase with a picture, and people may even report that it's "very desirable."

Importance (and verbal stimulus) implies rationality. People want to give the most rational response. They want to give a response they think the researcher wants to hear, a response they think will make them look smarter in the interviewer's eyes. *Desirability* is a less loaded word; add a visual, and the combination lets them be free to do whatever they want to do.

If we were studying a product category like ball bearings and working under the assumption the decision to buy or not is wholly rational, it would not make any difference whether we used an importance or a desirability scale. Yet while business-to-business selling tends to be more rational, it's not completely. The personality of the salesperson, the trust the customer feels in the salesperson, the seeming enthusiasm servicing the account, the way the support staff makes the customer look smart in front of the boss—these are all intangibles that affect the selection of many industrial products.

But in product categories that are heavily marketed and are driven by tangibles and intangibles, desirability and visual stimuli work better than importance ratings. Given that the turn-ons for some people are turn-offs for others, going with this symmetric scale as opposed to the traditional five-point scale works better.

Once consumers have rated the 75 to 100 attributes and benefits (or more) on this desirability scale, they then rate the company's product and its competitors' products on each of the same characteristics in terms of product performance or image using this five-point scale (fill in the blank with the name of the product category):

PERFORMANCE/IMAGE SCALE

5) Describes this_____ completely.
4) Describes this_____ very much.
3) Describes this_____ somewhat.
2) Describes this_____ slightly.
1) Doesn't describe this_____ at all.

The resulting measure of motivating power employs three underlying dimensions of attitude—the affective, the cognitive, and the behavioral (see Fig. 5.2). The affective component is simply the self-reported desirability, how desirable the feature or benefit is to the individual.

The cognitive component is the gap between buyer desires and product performance.

But we attempt to go beyond people's reports of what they want by probing beneath the surface to discover what they really want, an analysis done by correlating brand and image characteristics with actual behavior for each respondent—the behavioral component.

Figure 5.2 *Three-Dimensional Model of Motivation*

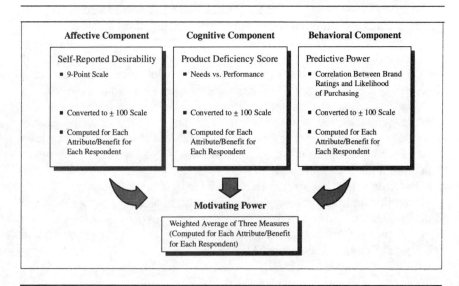

If a study has 800 people and 60 attributes and benefits, this involves 48,000 different analyses. The computer scales each of these measures from zero to +100 for positive motivation or –100 for negative motivation (sometimes called *demotivation* or *repellence*). Finally, the computer weights each measure to construct an overall measure of motivating power for *each* attribute and benefit for *each* respondent.

To indicate how these measures of "motivating power" can be used, consider five different effects in the automotive field:

AUTOMOBILE CHARACTERISTIC MOTIVATING POWER

Type of effect	Example
High positive	"Automobile that makes you feel younger than you really are."
Low positive	"Automobile that is economical to drive."
Neutral	"Automobile with air bags on driver side."
Low negative	"Automobile with a four-cylinder engine."
High negative	"Automobile with a reputation for unreliability."

In strategic cube analyses, we group the two "high" effects—both positive and negative—together and label them "high" in motivating power. Likewise, we group the two low effects, and label them, for lack of a more scintillating term, "moderate" in motivating power. Finally, the neutral effects, the attributes and benefits that neither attract nor repel, are labeled "low" in motivating power.

This technique examines where each attribute and benefit falls for each respondent individually. Benefit 2 in Figure 5.3, for example, captures the "Ponce de Léon" effect; it promises to "make you feel younger than you really are." Let's look at an individual example. For 57-year-old George T. Jones, this is "high" in motivating power, "high" in perception of client performance, and "low" in perceptions of competitive performance.

The strategic cube is both a means of looking at different attributes and benefits in a product category and a measurement methodology. By examining the motivating power and perceptions of a company's product or service and competitive products simultaneously, the cube reveals insights into promising positioning strategies. Attributes and benefits that are high in motivating power and where the company's product enjoys an edge over the competition represent wonderful opportunities for positioning and for message strategies.

To the extent that consumers are increasingly unable to differentiate competing brands in the same category by way of product function and imagery, companies have a positioning problem. The major difficulty today is that more and more brands are communicating the same posi-

Figure 5.3 *Microlevel Analysis: Respondent George T. Jones, Age 57*

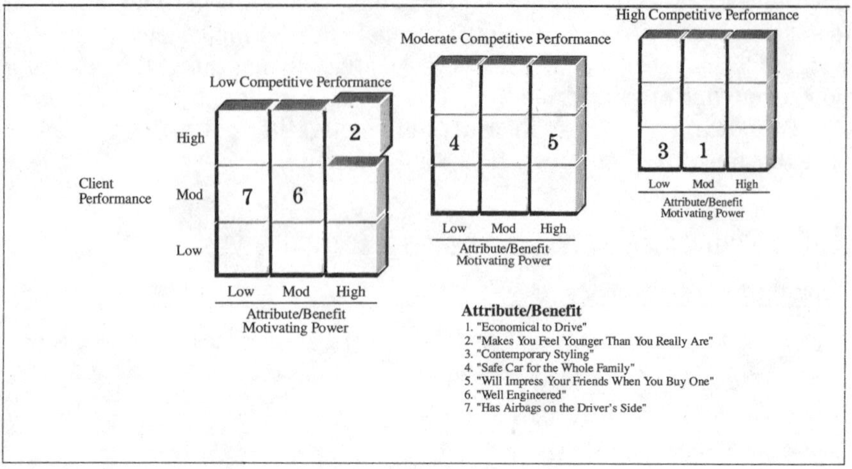

High Competitive Performance

Moderate Competitive Performance

Low Competitive Performance

Client Performance

High

Mod

Low

Low   Mod   High

Attribute/Benefit
Motivating Power

2

7   6

4   5

Low   Mod   High

Attribute/Benefit
Motivating Power

3   1

Low   Mod   High

Attribute/Benefit
Motivating Power

Attribute/Benefit
1. "Economical to Drive"
2. "Makes You Feel Younger Than You Really Are"
3. "Contemporary Styling"
4. "Safe Car for the Whole Family"
5. "Will Impress Your Friends When You Buy One"
6. "Well Engineered"
7. "Has Airbags on the Driver's Side"

tioning; it is just hard to separate them. If we took Pepsi Cola's advertising and slapped Coke on it, we'd bet no one would know the difference—an interesting test that could be applied to most product categories.

Worse are brands, that in an effort to differentiate themselves, move away from the core, essential positionings that made them great, and begin to work on secondary or even tertiary claims. Instead of the frozen lasagna which is based on Mama Italiano's family recipe, it's the frozen lasagna which has the magic dial that tells you when the product is cooked. The fact is, people are much more interested in the famous recipe, but we've moved away from that and are talking about peripheral things like the packaging.

Since positioning involves the packaging, distribution, pricing, advertising, point-of-purchase material—everything about the product—the basic issue is: what does a company want to communicate about its product to its prospective audiences—not just the ultimate consumers, but the distributors who will stock the product, the retailers who will sell it, and the person who will buy it? When marketing executives think of positioning, they generally think in terms of advertising, but that's much too narrow.

At the end of a positioning study, a company would like to have the sort of blueprint for action illustrated in Figure 5.4. The motivating power extends from low to high and the company versus the competition extends from superior to inferior.

Ideally we'd like to find ourselves in the upper left hand box with an immediate positioning opportunity. Not only is the item high in motivating power—in styling, in price, in clarity, in taste, in softness, in what-

Figure 5.4 *Blueprint for Action*

		Client versus Competition			
			Parity		
		Client Superior	Both Excel	Neither Excels	Client Inferior
Motivating Power	High	Immediate Positioning Opportunity: ■ Enhance	Price of Entry ■ Maintain	Potential Opportunity for Someone ■ New Product?	Key Weakness ■ Fix If Possible
	Low	Potential Positioning Opportunity ■ Increase Salience?	Over Investment ■ Cut Costs	No Action	No Action

ever counts—but our product is superior. All we have to do is enhance our superiority.

More usually, we find ourselves in one of the two middle boxes; both we and the competition excel, or neither one of us does. If we both do, we have to maintain the positioning to keep the price of entry high to potential competitors. If neither we nor the competition excel—if all portable computers weigh more than 20 pounds—there's an opportunity for a new product.

If we're in the top right box, and our prices, for example, are too high, or we're not offering a key feature, we have to fix it.

Perhaps the most interesting place to find ourselves is in the lower left hand box. We have a benefit that is low in motivating power, but we are superior. This is an opportunity to increase the importance of the benefit. Until Frank Perdue came along, the brand name on a package of chicken had very little motivating power. Now it does, and Frank Perdue is a wealthy man.

But only when the company has identified the consumer's problems—found the issues that are highly motivating—can it hope to introduce outstanding new products or give an existing product an effective positioning. Unfortunately, too many companies today rely on inadequate tools—focus groups being the most widely-used—to tell them what they need to know to market in the 1990s.

Clean-slate marketers in the 1990s will reject the past and use new technologies such as the strategic cube to develop a motivating positioning strategy.

☰ Elements of a Successful Positioning

Every successful new (or restaged) product or service must have a powerful, compelling positioning—which drives current and prospective buyers toward it and away from enemy brands.

The development of a successful positioning begins with a knowledge of the marketing environment and the optimal marketing target.

This step is followed by a rejection of death wish research tools masquerading as helpful methodologies. The natural urge to do focus groups, gap analyses, perceptual mapping, choice modeling, and other misguided approaches must be suppressed.

Once this urge to do something dumb is brought under control, a serious strategic research project must be undertaken in order to uncover:

- The critical *motivating factors* that explain why people buy your product category. (By "motivating factors" we mean those tangible and intangible attributes and benefits of a product which are "true" drivers of behavior.)
- Promises that your product/service in fact can deliver—factors or dimensions on which your product/service *performs well.*
- Promises where your product/service enjoys a *competitive edge*—factors and/or dimensions on which your brand has (or could have) a competitive advantage, scoring higher than major competitors.

6

THE MOST APPEALING PRODUCT IS ALWAYS THE LEAST PROFITABLE

The best product or service isn't necessarily the one that has the most consumer appeal.

Of course, any product that doesn't appeal directly to the target market is a dumb product. Similarly, any product that does not reflect the positioning is dumb. Why? Because such products or services are being marketed in a vacuum.

We sometimes see products that exist—even after Theodore Levitt's ideas in *The Marketing Imagination* have spread widely—only because a company's laboratory has developed them and the firm can manufacture them, not because anyone wants them.

More often we see both consumer and business-to-business products that companies have created with no feeling for the larger social or business context. For example, Miller Brewing Co. began rolling out its Matilda Bay Wine Cooler in September 1987, after the peak summer season and about six months after wine cooler sales had begun an industry-wide decline. Furthermore, they entered the market at a time when the trade was distressed; more than 100 cooler brands were on the market and the shakeout had begun. By the end of 1989, Miller had essentially abandoned the product.

If we haven't refined our product after having gone through the environmental analysis and targeting and positioning exercises we've described in the previous chapters, we're running the risk that our product may appeal to the people who created it, but not sell very well.

A CEO who is working on the basis of clean-slate marketing must ask the right questions about product design, and marketing management must be prepared to answer those questions:

THE BOTTOM LINE: WHAT A CEO WANTS TO KNOW

1) Are we in sync with the environment?
2) Is the product or service designed with marketing intelligence concerning the target and positioning in mind?
3) Did we examine a constellation of alternatives?
4) Did we go beyond traditional concept testing and other death-wish approaches that don't accurately estimate sales volume?
5) Did we take manufacturing costs into account in order to examine all the alternatives in light of their profitability?
6) Did we select a financially "optimal" product or service design?

≡ Broke or Not, It Ought to Be Fixed

We run across at least two common problems in new product development—the concept that just won't die and, far more common, the concept that needs help. There's also the concept that can't get heard.

Occasionally a product manager or marketing executive comes up with a product improvement, line extension, or new product idea only to be told by his management, "We're doing fine. If it ain't broke, don't fix it."

Yet, as we've already said, most brands *are* broke. While most markets are growing only at the same rate as the population, companies continue to introduce new products that take business away from established brands. Today, most entrenched brands, from cars to breakfast cereals, are slowly eroding as new products come into the marketplace, a trend that will accelerate in the 1990s. The question top management should be asking is not, "Why tinker with success?" but "How can we stop sliding into oblivion? What should we do?"

The answer, of course, is to change the formulation or introduce a new shape, a new package, a new color, a new size, a new function, or an entirely new item.

What is the right way to develop a new product or redesign an existing one?

1) Figure out each one of the possible feature alternatives—big box or small, red label or blue, air bag on passenger side or driver only, plain paper or coated.

2) Almost simultaneously with step 3, survey prospects and establish the market response to each of these individual features. We want the incremental (or decremental) demand associated with each of these possibilities.

3) Determine the incremental costs of each feature.

4) Use computer-aided design to take all this data—as many as 10 million alternatives—and calculate the financially "optimal" product or service.

Not long ago an airline, we'll call Globewide Air, approached us for help. It was doing all right, not losing money, but several competitors had come in with new services and seemed to be doing well with them. One key competitor seemed to be having great success with one class of service in the domestic market. That event caused Globewide's management to think about what it was doing with service: What do they know that we don't? How can we defend our turf?

Globewide's management began to wonder about one class of service, speculating that one class might simplify things. This, in turn, made it consider various ways to view one-class service: as first class or economy, with all the permutations between. Because there are many ways to do two classes as well, it undertook a general search to find the best way to configure the service, which it then extended from the domestic to the international market.

At the beginning, our work was helping Globewide see all its choices, which is typically something of a revelation for a client. They rarely realize that they have many alternatives. In the case of any service like an airline or a hotel (which we describe at the end of this chapter), this process takes a couple of months because there are so many options.

Once Globewide began to see all the alternatives, it began to examine how it currently was making choices.

In both the hotel and the airline industries, most choices were made on the basis of judgment. Judgment usually meant, "Give people lots of options." The tendency is to add more good stuff to the product because we think "more" will make the product more appealing.

Furthermore, Globewide had been pricing its service with little or no thought. In fact, of all the things they had been thinking about, price was the last considered and then on a cost-plus basis.

For this project we studied thousands of ways to do a one-class service, and tens of thousands of ways to do a two-class service. We learned that one class of service will never deliver the revenue of a two-class service. Even in its most appealing form—essentially first class for everyone—revenues continue to equal the average two-class service. There are two-class products that produce less revenue, but many more two-class products generate higher revenue than the best one-class product.

We then looked at costs, and the math suggested that there was no way a one-class service could be as profitable as two classes. The rest of the assignment was to decide how to configure the two classes. In certain instances, Globewide needed to improve features—notably food. But in other areas—particularly some of the lounge and gate-related services—the most appealing design was not going to produce a return on investment. Ultimately the computer evaluated more than 2 million alternatives to find the most profitable.

Our solution turned out to be a new configuration and not something Globewide was doing already. We recommended a mix of features and services it would never have guessed to compose the new configuration. Later in this chapter we'll show you how to find these breakthrough, often counterintuitive, product and service designs.

≡ Cannibalism Isn't Considerate

Before we talk about developing and testing product concepts, however, we want to touch on an issue we run into all the time: the problem that a new shape, flavor, size, or color takes sales away from the company's existing products. This is mainly a line extension problem and occurs with products designed to fill niches the company is not currently reaching.

Management wants to make sure that when it introduces a line extension for an established product the new version does not cannibalize the current brand excessively. This is no problem when the firm is entering a new business, but we regularly see cases where a line extension is forecast to obtain, say, a 3 percent share of market, and that share in that market looks like a big success. But when we analyze the situation, we find that of the three percentage points, 2.5 of them come at the expense of the brand it was designed to flank and only 0.5 percent is truly incremental business. Given the line extension's production and marketing costs, it's just not worth the investment for that tiny piece of new business. And this is why the idea that a line extension is the least risky way to introduce new products is a myth.

True, some categories—soft drinks, cigarettes, and beer, to name three—are so big and profitable that one could argue that a company should not mind if it cannibalizes its current business. As long as it takes some share away from competitors—even a disproportionately low amount—it can still make money. Anheuser-Busch may not care if Bud Light and Bud Dry take share away from Budweiser as long as they also take sales away from Coors, Miller, and Stroh.

Even if a line extension *does* cannibalize the existing brand, it may be a good move. The marketer of a well-known headache remedy introduced a line extension designed to relieve cold symptoms as well. The company expected the new formula to supplement its flagship product, but consumers saw it as a more powerful analgesic and bought it, abandoning the company's flagship product. Since the old product was dying a slow, terrible death anyway, the new version, even while it took sales from the flagship product, could be seen as a brilliant strategic move to prolong the brand's life.

We find that when companies come to us to talk about introducing a line extension, they say something like, "Tell us whether this is a 5 million unit brand." We have to explain that whether it's a 5 million unit brand or not is not the real question.

The real question is, "What are the incremental units or the incremental dollars this product will produce over the sales we achieve with existing products?" The corollary to this asks, "And is gaining this incremental share worth the additional costs?" A company that has a large snack cracker business came to us recently to run simulated market tests for new flavors they were thinking of introducing. We had to make sure that they understood and that we researched the effect on the entire category and not simply the new product's forecasted unit sales.

A related problem we often recognize as outsiders and one to which top management should be sensitive is what we call the Patton/Montgomery Syndrome. Both General Patton and General Montgomery would have liked to have won all the major battles in Europe in World War II. Eisenhower's task was to ensure that the Allies' joint objectives—winning the war—were achieved, and these objectives were not necessarily the individual goals of the separate commanders.

We find this syndrome in corporate America in two forms. In one, the new product brand manager would be delighted to take business away from another manager in the company as long as he or she received credit, although he would never admit to the impulse.

In the other, the product manager for the company's major brand constantly suppresses potential forays of the company's junior people onto his turf. He or she will do whatever possible to stop any new product or line extension that may take business away from his brand, not because he is thinking of the organization's needs but because he's thinking of his year-end bonus check, and he has the power to check the upstart because his brand is so important to the company.

≣ Line Extensions Are Easy to Research

As an aside, a new service idea tends to be more difficult to research than a product, and a truly new product tends to be more difficult to research than a line extension. Among packaged goods, for example, people can easily identify with a product that has, say, lower salt. They can identify with a new vitamin that produces 100 percent minimum daily requirements. These concepts are easy to communicate; people understand them, and they can make a decision to buy or not to buy. If the product does what it says it is going to do because the concepts are so easily communicated, the company can anticipate repeat purchase levels. If a new product promises to be less salty, and the product is in fact less salty, people will respond to it, like it or not as the case may be, and continue to behave in certain ways.

But with a new service, it is often difficult to communicate the concept, people do not understand it clearly, and their decisions to buy or not to buy are less predictive of real-world behavior. Not until the company actually begins to deliver the service does it know whether it is acceptable or not. The connection between a service concept and reality is more tenuous than it is between a consumer packaged goods or consumer durable concept and reality—not always, but generally speaking.

Similarly with a truly new product, it is sometimes difficult to communicate effectively what the product is all about unless the prospect actually has one in hand. Again, this is not always true. The video cassette recorder was very easy to communicate: it's a machine that permits you to play movies at home on your television set and to record programs off the air the way an audio cassette recorder takes songs off the air. The compact disk player was another new product that was easy to communicate: the disk that you put into the machine will give much higher sound quality than tapes or records.

As a general rule, it is easy to communicate a new product or service concept when something similar exists or when consumers are already predisposed to look for solutions to their problems. When a company wants to introduce a truly revolutionary new product for which nothing analogous exists or where the consumer need is not clear or both, the research becomes much more problematic.

It is possible to create a matrix to see where different products would fall.

NEW PRODUCT NEED/COMMUNICATION MATRIX

Consumer need	Ease of communication		
	Difficult	_Moderate_	_Easy_
Great	Medical insurance plans	Air bags	Video cassette recorder
Moderate	Keogh retirement plans	Antiplaque mouthwash	TV remote control
Low	Electric vegetable peeler	Book club	Microwave popcorn

The electric vegetable peeler failed because not only is the consumer need low, but the communication challenge was insuperable; the company was never able to convince people the device was safe. While there is no necessary connection between need, ease of communication, and sales, in general, the greater the consumer need and easier the communication, the greater the sales.

We have worked with two types of emerging product categories, which we've labeled as _evolutionary_ growth and _revolutionary_ growth products. Knowing into which column your new product falls can help clarify your thinking about market planning. The box on the next page shows the characteristics we've observed among these two kinds of products.

If these are the characteristics of evolutionary and revolutionary growth products, some specific examples of such products are shown on page 125.

≡ Appealing Is Not the Only Issue

The incentive for a product change usually comes from research and development or from the marketing management. The R&D people come up with a convenient new package by which to deliver, say, spray starch or a wonderful new formula that beats the current product's holding power by 43 percent.

Or marketing management, seeing a share decline, suggests focus groups or other research to provoke new ideas, new approaches, new

CHARACTERISTICS OF EVOLUTIONARY VERSUS REVOLUTIONARY PRODUCTS

Evolutionary growth	*Revolutionary growth*
Category characteristics (type of growth)	
Tempered (10%–20% or less)	*Explosive (30%–40% or more)*
Clearly a new subcategory	*Clearly a new category*
Low ceiling on demand	*High ceiling on demand (often 40% of population or more)*
Multiple brands don't necessarily expand category size	*Multiple brands generate "contagion effect," which expands the category*
Product characteristics	
Address minor or moderate consumer problems	*Address major or serious consumer problems*
Entries are seen as substitutes for one another	*Entries seen as complements to one another*
Perceived as another new product or "commodity" orientation	*Perceived as a breakthrough innovation*
Consumer characteristics	
Low involvement	*High involvement*
Benefits sought are moderately motivating	*Benefits sought are highly motivating*
Weak brand loyalty or willingness to switch	*Tendency to stay with first brand if it achieves customer satisfaction*
Marketing characteristics	
Word-of-mouth and public relations almost nonexistent	*Word-of-mouth and public relations accelerate demand*
Advertising and promotion important to competing brands	*Advertising and promotion less important as category seems to grow spontaneously*
Difficult to communicate	*Easy to communicate*

products. In either case, at some point a new product concept is developed, ready to be tested.

At this point, some companies simply take the product concept into test market. That's chancy because (a) it may not be the best design and (b) trying to fix a product already in test is like trying to repair a flat without stopping the car.

Other companies develop three or more—at the most ten—variations on the product and hire a research company to run concept tests.

We argue that computer-aided product design, which tests hundreds, thousands, even millions of variations, is better than either test

EXAMPLES OF EVOLUTIONARY AND REVOLUTIONARY GROWTH
PRODUCTS

Evolutionary growth	*Revolutionary growth*
Consumer electronics	
Transistor radio	Nintendo games
Memory phones	High-speed fax machines
Video cassette recorders	Cellular phones
Other consumer durables	
Expensive Japanese luxury sedans in the late 1980s (Lexus, Infiniti)	Low to mid-price Japanese sports cars in the late 1980s (Nissan 200ZX, 300ZX, Mazda Miata)
Large screen television in the 1970s	Microwave ovens in the 1970s
Juice blenders in the 1970s	Food processors in the 1970s
Packaged goods	
Pump toothpaste (e.g., Colgate)	Antiplaque cleaners (e.g., Plax)
Food products	
Oat bran hot cereal	Oat bran phenomenon
Shelf-stable entrées	Microwaveable entrées
Nutrasweet-added beverages	Juice boxes

marketing or concept tests. For one thing, the computer-aided design is virtually always more profitable than management's favorite concept at the project's start. In our experience, after hundreds of tests, management's favorite concept—the one they wanted to take into test market before any research—tends to be only average in consumer appeal and below average in profitability. The difference between the optimal concept and management's favorite can be substantial. In one study, we estimated the optimal concept to be more than eight times more profitable than management's—the difference between a major marketing success and a catastrophic failure.

Perhaps the most interesting finding has been that the most appealing concept is always the least profitable. This refutes the myth that the more appealing a new product is—that is, the more people who say they intend to buy it—the more likely the product will be a success. But offering the most appealing concept is like offering a quadruple scoop ice cream cone with chocolate sprinkles for a dime. The product has enormous appeal but is no way to make money in the ice cream business.

That's an extreme example, one all managers comprehend immediately. They often do not understand that *their* new or repositioned product is like that dime cone—appealing but a money loser. Or, somewhat more commonly, the product will not actually lose money, but it will not be making what it could.

Also, new products and services, line extensions, and repositioning efforts regularly fail because many—perhaps most—fail to ignite consumer interest. New concepts animate brand managers (they should), but they bore most prospects. Nevertheless, companies spend thousands of dollars every year on concept tests. They select the winning products, packages, and sizes for market introduction, then stand back as the products fail to live up to expectations. Two years and untold dollars later, they mercifully put them to sleep. What's wrong?

Concept testing is plagued with problems. Almost every marketer and researcher has done one (if not hundreds) of these tests, yet such tests often raise as many questions as they answer. We hear marketing executives ask questions like, "Is 17 percent in the top box ['Definitely Will Buy'] a good score?"

Or they say, "We studied three pricing variations. How could they *all* get 17 percent in the top box? Is there a *fourth* variation we should offer?"

Or, "If we changed the price [or the formulation or the packaging], how much will trial increase?"

To put the concept testing problems into perspective, let's walk through a typical exercise, suggesting ways traditional research can be improved. Then we'll describe a new variant of conjoint analysis as an alternative to traditional methods, and finally we'll describe in some detail a fairly complex example in which the computer looked at 2 million alternatives to find the most profitable one. This final example is fairly heavy going, but we believe it is worth the effort. We are convinced that only by evaluating many, *many* possibilities can management hope to find the concept that offers the greatest sales and highest profits, and the hotel example demonstrates why.

≣ The Concept Test—And Why It's Not Effective

An enthusiastic marketing manager triggers the traditional concept test when she asks, "What's the potential for this big new idea?" The idea might be a new coffee, or a new laptop PC, or, for the sake of this example, a home-baked pretzel.

The marketing manager goes on to observe that this new, home-baked pretzel could be positioned two different ways: the pretzel for serious bakers, or the pretzel for people who don't bake at all.

Each of these two positions could emphasize one of three different benefits: pretzels are nutritious; pretzels are fast; or pretzels are fun. The marketing manager is tossing out suggestions almost as fast as they can be recorded, and she's now describing six different concepts.

But she immediately points out that each positioning or benefit option could be based on one of four different product attributes, or reason-why stories: the salt (salt nuggets, salt-free), the mix type, the vitamin content, or the Old German Recipe. Now we're up to twenty-four different concepts.

Moreover, price remains problematic. The company's experience suggests five different price points, and the manager is unsure of what to charge. In either event, the concept now has five prices for the serious-baker pretzel; and five prices for the nonbaker pretzel. Within a ten-minute conversation, the marketing manager transformed one concept into 120 different concepts, a process that takes place all the time.

Worse, most companies are too clever to stop at 120 different combinations, and every new variable multiplies the number of possibilities. Sometimes researchers who are supposed to test the concepts leave a meeting bewildered by the number of possibilities: thousands, hundreds of thousands, millions of concepts could be tested. But what company would pay for such a test? Even if a company were willing to test an enormous number, traditional concept testing has serious limitations, including the following:

• *Sample limitations.* Research companies generally employ small (75 to 200), nonprojectable groups of men and women wandering through shopping malls and willing to answer questions for the research. Further, they tend to use only about three nonrepresentative malls and markets for a given study. (Unbelievably, one new firm has sparked some interest in the industry by testing as many as 200 concepts—with no rotation of the order of concepts tested—among 100 people at one point in time in one city and then using this questionnaire data to make volume forecasts. This is positively nutty.)

• *Measurement problems.* Researchers often use purchase intention and other rating scale measures with unknown reliability and validity. The scales miscarry because researchers don't know (a) whether they would obtain the same results if they repeated the study, or (b) whether the results actually reflect what they want to learn. It is as if they were measuring IQ by wrapping an elastic tape measure around the head. The results would vary with every measurement and wouldn't indicate intelligence anyway.

• *Alternative possibilities.* Few researchers are able to ask "what if" questions concerning variations in concept features and benefits efficiently. What if the package is red? Green? Teal? What if the price is 98¢? $1.98? $2.98?

• *Ignorance of costs.* In our experience, marketing managers seldom know the fixed and variable manufacturing and marketing costs, and researchers never know them. It is as if the folks in accounting want to reserve this esoteric information for themselves. But without knowing costs, a marketing manager cannot estimate profitability.

• *Limited models.* Finally, few researchers offer a valid model of the marketing mix into which to feed concept scores to predict sales and profitability. Researchers present concept scores to management as if they were discrete pieces of information in themselves: "This one got a 33 percent top two box score, beating the control concept by almost two to one." Great. But will it sell? And if it sells, will it be profitable? Blank looks from the researcher.

Can companies overcome these problems? We don't have all the answers, but we do have some ideas based on our research and on the work of other researchers and firms.

1) Begin with a larger, more projectable sample of prospective buyers (300 to 500) in more locations than the ones traditionally found for such tests. These people should be serious respondents, people recruited via random digit dialing and then brought to a central location, not the first bodies willing to stand still in a shopping mall.

2) Expose this sample to the big idea—a full description of the concept, complete with the name, positioning, packaging, features, and price (it's surprising to us how many concept tests ignore price). Present the concept in its competitive frame—that is, with competing products sold in the market at their actual prices. Experience shows that the more a test simulates, models, or mirrors reality, the more accurate the forecast.

3) Have consumers rate the concept in terms of purchase probability using a scale that is superior to traditional three-, four-, or five-point purchase intention scales for predicting likely market response. We have successfully used an eleven-point scale, created thirty years ago by Dr. Thomas Juster, then of the U.S. Department of Commerce. The scale couples word meanings with probability estimates to enhance serious thinking on the part of respondents. We've discovered through extensive experimentation that it predicts real world behavior more effectively than the alternatives, especially for mixed- and high-involvement decisions. The respondent can choose one of eleven levels shown on the next page.

Like all self-reported measures of consumer buying, this eleven-point scale overstates the actual purchasing that takes place. Much of this overstatement comes about because the research environment assumes 100 percent "awareness" and "distribution," something a company never realizes in the real world. Researchers assume all prospective consumers will be aware of the product (which never happens) and all those aware of it are able to buy it (which never happens).

JUSTER PURCHASE PROBABILITY SCALE

1) Certain will purchase (99 chances in 100)
2) Almost certain will purchase (90 chances in 100)
3) Very probably will purchase (80 chances in 100)
4) Probably will purchase (70 chances in 100)
5) Good possibility will purchase (60 chances in 100)
6) Fairly good possibility will purchase (50 chances in 100)
7) Fair possibility will purchase (40 chances in 100)
8) Some possibility will purchase (30 chances in 100)
9) Slight possibility will purchase (20 chances in 100)
10) Very slight possibility will purchase (10 chances in 100)
11) No chance will purchase (0 chances in 100)

Even taking the 100 percent awareness and distribution fallacy into account, people are more likely to say they will "buy" than in fact do buy. This is true in all product categories we have investigated. We have closely examined the relationship between people's reports on the eleven-point scale and awareness-to-trial (among people who were aware of the product and for whom product was available to be purchased) for numerous consumer packaged goods. And we have looked at this relationship in durable goods and financial service cases, including a hand-held microcomputer, a color television set, a charge card fee increase, long-lasting light bulbs, new car dealer visits, overnight messenger services, a new premium charge card, personal computers for the home market, and a new clock radio.

Our experience indicates that usually no more than 75 percent of the people who are convinced they will "buy," actually do buy. This figure declines as self-reported purchase probability declines, but the ratio is not constant. Indeed, the higher the level of self-reported behavior probability, the greater the ratio of reported to actual probability. Also, depending on the product category and the situation, virtually none of the people at the low end of the scale—from "Some possibility will purchase" on down—will actually buy the product or service. The graph in Figure 6.1 illustrates this relationship between actual and self-reported probability.

This led us to make three kinds of adjustments—for low-involvement categories, mixed-involvement categories, and high-involvement categories. Conventional wisdom says that purchase involvement is a function of the product or service; the more expensive, complex, or unfamiliar, the more time and deliberation the consumer gives the purchase. An automobile, by this view, is a high-involvement decision product; toothpaste is low.

Figure 6.1 *Relationship between Self-Reported and Actual Behavior Probability*

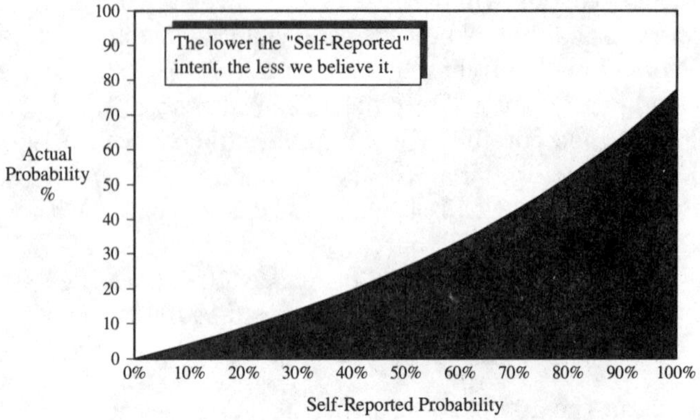

In fact, *purchase involvement is not a function of the product but of the consumer.* Some toothpaste purchasers who score high in compulsive neuroses will spend more time in front of a supermarket display deciding between brands, sizes, and packages than some car buyers do in deciding on a new car. We once found that the product that provoked the highest consumer involvement was bathroom wallpaper—not an expensive, complex, or unfamiliar product. In our work, therefore, we measure the consumer's involvement rather than assume anything about the product or service.

≣ Affective and Cognitive Measures Improve Forecasts

By taking purchase probabilities and involvement into account, we developed a method of weighting the numbers based on empirical evidence to produce a reasonably valid estimate of actual sales (i.e., the percentage of consumers who would buy the product at least once). The results, however good, were not overly impressive. Forecasting errors (adjusting for consumer awareness and product distribution) averaged around 21 percent, which meant that if a survey found that 30 percent of all consumers were predicted to try the product, the actual percentage could be as low as 24 percent or as high as 36 percent. This forecasting performance is fine but could be better. Purchase intent, as we learned, is an essential but insufficient predictor of market response, especially for mixed- and high-involvement products.

To help improve our forecasting ability, we developed two other types of measures in addition to purchase intent—one to capture affective and one to register the cognitive components of consumer attitudes.

THE AFFECTIVE COMPONENTS

These are the individual's emotional, or intangible impressions of a product. The affective measures include the following:

- *First impression.* We ask questions like, "What is your first impression of the idea for Home Baked Pretzels?" The seven-point scale runs from "terrible idea" to "terrific idea."
- *Personal identification.* "Based on what you have just seen and read about Home Baked Pretzels, what types of people do you think would like this new product?" The scale runs from "totally different than me" to "exactly like me." Also, "In terms of the members of your household, what types of people do you think would like Home Baked Pretzels?"
- *Uses and applications.* "Can you think of specific use occasions you might have for Home Baked Pretzels?" Choices range from "can think of no use occasions" to "can think of numerous use occasions."
- *Likes and dislikes.* "Which of the following best describes the degree to which you like or dislike anything about Home Baked Pretzels?" Choices range from "dislike everything about it" to "like everything about it."
- *Overall impression.* "*Overall* how would you rate Home Baked Pretzels?" From "terrible" to "excellent."

THE COGNITIVE COMPONENTS

These are a person's intellectual impressions of the product, including:

- *Uniqueness.* "How would you rate Home Baked Pretzels in terms of its uniqueness—that is, its similarity to or difference from other snacks on the market?" From "not at all unique" to "totally unique."
- *Superiority.* "How does Home Baked Pretzels compare to other products that currently exist?" From "clearly inferior" to "clearly superior."
- *Helpfulness.* "How helpful do you think Home Baked Pretzels would be in solving any problems you may currently experience with regard to these types of products?" From "not at all helpful at solving problems" to "extremely helpful at solving problems."

- *Value.* "What do you think of the value of Home Baked Pretzels in terms of value for the money?" From "extremely poor value for the money" to "extremely good value for the money."
- *Price.* "What is your opinion of the price of Home Baked Pretzels?" From "extremely high price" to "extremely low price."
- *Clarity.* "Which of the following describes the degree to which you find anything about Home Baked Pretzels confusing?" From "everything about it is confusing" to "everything is clear."
- *Believability.* "Is there anything about Home Baked Pretzels that you find hard to believe?" From "everything about it is hard to believe" to "everything is easy to believe."

By comparing people's reactions to new products and services with their actual behavior, we developed a three-dimensional, six-factor "behavior prediction battery" (see Fig. 6.2).

Ultimately, we employ a multifaceted equation to estimate real world behavior for each individual in the study (for more on why we look at every individual rather than groups, see Chapter 5; we don't want to commit the aggregate fallacy here).

This approach reduced forecasting error from 21 percent to about 14 percent so, if a survey predicted 30 percent trial (always assuming consumer awareness and product distribution), the actual might range from a low of 26 percent to a high of 34 percent.

Figure 6.2 *A Behavior Prediction Battery*

Affective Measures	**Cognitive Measures**	**Behavior Measures**
■ First Impression	■ Price	■ 11-Point Purchase Probability Scale
■ For People Like Me	■ Value	
■ For Occasions I Experience	■ Clarity	
■ Likeability	■ Believability	
■ Overall Impression	■ Uniqueness	
■ Helpful at Solving Problems	■ Superiority	

$$[b1(Factor1) + b2(Factor2) + b3(Factor3) + etc.] + [b_{13}(11\text{-Point Scale})] = \text{(Behavior)}$$

We think this approach improves the odds of forecasting what will actually happen. Some sixty-two validation studies that compared forecasted awareness-to-purchase conversion to genuine sales suggest that the method is reasonably valid—not perfect, but a major improvement over what is typically done in the industry. Figure 6.3 shows validation performance scores for those studies.

Often, however, the marketing manager is not sure what concept to test or how to describe the product exactly, what features and benefits to stress, or even what price to charge. Sometimes the number of possible product configurations seems limitless. But each concept test requires a fairly large sample size (300 to 500 people), and this means money. However, an alternative exists.

≣ Evaluating Many Concepts Simultaneously

Beginning in the mid-1970s, Professor Paul Green of the Wharton School of Business at the University of Pennsylvania pioneered a new research methodology that made the task of evaluating many concepts more efficient. His work clearly represents one of the major scientific advances in marketing during the past two decades. This technology, *multiple tradeoff analysis,* also known as *conjoint measurement* (we use the terms interchangeably) enables a researcher to evaluate many different concepts using approaches borrowed from experimental psychology.

Essentially, the researcher designs an experiment to test multiple factors—name, positioning, key benefits, size, shape, color, price, and

Figure 6.3 *3 x 3 Validation Table*

Actual Performance	Predicted Performance		
	Weak	Acceptable	Strong
Weak	83%	12%	10%
Acceptable	17%	71%	15%
Strong	—	17%	75%

more—by showing different combinations to different people. By applying multiple tradeoff analysis, a researcher can capture the main effects of, say, seven factors by exposing consumers to a relatively small set of concepts (often sixteen or fewer).

In practice, this means the research can evaluate thousands of potential concepts at a price comparable to a traditional test of perhaps five concepts. The researcher's real hurdle in using conjoint analysis has often been company management. Managers don't understand the procedure and often don't *want* to understand. Indeed, in our marketing IQ survey, more than 88 percent responded "don't know" to the statement, "Conjoint measurement and tradeoff analysis are different names for the same type of research."

By the late 1980s, however, marketers began to see that tradeoff studies had their own problems. They produce unreal measures of sales potential reflected in a questionable track record in predicting real world sales. Also, they tend to be limiting. Although they measure several hundred combinations, marketers in the 1990s have, not hundreds, but hundreds of thousands of options—and the standard approaches can't handle this well.

More seriously, traditional tradeoff studies tend to be misleading because they focus on the *most appealing* product. But as we have said earlier, the most appealing product is never the most *profitable* product.

Neither scores on purchase probability scales nor multiple tradeoff analysis utility scores address the key question: Will the new product or service be *profitable*? And in the 1990s, when most new products and services sink soon after launch, that's what smart managements want to know.

Fortunately, we do have an alternative in *computer-aided new product design*. This unique tradeoff analysis helps marketers design optimal products and services. The optimizer itself has several features: it predicts real-world behavior and sales; it covers millions of concepts; it identifies the most profitable concepts; the marketer can personally play out "what if?" scenarios; and it offers targeting and positioning guidance. The model is able to estimate trial for more than 10 million different product configurations. Combine this information with a company's knowledge of its market, and the computer can convert the trial figures into demand estimates.

To use this optimizer, you feed the company's estimates of consumer demand into a nonlinear optimization computer model, and it selects the "optimal" product. You temper the estimates by judgments about the marketing plan and cost considerations.

Take the home-baked soft pretzel example. Assume that we tested eight different factors by exposing respondents to a carefully selected set of sixteen scenarios. Four of the factors are *positioning* (serious bakers/nonbakers), *key benefits* (nutritious, fast, fun), *product attributes* (salt nuggets, mix type, vitamin content, Old German Recipe), and *price points* ($1.09, $1.19, $1.49, $1.79, $1.99).

To forecast demand for each home-baked pretzel combination, the company calculated the average demand for each of the sixteen concepts and learned that 22 million households are prospects for Home Baked Pretzels. Demand for any *one configuration* is then equal to the base level—22 million—plus or minus the effects of each individual factor, plus the interactions between factors. (This will become clear in a minute.) The demand (in total number of households) multiplied by the price equals total dollar demand.

Conjoint analysis permits us to address the question of which factors have the greatest effect on behavior. Couple the behavior forecasts with manufacturing cost information and, for the Home Baked Pretzel, the computer found that the optimal concept was to "appeal to occasional bakers as a great-tasting, fast-baking snack made from an Old German Recipe including the baker's own fresh milk and eggs. Offer it with European salt nuggets in the eight-pretzel size at $1.19." The market share potential was 9.5 percent; the profit potential was $16 million.

≡ How to Apply Computer-Aided New Product Design

To develop the most profitable product (or service) at an "optimal" price, we have to look at four things: the product's tangible features, its intangible benefits, price sensitivity (which we'll discuss in detail in the next chapter), and the return on investment. Today, with the computer, emerging new technologies represent the first applications of computer-aided design of new products and services in marketing.* The computer can manipulate all the raw data fast enough and inexpensively enough to give marketing executives the information they need to make intelligent decisions.

Here's an actual (if simplified) example to illustrate. Let's take a full profile tradeoff example, one that predicts real-world sales, and we'll use as an example a new hotel for which we consulted.

The new hotel idea had nine elements, and management originally suggested these alternatives as the "core" concept:

- Restaurant   2 restaurants
- Staff service   Moderate

*The authors want to thank Paul Berger, professor of marketing and quantitative methods, School of Management, Boston University, for his contributions to developing this technology.

- Pool   Yes
- Fitness center   No
- Room size   Small
- Business services   Yes
- Bath size   Small
- Shuttle service   Not offered
- Room rate $50

Customers had three other hotels available to them in the area: a Days Inn, which charged $40 for a double and $35 for a single; a Holiday Inn, $60 double and $50 single; and a Hyatt, $85 double and $75 single.

With the company's marketing plan in hand, we were able to forecast the performance of such a hotel. We surveyed prospects who answered questions about the "core" concept, the one the company's management would have selected on judgment alone. To stimulate real-world decision making, consumers saw the concept in a competitive context. Based on such a survey and the company's cost data, we obtained the following projected results:

- Trial*   29%
- Market share   4%
- Sales revenue $1,000,000
- Costs $1,200,000
- Gross margin   ($200,000)

As it stands, this hotel concept needs help because it will lose $200,000 the first year. Furthermore, no company wants to test just one concept, a hotel with these nine exact features. As we have said before and will be repeating throughout this book, companies need to test thousands of concepts—all combinations of all the various features. Only by evaluating all possibilities can a company hope to find the most profitable one.

≣ Profit Forecasts for Two Million Configurations

Our approach begins with the classic multiple tradeoff analysis. In other words, we show each respondent a special subset of concepts, often twelve to sixteen, since few consumers can discriminate among many more than sixteen possibilities.

We design these subsets carefully so that every respondent sees the

---

*Note that initial trial figures *always* assume consumer awareness and product distribution; if one or the other falls between the cracks, nothing else holds true.

same options for each factor in equal proportions, and the field interviewers do not present any one concept more often than any other. The results enable us to assess not only the main effects for each concept but also the demand for each combination of options.

To keep the example simple, imagine that, for this new hotel, management has to make only nine key decisions: restaurant type, level of staff service, availability of pool and a fitness center, business services, room size, bath size, shuttle services, and room rate.

There is, of course, nothing special about nine variables; a product or service may have more or fewer, and the computer doing the calculations does not care how many variables management includes. In fact, this hotel had many more variables; by the time we were finished, the computer had actually considered 80 million possibilities.

Imagine, again to keep this example simple, that management has only two choices in each area. (In the real world, of course, a given factor may have a dozen possibilities, but we're sacrificing verisimilitude for clarity here.) Since management has nine decisions, each with two choices, there are 512 combinations (2 to the ninth power). Of the 512 possible concepts, we show each respondent sixteen. This gives us the main effects for each individual of staff service, the effect of a pool, the effect of a fitness center, the effect of prices—every component individually.

With the survey data in hand, we isolate the "main effect" of each feature, which can be organized as in Figure 6.4.

Figure 6.4 *Main Effects of Nine Factors*

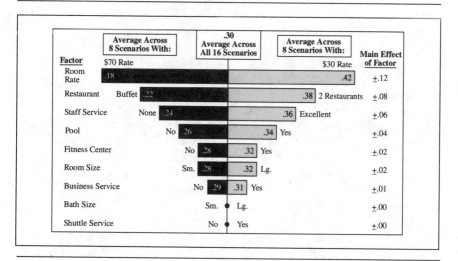

The "grand mean" of all sixteen scenarios is 0.30, which means 30 percent of all consumers, given awareness and distribution, would stay at the hotel at least once. The bar length indicates that room rate is by far the most important factor in a consumer's decision. The average across eight scenarios with a $70 room rate is 0.18, while the average with a $30 room rate is 0.42. So the room rate has an effect of plus or minus 0.12 (0.30, the average across all sixteen scenarios, 0.18 and 0.42). In other words, if the hotel charges $70 a night, trial will be 18 percent (the 30 percent base reduced by twelve points). If the hotel charges $30 a night, trial will jump to 42 percent.

If the hotel does not have a pool, the average across all eight scenarios is 0.26. If it *does* have a pool, the average is 0.34. So having a pool or not affects the offering plus or minus 0.04. In this example, neither the size of the bath nor having a shuttle service affects the offering one way or the other. (So why spend money on a large bathroom or a shuttle service? Why indeed?)

To estimate trial for all other concepts, we start with the "grand mean" of 0.30 and add or subtract the effects of each factor. The computer does this almost instantaneously and in this way finds the predicted score for any of the concepts.

The survey also shows not only how prospects rate each individual factor alone, but what happens when the factor combines with another. These are the *interaction effects*. Sometimes a factor's effect is not constant. It will vary depending on what's happening with another factor; consumers look at both simultaneously, not separately. For example, offering both a pool and a fitness center simultaneously does not increase trial as much as the "main effects" suggest. If the effects were additive, the trial estimate would be 0.36 (0.30, the average across all scenarios, +0.4, the effect of a pool, +0.2, the effect of a fitness center). The trial estimate is actually 0.34, because of the interaction effect. In fact, the fitness center has an effect only if there is no pool, and offering neither pool nor fitness center depresses the trial even more than the raw numbers would indicate.

But this approach can go well beyond 512 concepts. As we said above, usually there are more than two possibilities; imagine there are five levels for each of the nine factors. This means you can have 1,953,125 possible concepts (5 to the ninth power). The company may have a different number of levels for each factor: the arithmetic is a little different, but the principle is the same, and one usually ends up with an intimidatingly large number of possible concepts.

To deal with the need to test more than two possibilities for each factor, we take respondents through an additional questioning exercise where we assess every level one at a time (or, in research talk, *monadically*) in terms of its impact on purchase interest, including the levels tested earlier for which we know the main effects.

As a simple example, if two factors being tested were box size and box color, we might select a very large box and a small box, a blue color and a red color and expose people to all four combinations: a big blue box and a small blue box, a big red box and a small red box.

During the additional interviewing exercise, we would bring out the very large size box and have people rate it in terms of purchase probability. We would bring out a smaller box and have them rate it. We would bring out a medium size box, and have them rate it. We would even bring out a much bigger box than we ever tested and have them rate *it*.

In other words, we would have people rate a number of boxes, including the two boxes we measured in the tradeoff experiment. Using these two, as estimates of real-world appeal, we can then interpolate or extrapolate to estimate what the tradeoff scores would have been for box sizes we did not include in the experimental design.

Suppose that in the tradeoff experiment, people love the big box, and the big box forecasted a 30 percent trial level. They didn't like the small box very much, and in the tradeoff experiment we estimated that that would have a 10 percent trial level.

Later in the interview, on a different scale, respondent Smith rated a big box with a score of 5, a small box with a 3, and an intermediate box with a 4. If we know Smith's tradeoff score was 30 for the big box, and if we knew Smith's tradeoff score for the small box was 10, then, assuming linearity, 5 (the big box) is to 30 and 3 (the small box) is to 10 as 4 (the intermediate box) is to X, or 20.

For each factor, we then examine the specific demand curve. As one might expect in this hotel example, market share (always given awareness and distribution) declines as the room rate rises. In fact, where the company could anticipate a 42 percent share of the market at a $30-a-night room rate, share declines to 30 percent with a $40 rate; drops to 24 percent with a $50 rate; to 21 percent with a $60 rate; and to 18 percent with a $70 rate.

With the benefit of this "effects" data, we can forecast the performance of any concept including the most appealing one. But as we suggested earlier, who wants to market the most appealing concept—the four-scoop cone with chocolate jimmies for a dime?

In the hotel example, the most appealing concept to consumers looks like this:

- Restaurant   2 restaurants
- Staff service   Excellent
- Pool   Yes
- Fitness center   Yes
- Room size   Large
- Bath size   Large
- Shuttle service   Yes

- Business services　Yes
- Room rate　$30

This is an offer not many people could refuse. Indeed, our research indicated such a hotel would show the following performance:

- Trial　65%
- Market share　7.1%
- Sales revenue　$1,600,000
- Costs　$3,100,000
- Gross margin　($1,500,000)

Oh, boy, a 65 percent trial and a 7.1 percent market share. It sounds great until you look at the bottom line. Because the most appealing concept is a lot more expensive to offer, we estimate that the annual costs for such a hotel (based on the client's figures) would be $3,100,000, compared to the core concept's $1,200,000 cost. So the most appealing concept loses $1.5 million a year versus the $200,000 the core concept will lose—but neither proposal is one many managers would recommend to their boards of directors. This is the ten-cent quadruple-scoop ice cream cone revisited.

Somewhere in here, however, lurks a feature combination that will actually make the company some money. To tease it out, we have to obtain from the client all of the costs associated with each feature and level option, both the fixed and the variable. We consider any corporate objectives or constraints. For example, the company may set 20 percent as the minimum penetration level it will consider or assume the competition drops its price. The computer takes all this information—everything about costs, consumer preferences, the competitive situation—and searches for optimal, the most profitable, solutions.

In this place, at this time, the optimal hotel would have offered

- Restaurant　1 Restaurant
- Staff service　Excellent
- Pool　Yes
- Fitness center　No
- Room size　Moderate
- Bath size　Moderate
- Shuttle service　No
- Business services　No
- Room rate　$60

Our computer model says that such a hotel (given awareness and distribution) would enjoy the following results:

- Trial   34%
- Market share   5.2%
- Sales revenue $1,250,000
- Costs $950,000
- Gross margin $300,000

True, this hotel would not attract as many people who stay at least once as the most appealing concept, although it would do better than management's original proposal—34 percent versus 29 percent. Nor would it take as large a share of the market as the most appealing concept—5.2 percent versus 7.1 percent. But because its costs are so much less than both the most appealing concept and management's initial proposal, we forecast that it will return a profit.

≣ The Most Appealing Concept Is the Least Profitable

After eight years' work and more computer simulation runs than we'd like to count, we've discovered that inevitably the most appealing concept—the one offering the highest consumer trial—is the least profitable. This should not surprise anyone reading this book. But what may be a surprise is that marketing management's favorite concept—the one that sounds so logical, so right, that management may take it to market without any serious research—has been average in terms of demand, and below average in forecasted profitability (see Fig. 6.5).

Figure 6.5 *The Relationship between Concept Appeal and Product Profitability*

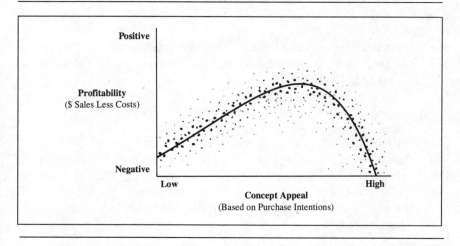

DEVELOPING THE OPTIMAL PRODUCT

To develop a *financially optimal* product or service, marketers must understand

- The marketing environment and where the product fits.
- The target for the product (how many of them are there, and where do they live and work?).
- The product's positioning strategy.
- The effect each potential benefit and attribute of the product (including price) has on expected demand.
- The cost of offering each potential benefit and attribute.
- The forecasted sales and profits of each of thousands, if not hundreds of thousands, even millions of alternative product and service concepts.
- The one concept that is optimal (which concept will produce the highest ROI?).

Erratum for page 142

While the traditional method—concept testing—remains the most common way to develop and test new product concepts, it's not necessarily the best approach to new product and new service development. A company can improve on its concept testing, but the technique remains limited if only because it cannot test a great number of concepts economically.

Tradeoff analysis, borrowing from experimental psychology, was an enormous improvement over concept testing. But in general, its goal remained the same as the goal of traditional concept testing: Find the concept that produces the highest level of consumer appeal and therefore the highest levels of purchase probability.

And that, of course, is not what a company really needs. What it really needs is the most *profitable* concept. We've found the difference in profitability between the optimal concept and management's favorite concept to be as much as eight to one. This difference means that marketing managers cannot, flying by instinct and gut feel, simply pick the most profitable product or service from among all the—often literally— millions of possible combinations.

They can use computer-aided product design to find that optimal combination. To do so, of course, will require a revolution in marketing thinking. It will require giving up the myths that a company must offer the most appealing and highest-quality products and services; that the greater the approval and the higher the level of quality, the greater the chances of marketing success. Without considering profitability and return on investment, such success can turn into financial disaster.

But how many companies price their products profitably?

DEVELOPING THE OPTIMAL PRODUCT

To develop a *financially optimal* product or service, marketers must understand

- The marketing environment and where the product fits.
- The target for the product (how many of them are there, and where do they live and work?).
- The product's positioning strategy.
- The effect each potential benefit and attribute of the product (including price) has on expected demand.
- The cost of offering each potential benefit and attribute.
- The forecasted sales and profits of each of thousands, if not hundreds of thousands, even millions of alternative product and service concepts.
- The one concept that is optimal (which concept will produce the highest ROI?).

7

YOUR PRICES AREN'T BASED ON STRATEGY OR RESEARCH? YOU MUST BE CLAIRVOYANT

"Price," someone said recently, "is a thermometer that measures how well you've done the rest of your marketing and management."

Yet most companies make their pricing decisions without any strategy or serious research. Our marketing IQ study corroborated this once again, since almost half (45.8 percent) of the executives thought the statement "Most pricing decisions are undertaken without any serious, formal research" was true.

We argue the revolutionary idea that to be successful in their pricing efforts companies ought to do six things:

1) Examine the environment (always).
2) Tie pricing to the target, positioning, and product.
3) Examine many alternative pricing strategies.
4) Study manufacturing and distribution costs and their relationship to product demand.
5) Undertake serious pricing research to develop a price elasticity curve that shows how sales change as price goes up or down.
6) Select the optimal price based on the best strategy, costs, and price elasticity curve.

If the marketing managers have done all of this before presenting the marketing plan to top management, they will be prepared to answer the bottom-line questions that concern CEOs:

THE BOTTOM LINE: WHAT A CEO WANTS TO KNOW

1) Are our prices in sync with the environment?
2) How exactly are our prices tied to the target and to our positioning?
3) What is our pricing strategy, and how did we arrive at it?
4) Did we formally evaluate a myriad of alternative price points?
5) What are our costs, and how did we determine them?
6) How will our forecasted profits change with changes in pricing?

≡ Strategies Rather Than Dumb Rules of Thumb

We do not argue "right" or "wrong" pricing strategies. A strategy may be appropriate or not, and a company may—and probably should—change strategies as circumstances evolve, as products and markets change or mature.

We *do* argue that a company should have some pricing strategy. A conscious, deliberate plan will always be better than expediency or following a dumb rule of thumb. We are regularly surprised, however, when we visit a major American corporation and find no pricing strategies. We became interested enough that we did some small-scale research to learn whether lack of strategy was prevalent just among the companies we knew or whether the situation was widespread.

Our research looked at all American businesses as fitting into one of four categories:

THE STRATEGY/RESEARCH PRICING MATRIX

	Serious strategy	*Little or no strategy*
Serious research	Sophisticated players	Radical empiricists
Little or no research	Gamblers	Losers

The companies in the top left box, the sophisticated players, are those that conduct serious pricing research (that is, primary research, not secondary analysis) and follow a serious pricing strategy. The losers in the lower right do little or no research and have little or no strategy.

Our research found:
- Only about 8 percent can be considered sophisticated players with both a pricing strategy and research to support it.
- Only about 4 percent are radical empiricists with research but no strategy.
- Some 47 percent are gamblers; they have a serious pricing strategy but do little or no research to support it.
- These results leave a sobering 41 percent of all companies with neither strategy nor research—the losers.

In other words, we estimate that more than half—55 percent—of all American companies *do* have a pricing strategy, but only 12 percent perform any serious pricing research to support the strategy.

McKinsey & Company's *Pricing Benchmark Survey* recently asked marketing managers from over 300 major North American companies, "In the past year, has your company done any research to measure or predict price elasticity?" Only about one-third said they had. Some 58 percent said they had not, and a dubious 10 percent said they were unsure.

Of the one-third who had done some research, almost half (48 percent) used historical data analysis, reported Michael Marn, a firm pricing consultant, heading McKinsey's Pricing Sub-Center. The remaining 52 percent (of the one-third or 15 percent of the total) used test marketing, self-administered surveys, conjoint analysis, and other research tools. Thus McKinsey's data dovetails nicely with our finding, confirming the rareness of primary pricing research (our 12 percent versus their 15 percent).

Some readers may wonder how it is possible for a company to operate with little or no pricing strategy and no pricing research. Surely, they will say, every company that puts a price on its products has *some* kind of strategy.

They have something, but to call it "strategy" stretches the word's meaning so far that it snaps. We say these firms are taking an expedient or dumb rule-of-thumb approach to their prices. Here are three examples of what we're talking about.

- *The cost-plus pricing approach.* Sometimes a company doesn't even know its true costs. A product or service's *actual* cost is a major cause of "marketer headache" and is the main reason that marketers give so little attention to pricing. *Companies don't know their costs.* It does not make a lot of sense to talk about margin or markup or return on investment if marketing management does not know the costs from which it is marking up or the actual investment. Sadly, in far too many cases, that's the way the world works. Many companies simply cannot calculate their costs accurately at the individual product or item level. Others either don't calculate them or don't share this information with marketing management.

However, even if a company cannot calculate actual costs, marketers can develop good approximations—but to do so takes work and cooperation within the organization between the marketing and finance people.

• *The old "match-the-competitor's-price" approach.* The problem with this approach is that a company cannot know—except at the most gross and superficial level from, say, an annual report—whether the competitor is making money. What company knows its competitor's costs when the competitor itself may not know them? And if you don't know costs, how can you calculate profitability?

• *The "beat it or raise it" approach.* This is where a company sets its prices lower or higher than a competitor's because—well, because it seems like the right thing to do. We've always felt this is more like Russian roulette than poker.

If those are pricing approaches without any strategy, what are examples of little or no research? This is where a company management takes a semiconscious or oblivious approach to pricing. We find that managers who do not want to conduct any marketing research make comments like these:

• *"What do you mean, 'research'?"* These managers cannot imagine any research technique that will help them make more effective, more profitable decisions.

• *"We can't afford any research."* The unspoken corollary here is, "We *can* afford the costs of screwing up." The argument includes the assumption, "Research isn't going to tell us anything we don't already know."

• *"Let's do it the way we did it last time: we don't need any research."* The assumption here—call it blind hope—is that the buyer hasn't changed; the competition hasn't changed; and the company and its product or service are identical to what worked the last time. If the executives think about the situation, they may agree the world *has* changed a little, but they will claim shifts are not significant.

• *"All right, we'll hold some focus groups."* This is, as we've been saying, a form of death-wish research—the unconscious, masochistic desire to destroy the brand, the company, oneself, or all three. Focus groups, by their nature, cannot tell management what it needs to know about prices.

• *"We'll do some research to establish the product's value."* This is another form of death-wish marketing, but because it is increasingly common, let's take a moment to see why.

The commonly used multi-attribute model and theory assume that if all the importance scores, multiplied by all brand ratings for a given brand's attributes, are added, they will equal the brand's "value." The product's price should be proportional to this "value." So that if the "value" of a new cola is 90 percent of the market leader, it should be priced at 90 percent of the market leader.

Here is the kind of table such research is liable to produce:

ZIPPY COLA EVALUATED AGAINST PEPSI AND COKE

		Evaluation		
Attribute	Importance	Pepsi	Coke	Zippy
Great taste	5	5	4	5
Right amount of carbonation	4	4	5	5
Popular brand	4	4	5	2
Not too sweet	3	4	2	5
Deep rich color	2	4	5	5
Weighted sum		77	76	78

This table says on the most important attribute, "great taste," respondents gave both Pepsi and Zippy Cola a 5. Multiply the importance ratings by the evaluations and add them up, and you reach the preposterous conclusion that Zippy Cola should be priced comparable to the market leaders.

While this example is deliberately extreme to illustrate the point, companies are today engaging in such faulty research to establish their prices. The research is flawed because it assumes that it captures all attributes, both tangible and intangible, which it does not.

It also assumes that importance ratings really measure "motivating power," which they do not. And it assumes the company can ignore the price of entry into the category, which it cannot. Zippy Cola would be competing not only against Pepsi and Coke's taste; it would be competing against decades of advertising.

≣ From Pricing Loser to Sophisticated Player

Until fairly recently, pricing was marketing's neglected stepchild.* Marketers gave the more lively and attractive children—advertising and

*The authors acknowledge with thanks the contribution of Thomas T. Nagle, Ph.D., associate professor, School of Management, Boston University, and managing partner, The Strategic Pricing Group, to this discussion of price sensitivity. For a much more detailed discussion, see his brilliant book, *The Strategy and Tactics of Pricing: A Guide to Profitable Decision Making* (Englewood Cliffs, N.J.: Prentice Hall, 1987). This chapter is based in part on a presentation, "Pricing Research: Theory and Measurement with Clear Management Implications," given by Kevin J. Clancy and Thomas Nagle at the American Marketing Association's 21st Annual Attitude Research Conference in Newport Beach, California, in January 1990.

product development—loving concern while parceling out minimal and almost grudging attention to pricing.

Anyone who passes Marketing 101 gives lip service to the Four Ps—product, price, place, and promotion—but in practice most companies have deployed pricing only tactically, to support promotional strategies or to launch new products. They have not paid serious attention to pricing strategy as an issue in itself. And should pricing require serious attention, they sent it over to the accountants, for whom pricing seemed to have a perverse fascination.

Studies in the 1950s found that almost all major American companies treated pricing as a purely financial decision, as though it had nothing to do with marketing. In a 1960s survey, less than half the marketing executives responding indicated they thought pricing an important marketing responsibility. By the 1970s, attitudes began to change; deregulation and international competition provoked pricing challenges that threatened many established company positions. Even then, however, these companies thought of pricing in terms of defensive tactics, not aggressive strategies.

By the 1980s, marketing executives—like the prince who meets Cinderella at the ball—began to recognize pricing's potential and significance as a marketing function. In fact, their appreciation developed into a fascination by the end of the decade. In two consecutive studies by Fleming Associates during the 1980s, top American marketing executives cited pricing as the most critical issue currently confronting them. And if this were a fairy tale, that's how it would end: The handsome price falls in love with the neglected stepdaughter; they marry and live happily ever after.

But it's not a fairy tale. It's life, where falling in love and getting married isn't the end of the problems. It's the start of a whole new batch of problems.

While marketing executives may say pricing is the most critical issue facing them—at least when answering a questionnaire—too few, as we've just seen, treat the pricing function as though it were truly critical. We are going to discuss pricing research and strategy, but to be sure everyone is speaking the same language, we want to discuss the elements that determine price sensitivity.

≡ What Determines Price Sensitivity

To make pricing decisions effectively, a company needs to know something about its customers and their sensitivities. For example, the more consumers value any unique attributes that differentiate a product from competing products, the less sensitive they are to a product's price. Does the product, therefore, have any unique—tangible or intangible—attributes that differentiate it from competing products? How much do consumers value those unique attributes? As an example, Tom Nagle cites Heinz, which developed a secret formula for making its ketchup thicker than the competition's and was able to increase its market share from 27 to 48 percent while still enjoying a 15 percent wholesale price premium.

Furthermore, can consumers recognize those unique attributes by observation, or do they have to buy and consume the product to learn what it offers? Is the product highly complex, requiring specialists to evaluate its differentiating attributes? Can consumers easily compare the prices of different suppliers, or do suppliers set their prices according to different sizes and combinations that make comparison difficult?

Consumers are more sensitive to the price charged by any one seller when they are aware of substitutes, which may be either competing products or competing sellers of the same product. When generic grocery products first became available, some supermarkets stocked them in special sections, and others placed them with competing branded products. Generic sales were much greater, and branded products correspondingly less, in stores where generics shared shelf space with branded products.

Just as consumers are more sensitive about price when they know about substitutes, they are less sensitive to a product's price when it is difficult to evaluate competing offers. Homemakers may know that other laundry detergents are less expensive than their usual brand, but unless they know those detergents will clean as effectively, they will not consider them as an alternative.

The greater the expenditure, in both relative and absolute terms, the more sensitive consumers are to price. They tend to spend more time shopping for a refrigerator than an electric iron.

Buyers are more sensitive to a product's price when they are sensitive to the cost of the end-benefit to which the product contributes and when the product's price accounts for a large share of the end-benefit's cost. An office equipment manufacturer, for example, buys sheet steel from which it makes desks. If desk buyers are highly price sensitive, the desk manufacturer will be highly sensitive to steel prices.

Consumers are less sensitive to the price of a product when they actually pay only a small portion. Boots Pharmaceuticals, for example, recognized that a low introductory price for its anti-arthritic prescription drug, Rufen, would be ineffective because insurance reimbursements cover a high portion of its price. Boots circumvented the problem, says Nagle, by attaching a coupon to the bottle that a buyer could send in for a $1.50 rebate. As a result, the consumer received the full benefit of the introductory price cut even though the insurance company paid a substantial portion of the cost. Rufen took a 6 percent market share in four months after introduction, an usually high penetration for this market.

Consumers are less sensitive to the price of a product when they have made a large "sunk" investment in anticipation of its continued use. Once a consumer has bought a fancy fountain pen, expensive camera, or laser printer, the costs of ink refills, film, and toner cartridges become less important. Nagle points out that in the early 1980s, many companies developed objectively superior word processors and priced them below the leading brands. Most failed because companies, having already invested in staff training, were not willing to make that investment again.

Consumers are less sensitive to a product's price when a higher price signals that the product is higher quality. These products tend to be image products, exclusive products, and unknown quality products. For example, Mercedes is able to command a higher price than a comparable automobile because it has a prestige image. Business travelers often fly first class for the prestige—"First on, first off"—not for the extra leg room, better food, or because the high price reduces the probability of sitting next to a small, noisy child. And consumers sometimes use a high price as a product quality cue. In one case, because consumers could not evaluate a new car wax's merits, sales lagged until the company raised the price from $.69 to $1.69.

Finally, consumers are more price sensitive in the short run when they can hold inventories of a product and believe the current price is temporarily lower than it will be in the future. Consumers will, for example, stock up on discounted canned tomatoes while they will not stock up on discounted fresh tomatoes to the same degree.

≣ Pricing Is an Art, Not a Science

Pricing, more than most other areas of marketing, is both an art and a game. It's a game because the pricing strategies of competing firms are highly interdependent. The price one company sets is a function of what the market will pay *and* what competitors charge. One firm's prices are often a response to competitive pressures as well as an effort to influence competitors' pricing behavior.

True, other marketing areas resemble a game as well. Almost as soon as Nabisco introduces Bearwich's, bite-sized, bear-shaped line-extensions of the company's successful Teddy Grahams, Keebler introduces Elfkins, a line of miniature elf-shaped sandwich cookies. But it takes time to develop a new product response; a company can establish a new price overnight.

While we agree that pricing is both an art and a game, we believe a product's price should be part of an overall pricing strategy, and we also believe, given our professional bias, that research has a decisive role in helping management make informed pricing decisions.

But before moving along to how we think companies ought to be making their pricing decisions, we want to sketch some traditional pricing strategies, if only to suggest a few possibilities to the 45 percent of all American companies that do not now have any strategy.

• *Cost-based pricing.* This covers both markup pricing and target return pricing and assumes that a company knows its variable costs, overhead, depreciation, and maintenance expense. If it does know these figures, the markup price formulas are straightforward. First, find the unit cost by adding the total variable costs to the total fixed costs and divide the answer by total unit sales. Once you have the unit cost, one way to calculate the markup price is to divide it by 1 minus the desired return on sales. So if each unit costs $8 and the company wants a 20 percent return on sales, the markup price is $10 (8 ÷ [1 − 0.2]).

Of course, this assumes that marketers know costs. Some years ago, when we began consulting for a major financial services company, we were surprised to discover the firm could not tell the profit contribution of individual customers because the firm didn't have a firm grip on its costs. The company assumed in those days that the profit contribution of all customers was about the same, that the customer who charged $50 a month in a restaurant was worth as much as the customer who charged $1,000 a month in airline tickets.

This assumption seemed so improbable to us that we pressed the marketing director. He admitted that perhaps it was unlikely that all customers contributed approximately the same profit, but the company did not have any method to measure that contribution on the individual customer level: they had, after all, millions of customers.

We suggested that if the company could measure the individual customer's contribution, the information might be useful. It could positively affect other marketing efforts—targeting, advertising, new products, positioning, pricing.

The marketing director said he would look into it.

Six months later we met to discuss the investigation's results, which had found, as we had suspected, a vast difference in profitability between customers. This information had a profound and far-reaching effect on the company's pricing strategies, among other things.

• *Target return pricing.* Target return pricing demands a similar grasp of fifth-grade arithmetic. To calculate a target return price, the formula is (total unit cost + [the desired rate of return × the invested capital]) ÷ unit sales. Assume that the company wants to make a 20 percent return on its $1,000,000 invested capital and, to keep the figures simple, also assume that it sells 100,000 units a year. If the unit cost is still $8, the target return price is the same $10. (If the total unit cost is $800,000 and the annual unit sales are 100,000, the formula looks like this: [800,000 + (0.20 x $1,000,000)] ÷ 100,000).

The math is simple, but markup and target return pricing share a major problem. Both assume the unit sales figure is a given, regardless of selling price, which, in the real world, is not true. In addition, product cost is virtually always a subjective opinion, not an objective number, since as we've seen companies do not know their costs. Product cost is a judgment call. As such, it may cover either full cost or out-of-pocket costs. It may reflect cost levels the company currently experiences or be based on an experience curve. It may be an estimate of future costs. It may include past R&D expenses. Which factors management uses depends largely on management's product and market objectives. That's fine until management begins to kid itself with unreal cost figures.

• *Pioneer product pricing.* For a brand new—pioneer—product, marketers typically use two strategies: skimming and penetration. The skimming strategy says, "We've got a unique, desirable product, and we're going to make as much as we can as long as we can." How long, of course, depends on how long it takes the competition to react with a similar product. Health food buyers, for example, are willing to pay more for foods without additives and sweeteners than most consumers. Health food manufacturers can earn more by skim pricing on limited sales to this segment than by cutting prices to attract more consumers.

The penetration strategy accepts lower profits over a longer time period either to gain market share or to keep competition out of the market. If you're the market leader and establish relatively high prices, smaller competitors can often crowd under your umbrella. If you're the market leader and set relatively low prices, smaller competitors have to find their own umbrellas. People Express Airlines used penetration pricing to enter the trans-Atlantic market, charging only $149 for a one-way ticket from New York to London. To avoid the kind of competitive response that killed Laker Airlines, People took no reservations, limited the number of flights, landed at Gatwick rather than more-convenient Heathrow, and provided only minimal comfort and service en route. As a result, People's flights were unattractive to most of the people who were already flying the Atlantic on other airlines; they filled their planes with people who would not otherwise have flown to Europe.

• *Product line pricing.* Product line pricing strategies include price bundling, premium pricing, image pricing, and complementary pricing. Price bundling offers a lower price on several items than the same things bought individually; examples include season tickets, all-you-can-eat restaurant buffets, and automobile option packages. Premium pricing examples include the rock concert promoter who charges more for seats close to the band, and the marketer who initially places a high price on a product, when it's selling to the price-insensitive people who want to be the first on their block with something new, and later lowers the price to attract price-sensitive consumers.

Image pricing occurs when a company introduces an identical version of a current product with a different name at a higher price. Manufacturers often have one price on their brand name jeans, washing machines, or vitamins and another on their private label counterparts. Finally, complementary pricing includes two-part pricing—where the company virtually gives away the razors so it can sell the blades—and loss leadership—dropping a brand name product's price to generate store traffic.

• *Competitive pricing* strategies include

1) *Penetration pricing,* where a manufacturer attempts to exploit its economies of scale by pricing below competitors in the market and thereby drive them out.
2) *Predatory pricing,* where a company already in the market cuts its prices in an attempt to hold off competition.
3) *Experience curve pricing,* which is similar to penetration pricing, except that the firm attempts to exploit economies gained through experience rather than through size. The firm prices below its competitors in a market in an attempt to drive them out.
4) *Price signaling,* which lets competitors know the company plans to defend its prices. When Goodyear went after a larger share of the radial tire market, its CEO gave numerous interviews explaining his strategy and why competitors could not hope to counter it. At the same time, Goodyear gave the press guided tours of a new, state-of-art tire plant that gave it the industry's lowest incremental production cost. Goodyear's weaker competitors felt they could not win a price war against such a determined adversary and withdrew without a fight.

≣Research That Leads to Better Pricing Decisions

So if these are the strategies, what kind of research leads to better, if not "optimal" pricing decisions?

To develop the most profitable product at an optimal price, we have to look at four things: the product's tangible features, its intangible benefits, price sensitivity, and the return on investment.

The best way we know is through experimental research: simulated test marketing or tradeoff analysis or a combination of both.

One tool marketers use extensively to evaluate different prices is the concept test. As we pointed out in the last chapter, almost every marketer and researcher has done one (if not hundreds) of these tests, yet they often raise as many questions as they answer. Tradeoff (or "conjoint") studies answered the concept test's problems. With a tradeoff study, the company is able to estimate the market potential of hundreds of concept variations but needs to test only a handful of concepts.

But tradeoff studies have their own problems. Traditional tradeoff models cannot measure sales potential with any degree of demonstrated validity. Moreover, they tend to be limiting; in the 1990s marketers have not hundreds, but hundreds of thousands of options, and the standard approaches can't easily handle this many alternatives.

Furthermore, traditional tradeoff studies tend to be misleading. They focus on the most appealing product, but as we've shown this is never the most *profitable* product. What management wants (or should want) is a method that maximizes profitability.

Fortunately, marketers do have an alternative in the computer-aided, new product design approach we described in the last chapter. The optimizer can predict real-world behavior and sales; it can cover millions of concepts; and it can identify the most profitable concepts. The marketer can personally play out "what if?" scenarios and obtain targeting and positioning guidance.

But how, exactly, does such a program work? Again, this example may be heavy going, but someone who understands the procedure is harder to bluff in a meeting.

Not long ago a major U.S. brokerage firm was weighing a new service that would permit customers to deal with the firm through their personal computers. Management felt that brokerage customers would pay a fee to have access to their accounts through their personal computers, but the company was not sure what features such a service should include or how much it should charge. The firm's basic problem was to identify the optimal combination of features and price. The more features the system included, the more it would cost to set up and maintain. The higher the price, the less attractive the service would be to customers. Management wanted to include only those features most attractive to customers and price those features properly to make a profit.

To understand how prospects felt, we interviewed 500 prospective users randomly selected from a master list of the firm's customers with investment balances greater than $10,000. We conducted forty-five-minute interviews in the customers' homes, during which the interviewer asked respondents to rate sixteen different combinations of features and prices in terms of buyer interest. Therefore, although the number of combinations totaled more than half a million, no one respondent had to consider more than sixteen.

These sixteen represented a carefully selected mix of six different factors:

- Hours of operation.
- Types of information the customer could request.
- Ability to move funds between accounts.
- Ability to place orders.
- Access to a personal line of credit.
- Monthly charge for the service.

The interviewers asked respondents to rate each configuration on the affective, cognitive, and purchase intent scales we described in the last chapter. (Affective measures, as we indicated on page 131 in Chapter 6, include things like first impressions: "What is your first impression of the idea for this new home brokerage service?" Cognitive measures cover elements like uniqueness: "How would you rate the new home brokerage service in terms of its uniqueness—that is, similarity to or difference from other services on the market?")

With these data, we were able to develop a "micro model" of the potential market. The brokerage firm could employ this model to estimate the number of consumers who, once they became aware of the service, would sign up for each one of the more than 500,000 possible feature combinations.

This tradeoff analysis showed that price determined consumer interest. Averaging across different feature combinations, the effects of price were as follows:

HOW PRICE INFLUENCES HOME BROKERAGE TRIAL

Monthly service charge[a]	Predicted percentage of customers who would sign up (assuming awareness and opportunity)
$5	30%
10	21
15	18
20	14
25	12
30	5

[a] We included only the $5, $15, and $25 price levels in the actual interviews. We were able to estimate the other levels by using a procedure discussed in Chapter 6 that estimates the demand for the intermediate prices. By so doing, it is possible to reduce respondent fatigue, sample size, and study costs.

The table indicates just what you would expect; as the price goes up, demand goes down. The figures are useful, however, because they put specific percentage usage estimates on each price point.

Because price was so important to the brokerage firm's customers, management wanted to be sure that the new service included only those features that justified their value to potential users. Management therefore paid particular attention to the utilities attached to various attributes.

A *utility*, in simple language, is the predicted increase (or decrease) in the proportion of prospects who would sign up for the service with different options. Utilities are useful because they can be added (or subtracted) to indicate how various factors combine.

Here's how utilities work: assume that the average of all factor combinations shows that 20 percent of all prospects are interested in this service. This figure, 20 percent, becomes the base against which to measure individual factors. Depending on the level of the factor, more or fewer than 20 percent of the prospects will sign up, and the utility indicates this difference.

For example, consider the factor of hours of service; the "level" of being open only eight hours a day has a −13 utility value. In other words, an eight-hour-a-day service would attract only about 7 percent of the potential market (20 percent minus 13 percent). In effect, the level of this factor would depress the 20 percent average by about two-thirds. On the other hand, a service open twenty-four hours every day has a +8 utility value. It would attract about 28 percent of the market (the 20 percent base increased by 8 points).

Here are the utilities associated with hours of operation:

HOME BROKERAGE SERVICE HOURS

Hours of operation	Utility [a]
8 hours, weekdays (9 A.M. to 5 P.M., Mon. to Fri.)	-13
12 hours, weekdays (8 A.M. to 8 P.M., Mon. to Fri.)	+1
24 hours, weekdays	+4
24 hours, every day	+8

[a] In this case, we scaled the utility values to represent increases or decreases in the predicted share of consumers who would sign up for this service (given awareness and opportunity).

The utilities associated with price are:

HOME BROKERAGE SERVICE PRICES

Monthly service charge	Utility
$ 5	+10
$15	-2
$25	-8

These figures indicate that if the service cost $5 a month, about 30 percent of the prospects would sign up (20 percent increased by 10 points).

With these figures, it is possible to determine that a service available twelve hours a day and costing $15 is slightly more attractive to prospects than one available eight hours a day and costing $5. The calculation to show this is straightforward. The utility of a twelve-hour service costing $15 is –1 (we add +1, the twelve-hour service's utility, and –2, the $15-a-month's utility). Therefore, approximately 19 percent of all prospects (20 percent minus 1 percent) would be interested in a $15, twelve-hour service product.

The utility of an eight-hour service costing $5 is –3 (add –13, the 8-hour service's utility, and +10, the $5-a-month's utility); this configuration would generate interest among 17 percent of prospects (20 percent minus 3 percent). In other words, taking only these two factors, it is possible to compare the various combination with simple arithmetic. And, incidentally, this example demonstrates once again that the cheapest product is not always the most appealing.

Consumers *do* find a service available twenty-four hours a day more attractive than one available only eight or twelve hours a day, but the smaller utility increases for twenty-four-hour weekday service (3 units, the difference between +1 and +4) and twenty-four-hour daily service (4 units, the difference between +4 and +8) indicate that customers would be less willing to pay an additional $10 for those features.

We are able to estimate utilities for more features and price levels than a tradeoff questionnaire actually includes. The more items a questionnaire includes, the more expensive the research, and the extra items are often unnecessary. In this case, if the company knows how people will respond to price points of $5, $15, and $25, it is possible to estimate how they will respond to intermediate prices of $10 and $20 as well.

With this research, the brokerage firm could forecast the gain (or loss) in sales for any price increase (or decrease) that might accompany a change in the features offered. By evaluating the gains and losses associated with various feature combinations, management was able to select an optimal combination of just those features whose cost was justified by the increased value they offered to potential customers.

≣Simulated Test Marketing's Pricing Applications

We discuss simulated test marketing in detail in Chapter 9, but it has a special application to pricing strategy.

A company can use simulated test marketing to test alternative prices or, better yet, identify an optimal price—the price that maximizes both sales and profits. A firm can also employ simulated test marketing to assess the effect on competitive pricing tactics. Usually management would like to know what would happen if the competitor held its current price, dropped it, or raised it.

Here's a simulated test market pricing example from our experience with a major Japanese consumer electronics manufacturer. Although we've disguised some of the details, the case is true.

The company was interested in assessing how different advertising and pricing strategies would affect market demand for a new multifunction product (a combination digital clock, AM/FM radio, and cassette player with a built-in memory calendar/date book). In addition to being a high-quality clock radio, the product enjoyed several unique features. The clock alarm could activate either a buzzer, the radio itself, or a cassette tape (a demonstration tape played the old song, "When the Red, Red Robin Comes Bob, Bob, Bobbing Along"). The computer memory was another unique feature; it permitted the user to program up to 500 key dates, times, or combination of both. With this system, the user could peek ahead in a given month or week to see key dates coming up or wait until the morning of the date when the programmed information would appear on a small screen.

The manufacturer asked two key questions. First, how should the company position the product in the television advertising: as an advanced clock radio or as a tabletop time management computer? Second, should the product be priced at $59 to attract a large share of the high-volume radio market; at $79 to compete with high-quality AM/FM radio-cassette players; or at $99 to signal the product's unique features and skim the consumer segment that valued those features most highly?

To answer these questions, we conducted a simulated test market experiment. In each of four markets, we randomly recruited 300 prospective buyers (men and women, age eighteen and over). We invited them into a research facility for the apparent purpose of previewing a new television program and seeing new home electronic products. The study design was very simple. We assigned each participant randomly to a group to be exposed to one of the two possible positionings with one of the three possible prices. Thus, we exposed six groups (2 x 3) of fifty participants each at each location to a different positioning and price combination.

We first exposed the groups to a new half-hour television program in which was embedded advertising for the new product, for competitive products, and for control products. Following this, we invited participants into an adjoining simulated electronics store where they had the opportunity to see the new product along with many competitive products, priced as they would be at local stores. Respondents could ask questions of store sales people and read available literature about the products.

All products in the store were for sale at a significant discount off the listed price. Approximately 40 percent of all participants actually made a purchase. We asked the nonbuyers a set of questions to estimate what they would have purchased if they had actually bought something.

The results of the study showed significant effects of both positioning and price on demand. Overall, 14 percent of all prospective purchasers bought the new product. Demand varied with positioning and price in the following way:

PERCENTAGE OF COMPUTERIZED CLOCK/RADIO PURCHASERS

Price	Advanced clock radio	Time management computer
$59	25%	20%
$79	19%	11%
$99	8%	1%

In other words, almost as many people bought the device as an advanced clock radio at $79 as bought it as a time management computer at $59. And while the percentage of people buying the device as a clock radio declined about 24 percent as the price went from $59 to $79, this revenue loss was more than offset by the price increase. And since profit is leveraged, profit went up by an even larger percentage.

While the company management loved the idea of selling the product as a time management computer and thereby advancing the firm's image as a company on technology's leading edge, it actually positioned it as a superior clock radio at $79 and enjoyed a considerable success.

≣ One and One Can Equal Five or More

Sometimes, however, a firm has more than two or three prices to test in a simulated test market, and this can get very expensive. When a major midwestern food marketer came to us with a pricing problem, for example, it was interested in testing five different prices for a new line of microwave entrées, ranging from a low price of $1.89 per unit to a high of $3.29.

A five-cell (five-price) simulated test market (STM) study would have been prohibitive—$400,000 or more. So we combined the best of STM technology and multiple tradeoff analysis (discussed in the last chapter). Basically, we conducted a two-cell, high- and low-price STM that gave us a precise fix on consumer demand at opposite ends of the price curve. But to measure the demand at five price points, each respondent went through a nontraditional tradeoff exercise in the STM interview.

We then "fit" the trade-off price elasticity curve to the fixed demand points (at $1.89 and $3.29) in order to estimate what trial demand would have been had we undertaken five different STMs. Thus, for the price of two cells, we were able to estimate all five (see Fig. 7.1).

Even better, we were able to fit a curve through all five price points to estimate an "optimal" price. This turned out to be $2.79, a finding that delighted the client.

≣ Your Cost Assumptions Make All the Difference

Our examples may suggest that if you do serious rather than death-wish research, finding the "best" price is easy. The truth is that good research helps, but it must be integrated with company knowledge about its own costs. The "most profitable price" is a function of consumer demand (as estimated by the research) and manufacturing and marketing costs.

Suppose we have a small home appliance—an air cleaner—we could sell at three different prices: $79, $89, and $99. We do the research and establish that the product will obtain a 10.1 percent share of the market

Figure 7.1 *Packaged Goods Pricing Application with Trade-off Added*

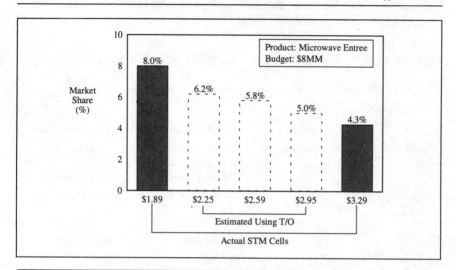

in units at the low price, an 8.5 percent share at the middle price, and a 7.1 percent share at the high price. Which is the best price?

Depending on our cost structure, however, the answer could vary considerably. Note the three different sets of assumptions in the following table. In each case we've assumed the same $20 million marketing investment.

- Under scenario 1, with an assumed cost of $42 per unit, the $99 price generates the greatest contribution.
- Under scenario 2, however, which assumes a variable cost structure ($42 for the first 750,000 units, $33 for the next 250,000, and $30 for all units above 1,000,000), the $89 price is marginally more promising.
- Finally, scenario 3 assumed that the firm would have to build a new $30 million plant to produce this product with a $10 cost per unit. Under these circumstances, the $79 price appears to be a winner.

The correct decision of which price is best obviously depends on the cost assumptions. This is a particularly troubling issue because of a problem we've discussed earlier—in many companies marketing executives are not privy to cost information.

In the 1990s we believe that more companies will move out of the loser box and into the sophisticated player corner with both serious pricing research and a serious strategy. More marketing executives will learn about costs, and more top managements will demand that every marketing plan include estimates of profitability and return on investment. More companies will in fact treat pricing as a critical marketing function.

And that in itself will be a marketing revolution.

HOW COST ASSUMPTIONS CHANGE PROFITABILITY FORECASTS

	Scenario 1	Scenario 2	Scenario 3
Assumptions:			
Market size	*10 million units*	*10 million units*	*10 million units*
Manufacturing costs	*$42 per unit*	*$42 for first 750,000* *$33 for next 250,000* *$30 for 1,000,000+*	*$30,000,000* *for plant* *$10 per unit*
Marketing costs	*$20,000,000*	*$20,000,000*	*$20,000,000*
Profit forecasts:			
$79 price	*$17,370,000[a]*	*$19,740,000*	*$19,690,000*
$89 price	*$19,950,000*	*$20,850,000*	*$17,150,000*
$99 price	*$20,470,000*	*$20,470,000*	*$13,190,000*

[a] Here's the arithmetic behind the figures:

First calculate the number of units the company would sell at each price point by multiplying the total market by the share estimates. E.g., 10.1% x 10 million units = 1.01 million units.

Next, multiply the number of units by the price to obtain a gross sales revenue figure. E.g., 1,010,000 x $79 = $79,790,000.

Next calculate the manufacturing costs for the number of units at each price point. E.g., 1,010,000 x $42 = $42,420,000.

Finally, subtract the manufacturing and marketing costs from the gross sales figure to find a net profit figure. E.g., $79,790,000 – $42,420,000 – $20,000,000 = $17,370,000.

THE PRICING ENVIRONMENT

- Take a close look at the marketing environment.
- Peg the pricing to knowledge of this environment, the target, positioning, and the product.
- Be a sophisticated player. Avoid being labeled a gambler, radical empiricist, or loser. To be a sophisticated player requires that you:
1) Consider and evaluate alternative pricing strategies.
2) Undertake serious pricing research—often employing experimental designs—in order to develop a price elasticity curve.
- Study manufacturing and distribution costs and their relationship to product demand.
- Select an optimal price based on an agreed upon strategy, a documented elasticity curve, and your cost structure.

8

THE CHECK IS IN
THE MAIL, I'LL STILL
RESPECT YOU IN
THE MORNING, OUR
ADVERTISING WORKS

Government agencies are continually asked to account for the performance of programs paid for out of taxpayer dollars. Did the Patriot missile really work? What about the Stealth bomber? Were they worth the money? Are Head Start Programs cost effective? How about the college loan programs, AIDS and cancer research, and environmental programs? Questions about accountability and return on investment should be asked.

As we said in Chapter 1, $130 billion was spent on advertising in the U.S. this year: *no one* knows if it was worth the investment, and few people seem to want to know or even care. If you ask a marketing director the return on the $125 million advertising budget he administers for his company, he'll mumble, turn away, and say, in effect, "Trust me."

We believe that for advertising to "work," it must produce a clear return on investment. No evidence currently exists, however, to support the relationship between advertising expenditures and ROI.

Whittle Communications exploited this unhappy situation with a much discussed print advertising campaign (see Fig. 8.1).

Figure 8.1

We also believe that

- Advertising currently is in a dismal condition.
- Companies must improve their advertising messages by using the tools now available.
- Advertising, far more than promotion, has the potential to create demand for a new product and to maintain an established product's health.
- Companies also must improve their media spending to increase its effectiveness by measuring cost per thousand *impacted* viewer rather than simple cost per thousand.

As we have been saying all along, to be effective requires a *clean slate*. We need to start the advertising planning process with no assumptions and no propensities. A CEO working on the basis of *clean-slate marketing* asks the tough questions about advertising:

THE BOTTOM LINE: WHAT A CEO WANTS TO KNOW

1) What kind of financial return are we getting on our advertising investment?

If the answer is, "I don't know" (and it probably is), ask the next six questions:

2) Are our ad strategy and tactics clearly linked to the environment, the target, the positioning, the product, and pricing?

3) What have we done to ensure that our message strategy is motivating and memorable?

4) Have we evaluated *many* alternative ad executions using criteria that predict sales?

5) Have we selected media vehicles based on their *impact* rather than the conventional criterion of number of people reached?

6) Does the media schedule reflect knowledge of the relationship between type of product, frequency of product purchase, competitive effects, and other factors that are proven to interact to affect sales?

7) Does our ad performance tracking system go beyond simple awareness and purchase measures to provide genuine marketing intelligence to facilitate constant improvement in the campaign?

≡ What Do the Bermuda Triangle, the Loch Ness Monster, and Advertising with Proven ROI Have in Common?

When Kevin Clancy first went to work for BBDO advertising more than twenty years ago, the agency's executive vice president E. E. Norris put Clancy on a special assignment. Norris wanted the agency to publish a book on great advertising—examples of advertising that had dramatically affected sales and had produced a clear return on investment. Norris asked Clancy to scour the agency files, talk to clients, read the academic and business literature, and even interview competitive agencies. Norris's assumption, of course, was that these cases would be easy to find. After all, this was the heyday of American advertising. Creativity was at its zenith, and advertising was a frequently discussed topic of dinner and cocktail party conversations. Creative shops such as

Doyle Dane Bernbach, Leo Burnett, and Ogilvy & Mather were turning out increasingly more exciting work; strategy- and research-oriented agencies such as BBDO, Grey, Ted Bates, and Young & Rubicam were becoming famous for their powerful positioning strategies; and mega-agencies such as J. Walter Thompson and McCann Erickson were continuing to produce good stuff.

After months of research, Clancy turned in a disappointing if not depressing report. Great sales-producing advertising is hard to find. Few cases existed. Clancy could point with pride at work BBDO had done for Chiquita Bananas, Chrysler, Pepsi Cola, and Schaefer Beer, but, by and large, advertising with proven sales results was as rare as deer in Manhattan. No book was written.

But that was two decades ago. What about today? Just how bad is advertising's current state? David Ogilvy talked to an interviewer* at the beginning of 1991:

> The other day I was at a meeting where they showed me about 100 television commercials from all over the world. I was shocked. In many cases, I could not understand what they were trying to sell. They didn't tell. Neither did they say what the product was supposed to be good for. They didn't give me one reason for buying.
>
> Today, the people who are paid to write advertising are not interested in selling. They consider advertising an art form. And they talk about creativity all the time. I'm a salesman. I don't care whether what I do is arty or clever. I want to sell products, but advertising people today, they want to win awards. They use advertising to promote themselves, so they can get better jobs and higher salaries. It's a scandal.

In a recent speech to the Advertising Research Foundation, Chris Whittle talked about having met privately over the past three years with a number of research and media heads of America's biggest advertising spenders and with some of the heads of their biggest research suppliers. To a person they said they no longer had any proof (assuming they ever did) that the great bulk of advertising worked. One said, "We don't measure one medium against another because we don't think either will work." Said another, "We stopped doing effectiveness research years ago."

Whittle also related that not long ago a company was sued for including false claims in its advertising. Their attorneys argued rather convincingly in court that no damage could have possibly resulted because there was no evidence that the commercials affected anyone. So why, one

---

*Kenneth Jacobsen, in *Adweek magazine*, January 28, 1991.

might ask from another perspective, was the company running the commercials in the first place?

Today, only one out of three marketing dollars goes into advertising. The rest goes to promotion—coupons, specials, rebates, and other short-term efforts. Twenty years ago the figures were reversed. Promotion has done so well because most advertising has been unable to demonstrate a convincing connection between advertising and sales results. Perhaps that will change as research technology improves. Several companies are now recording both the television commercials to which consumers are exposed *and* the products they buy at supermarkets and drug stores, to see if there is a relationship between exposure and purchase.

Magrid M. Abraham, president of product development and marketing at Information Resources, Inc., a Chicago-based vendor of syndicated single-source data, and Leonard M. Lodish, professor of marketing at the Wharton School, have reported in the *Harvard Business Review* that, in 360 tests, increased advertising led to more sales only about half the time.

Perhaps more significantly, they found that *only* 16 percent of the sixty-five trade promotion events they studied were profitable, based on incremental sales of brands distributed through retailer warehouses. They found, in fact, that in many promotions, it cost more than a dollar to obtain a dollar's worth of incremental sales. So promotion is not the answer either.

In 1980 the Advertising Research Foundation decided to undertake the biggest study ever done to establish the validity of different advertising research tools. The study designers (Kevin Clancy among them) believed that, to demonstrate copy testing validity, the ARF would have to compare advertising research scores with real-world sales results to reveal the types of advertising research studies that predicted marketplace results.

It was initially felt that this would be easy. After all, so many different campaigns were producing supposedly different performance levels that it should be possible to identify them. At first, advertisers were quite positive. A large number said they had two different campaigns that produced different results for the same product, but when the ARF tried to obtain the campaigns and the evidence that one was indeed better than the other, it ran into problems. Not that companies refused to cooperate, but the campaigns did not exist. After five years, the ARF had found just five cases where two campaigns for the same product produced significantly different sales results.

This is a sad commentary on the state of advertising. If advertising is as powerful and as effective as many people think it is, it should be easy to find lots of cases—hundreds, thousands—where two campaigns had different effects on sales.

The ARF's experience was not unique. The Magazine Publisher's Association spent months pretesting magazine ads to use in a print/TV advertising effectiveness study. It finally found three—Kraft Miracle Whip, Reynolds Plastic Wrap, and e.p.t. Pregnancy Test—that showed enough power to communicate *any* message. As Robert Warrens, a senior vice president and director of U.S. media resources and research at J. Walter Thompson/Chicago remarked about the MPA effort,

> We found, looking back at previous research, that you really had no sense of the creative impact, or how well the creative was doing in terms of communicating the product's specific attributes. So many of the tests are littered with advertising that really didn't work at all—let alone trying to show some incremental effect. So when we say this project shows that advertising works, and that print and television together work better than either one alone, we are really saying *good* advertising works.*

We are not, in this book, going to argue for advertising and against promotion or the other way around. We do believe advertising is necessary to build a brand. The challenge to marketers is not to abandon advertising, since advertising is, in essence, communication and marketers will always have to communicate with prospective customers. The marketer's challenge is to produce more memorable and effective advertising and to place it where it can have the greatest impact. We want to help make advertising the powerful marketing weapon it can and should be.

≡Too Many Ads, or Too Many Dull Ads?

We have been collecting data for two decades that suggest that new product and new service awareness and penetration—both the result in large part of advertising—are increasingly difficult to achieve. Therefore performance per dollar is slipping. The consumer's increasing inattention to advertising explains, in part, why copy test and persuasion scores have been dropping by 1 to 2 percent a year for more than a decade. And this drop explains, in part, why advertising awareness and new product awareness scores have also been dropping.

---

*Wally Wood, "Fine-Tuning the Print-TV Findings," *Marketing & Media Decisions*, August 1990, 84.

In a study we conducted in 1990, we found almost as many Americans (40 percent) saying they dislike the advertising they see today as assert they like it (47 percent). This dislike has been growing steadily and may be related to the general antibusiness sentiment spreading throughout the land. Four-fifths of all Americans said there is more advertising today than five years ago—more mail sent to the home, more commercials on television, more ads in magazines and newspapers and on the radio. Most people (69 percent) estimated the typical prime time television hour contains far more commercial minutes than it actually does, and some (16 percent) believe commercial messages consume more than 20 minutes in each hour. (It's really about eight minutes.)

Not only do people believe television carries many, many, many, many commercials, they overestimate commercial length. More than two-thirds of the population (70 percent) believes commercials are longer than 30 seconds, and a sizable percentage (44 percent) think the typical commercial is longer than a minute. (Most commercials today are 30 and 15 seconds in length.)

Our study found only about a quarter of the population saying they actually watch a commercial when it appears. Fourteen percent say they leave the room; 27 percent zap it or change the channel; 30 percent pay attention to something else. The missing percentages don't know or don't say what they do.

In 1990, 28 percent of all television viewers told the Roper Organization that they "often" switch to another channel during commercials—twice the number that responded similarly in 1985.

People do respond to different commercials in different ways. The Pretesting Co., an Englewood, New Jersey, research organization, found that 39 percent of insurance companies' target audience switches channels when insurance spots come on. Only 15 percent of the soft drink audience switch, indicating perhaps that soft drink ads are more engaging than insurance spots.

Magazine advertising does not make out any better. Our study found only 11 percent saying they read a publication's ads. The same percentage, however, assert they never read the advertising; they *always* turn the page without reading. Another 44 percent say they skip the ads most of the time, while 32 percent say they skip the ads only sometimes.

Asked whether the overall amount of advertising they see or read bothers them "a lot" or "a fair amount," a sizable minority (40 percent) says it does. Only about a fifth (22 percent) say they are not bothered at all, while the rest are bothered only a little (37 percent) or are not sure. What's going on? Several things.

≡ Inefficient, Poorly Targeted, Weak Messages

Media inefficiency is one issue. In 1976 the three television networks accounted for 91 percent of the prime time viewing. It's been downhill since. By 1986 the figure had fallen to 74 percent and by 1990 to almost 61 percent. David F. Poltrack, senior vice president of research for CBS, said he had projected that this decline would begin to slow sharply in 1990, with the networks losing only another two percentage points by 1995. But according to the *New York Times,* the numbers indicated the opposite. "We're already lower than our projection for 1995," said Poltrack at the end of 1990. "Now we have to think about a three-network share in the mid-50s by then." Meanwhile, costs have continued to rise, so advertisers are paying more while getting less.

Poor targeting is another issue. Many advertisers select target markets without sufficient thought—the problem we discussed in Chapter 4. We find it hard to believe that advertisers are still targeting eighteen- to forty-nine-year-old women and heavy users the same way they did twenty years ago, but that's what's happening. People who are not in the target audience tend to screen out the ads aimed at that target. Putting it another way, advertising lawn mowers to apartment dwellers wastes money.

The advertising message is the third issue. Too many advertising executions today are more likely to be ignored or forgotten than remembered and acted on. These are me-too message strategies that fail to tap consumer needs and, consequently, fail to motivate the consumer to buy. It's not unusual to see different brands in the same category using the same message strategy and, often, not a very good one at that. "Stay at a Holiday Inn Hotel and Drive Away with a Brand New Lincoln [illustrated with $5 bill]" was a headline in a spring 1990 print ad. "Stay at a Red Roof Inn and drive off with a brand new Lincoln [illustrated with $5 bill]" was a January 1991 print ad. A Red Roof agency spokesperson said, "We never saw their ad. Our ad was the result of brainstorming. No one who worked on the Red Roof ad has ever worked on a Holiday Inn account."

In theory, effective advertising is not that hard to produce. Take a motivating message, give it a memorable execution and proper exposure, and you have advertising that provides a healthy return on investment. Unfortunately, that sounds like the advice on how to make money on Wall Street: just buy stocks that go up; if they don't go up, don't buy them. Although the secret to advertising is a powerful, motivating message strategy, unlike stocks, marketers *can* identify a motivating message.

Because "message strategy" means different things to different managers, let's make sure we're talking about the same thing. The common theme is the notion, explicit or implicit, that the company wants to tell buyers something about its brand, product, service, or company: "A message strategy is your basic selling proposition—the reason consumers should buy your product rather than someone else's." That something should positively differentiate your product or service from the competition's. If the company differentiates this well, it will ring up a sale. So, first, how can the company develop a message strategy at all? Then, second, how can it do it well?

In broadest outline, the task is the same one we talked about in the targeting chapter, the product design chapter, and the positioning chapter: Look at hundreds, if not thousands, of alternatives to find the most powerful one. Using this procedure, a company and its advertising agency creates, screens, and evaluates numerous alternative message strategies to find the one that maximizes sales response.

We routinely talk to advertisers who think they already have a system that produces message strategies that maximize sales response. We're skeptical. Indeed, the contradiction between what many advertisers *think* they have and what we're convinced they *really* have is worth a brief digression into how companies typically make advertising message decisions. Then we suggest ways to do better.

≡Preposterous Approaches to Message Development

Companies take some of the same approaches to message development that they take to positioning.

Focus groups are among the most preposterous approaches to message development. Yet companies love a good group, particularly if it's done in an interesting place. They take this approach all the time. While focus groups may be a place to start, unfortunately it's where many companies end as well. The unquantifiable, unstable opinions of paid informants become the basis for message strategy.

As a case in point, not long ago, reported *Forbes* magazine, Brown & Williamson wanted to know something about blue-collar males between the ages of twenty-one and thirty-five, the target market for Prince, a new cigarette with strong tobacco and flavor. The company's advertising agency sent two researchers to Little Rock, Arkansas, where the brand was being test-marketed.

The researchers hired a local focus group recruiter to round up a dozen subjects—described by one researcher as "blue collar, but articulate enough to say more than 'yup' and 'I dunno.'" As *Forbes* stated, "It wasn't easy. The research happened to coincide with the first weekend of deer-hunting season. Many of the prospects turned down the offer of $50 for two to five hours of conversation and photographs and took to the woods instead." The agency finally settled on nine focus group participants.

Back in New York City, said the magazine, the researchers concluded that "blue-collar, Arkansas males were poor, sexually frustrated, and feeling hemmed in, to which they responded by getting together in groups and lighting up." The Prince advertising theme, "Make your move," was a phrase one researcher described as a "call to action to reassert control over their lives."

While such focus group research is quick and cheap (the agency spent about $10,000), even the researchers knew it was preposterous. *Forbes* quoted one agency researcher as saying, "You have a week, so you take short cuts. Of course it troubles me, but I'm pragmatic enough not to fall on my sword about it." Brown & Williamson might argue that such an approach is good enough for a test market; why spend big bucks on a product that may not fly? Yet *Forbes* observed that if Prince should make it into national distribution, "what plays in Arkansas will have a major role in deciding what should play elsewhere." Presumably one focus group could determine a national campaign.

We argue that one objective in test marketing is to give the product the best possible opportunity. A company that wants to save money on the test market can save even more by not testing at all.

Importance ratings is the second preposterous approach companies use in both positioning and message strategy development. The company asks people to rate twenty product or service attributes and benefits on a five-point importance scale. These are attributes like, "For me, the fact that an antacid is easy to swallow is 5. Extremely important. 4. Very important. 3. Somewhat important. 2. Slightly important. 1. Not important at all." This approach soothes managers because the results are so predictable. The generic, rational, and tangible answers come out the winners every time, and advertising based on the results tends to be generic, predictable—and forgettable.

Perceptual mapping is another preposterous approach, especially when a company uses it as a planning guide. As we pointed out in Chapter 5, a perceptual map may offer some insight into where consumers place a product or brand relative to other products. Even if perceptual mapping violates responsible research practices, however, it may produce interesting insights and stimulate creativity.

But when management begins to draw inferences concerning the future based on the procedure—when, for example, executives decide they should try to move a product from one spot on the map to another—we become concerned, because, for all the reasons we outlined, the technique is akin to taking Laetril to cure cancer.

Gap analysis is perhaps the most popular message strategy tool. As we demonstrated in Chapter 5, gap analysis is able to miss as many as half the people who want a product attribute but aren't getting it. Gap analysis discloses the right answer to a positioning or message strategy question only some of the time, and no one can tell whether this was one of the times. Based on this fatal flaw and its widespread marketing use, gap analysis gets our vote as the craziest approach to message strategy decision making.

Pedestrian approaches are not nearly as bad as the preposterous, but they're still inefficient or ineffective:

Advertising concept testing leads this list. It's simple to do, relatively inexpensive for each concept tested, but too complicated and too expensive when a company wants to test many alternative strategies.

Tradeoff analysis reduces the expense of testing many alternative concepts. Unfortunately, companies usually take only the most mundane, pedestrian factors and levels into a tradeoff (or conjoint) study. The results are only just a step beyond concept testing but a step beyond management comprehension as well.

≣ A Preferred Approach to Message Development: Message Engineering

After more than ten years of work with a wide variety of companies, we have found the preferred approach to an effective message strategy is a three-step process:

1) Create a definitive and creative list of product or service attributes and benefits that might form the basis of a message strategy. This is the message audit phase, designed to uncover all possible messages.

2) Screen this list to determine potentially strong messages. This message screening phase identifies the most promising attribute and benefit messages.

3) Evaluate each attribute and benefit combination in terms of forecasted sales response.

Steps 1 and 2 are the same two we took at the end of Chapter 5 to establish the product's positioning. The company that has conducted a positioning study can build on those results to construct the advertising message. Once management knows how it wants to position its product or service in people's minds, the question becomes, "What is the precise advertising message we need to do so?"

If a company already has a positioning study, it need not repeat the first two steps for a message maximization study. But because some companies are more interested in an advertising message than in positioning, we'll discuss all three steps, albeit from a slightly different perspective than in the positioning chapter.

≣ Step 1: The Message Audit

The basic object here is to generate a long list of attributes and benefits that might form the basis for a powerful message strategy. To help uncover these attributes and benefits, a company might do a category scan, exploratory research, personality assessment, social values analysis, emotional exploration, or some combination. (Note that companies use these techniques to uncover strong positioning statements as well. Also note that the techniques are just as appropriate for business-to-business marketers as for consumer marketers, and as appropriate for products as for services.)

A *category scan* is a close review of all attributes and benefits, tangible and emotional, competitive brands in the category employ.

Exploratory research could include focus groups, in-depth interviews, or both, using laddering, projection tools, or other methodologies. The focus groups do not produce the advertising's message—at least not until the message travels through steps 2 and 3. In other words, the company cannot just take what comes out of a focus group, no matter how productive or passionate, and run with it.

Laddering is the term given to a questioning approach that researchers use to uncover underlying associations with a given stimulus. The questions are a series of probes, usually beginning with a question such as, "What is the advantage to you of_____?" which might be "an antacid that's easy to swallow." When the respondent replies, "I don't have to chew," the next question probes his or her response, "What is the advantage of not having to chew?" That response is similarly probed: "What is the advantage of not having to taste the antacid?" The process continues until the respondent can no longer volunteer advantages.

Laddering analysts look for the respondent's tendency to relate ideas, values, characteristics, and the like. When many respondents have strong associations, the conclusions are usually interpreted to mean there are "natural" relationships that communications can employ.

Projection tools are like parlor games: If RC Cola were an animal, what kind of animal would it be? If Dr. Pepper were a sport, what sport would it be? If 7Up were an automobile, what automobile would it be? Or tell me a story about Orange Crush. Or if you were the president of Hires Root Beer and could make one change in the product to make Americans happier with it, what change would that be? If you were president of Pepsi Cola's advertising agency and could say only one thing about the product to motivate more people to buy, what would that be?

Personality assessment—an analysis based on primary or secondary data of the key personality traits that may potentially underlie behavior in the product or service category—can also be helpful. For example, to do a study for an over-the-counter drug, you would like to include a measure of hypochondriasis (what hypochondriacs suffer from) since it explains a significant variance in over-the-counter drug use. To do a study on a cosmetic without including a measure of narcissism would be a mistake. Since there are literally thousands of potential personality traits, it takes an expert to provide some insight into which ones might be relevant in the product category and to help select the measures of those relevant traits a study ought to include.

Social values analysis and *emotional exploration* are techniques companies employ less often than other methods, although they offer tremendous potential. The late Professor Milton Rokeach was a pioneer in the study of social values and how social values drive human behavior. We have distilled the work of Rokeach and others into eight critical dimensions:

- Achievement
- Security
- Sense of belonging
- Love
- Excitement
- Fun and enjoyment
- Self-esteem
- Social recognition

It may seem an oversimplification to reduce all social values into eight categories, but, just as a rainbow contains all shades of color with a relatively few apparent, these eight values represent the common denominators for all emotional shades.

You can establish how relevant each of these values is to consumers and others either directly—by measuring relevance in a research study—or indirectly—by inspecting secondary sources closely. In the audit phase, we use this grid of critical values and *Yankelovich Monitor* insights to help us focus on which particular values might be relevant for a given product and to provide ideas of how to measure each one.

For example, to identify items that link a consumer's need for achievement to his or her automotive requirements, you might ask this question and offer various possible answers:

How desirable is it that the next car you buy will

- make you feel prosperous and financially successful?
- provide you with a sense of accomplishment?
- convince your neighbors that you've really made it?

Emotional exploration looks at people's psychological needs and how a particular product or service category addresses them. Professor Robert Plutchik, a professor of psychiatry at Albert Einstein University, has written the definitive work on the measurement of emotions and has shown that eight basic emotions (not to be confused with the eight social values) drive behavior (see Fig. 8.2). The eight basic emotions are

- Joy
- Acceptance

Figure 8.2 *Wheel of Emotions*

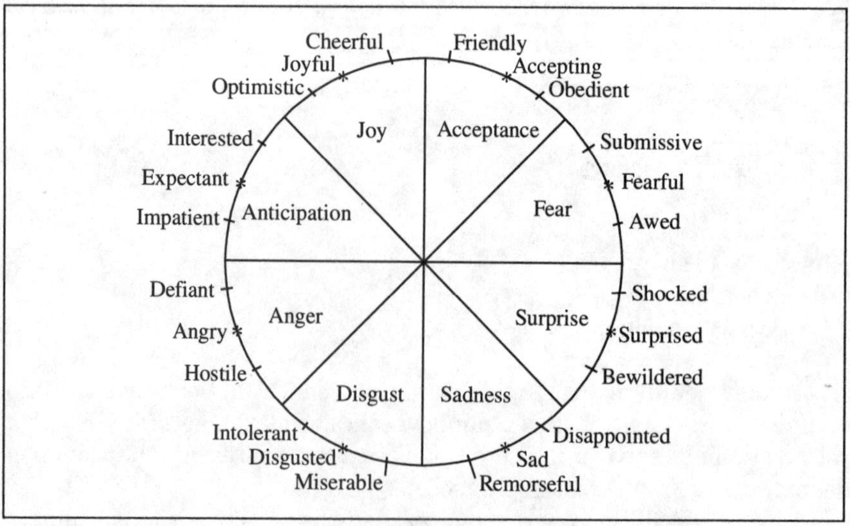

- Fear
- Surprise
- Sadness
- Disgust
- Anger
- Anticipation

The problem is to translate the theory into practical application. How, for example, might the dimension of joy be defined to reveal the consumer's feelings about an automobile?

It's not especially difficult. Plutchik's analysis yields multiple items, not just for joy but for all eight dimensions. To trace joy, a questionnaire might include items such as this:

How desirable is it that the next car you buy
- gives you a feeling of enthusiasm and excitement?
- makes you feel happy, contented, and pleased with life?
- keeps you entertained and amused?

The goal, as we said in the positioning chapter, is an exhaustive list of attributes and benefits, both tangible and intangible. The task is to fill out a matrix, like the one we began in Chapter 5, with a rich, promising collection of possibilities, a list that includes creative, thought-provoking, innovative attributes and benefits.

SPORTY NEW CAR ATTRIBUTES AND BENEFITS

	Attributes	Benefits
Tangible	Removable hard top	Like two cars in one
	Short-throw, five-speed transmission	More fun to drive
	Dealer handles all details, including getting you to and from work	No time wasted dropping off and picking up car for servicing
	Etc.	Etc.
Intangible	Manufacturer known for quality	You feel better about driving it long distance
	Car bought by successful people	Evokes an image of achievement
	Car preferred by people under thirty-five	Makes you feel and look younger than you really are
	Etc.	Etc.

·   Ideally, this first step produces 75, 100, or more tangible and intangible product or service attributes and benefits that might form a powerful message strategy. The next step is to reduce these to a more manageable number.

≡ Step 2: Screen the Messages

We believe the strategic cube analysis we described in Chapter 5 is the best way to screen the message (see Fig. 8.3). The cube assesses the motivating power of each rational and emotional attribute and benefit in three dimensions—its power to motivate, how consumers rate the company on the attribute, and how they rate the competition on the attribute. The most promising message opportunities, like positionings, should be highly motivating, credible for the company's product, and possible for the company to establish before the competition does so.

The strategic cube is a way to look at different attributes and benefits in a product category. By examining the motivating power and perceptions of a company's product and competitive products simultaneously, the cube reveals powerful message strategies. Attributes and benefits high in motivating power, and in which the company's product enjoys an edge over the competition, represent wonderful message strategy opportunities.

Figure 8.3 *The Strategic Cube*

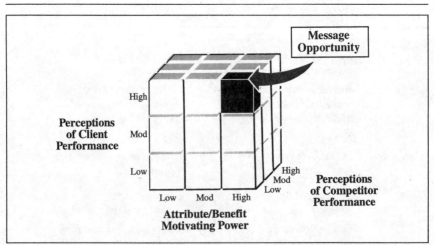

Each cube results in a blueprint for action, as shown in Figure 8.4. In the upper left corner are the attributes or benefits or both that are high in motivating power and in which the company is perceived as superior—an immediate strategic opportunity. Attributes and benefits in the lower right corner are low in motivating power *and* are areas in which the company is perceived as inferior. Since these are attributes and benefits on which a competitor might focus, the company should monitor their use in competitive strategies but should not use them.

In summary, strategic cube analysis is the best tool we know of for helping identify a great positioning strategy and for screening candidates for an advertising message strategy. What the cube cannot do, however, is tell a marketer how to *combine* motivating attributes and benefits into a compelling story for advertising copy. Thus, we need to move on to another step.

≣ Step 3: Message Engineering

Finally, and most important, advertisers need to combine the "winning" attributes and benefits and test them in a measurement model designed to identify the most powerful, most motivating message strategies. We call this *message engineering*.

This technique evolved during the past ten years from three differ-

Figure 8.4 *Strategic Cube Analysis Results*

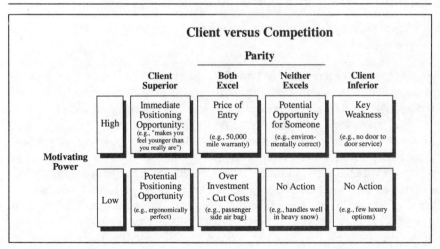

		Client versus Competition			
		Client Superior	Parity		
			Both Excel	**Neither Excels**	**Client Inferior**
Motivating Power	**High**	Immediate Positioning Opportunity: (e.g., "makes you feel younger than you really are")	Price of Entry (e.g., 50,000 mile warranty)	Potential Opportunity for Someone (e.g., environmentally correct)	Key Weakness (e.g., no door to door service)
	Low	Potential Positioning Opportunity (e.g., ergonomically perfect)	Over Investment - Cut Costs (e.g., passenger side air bag)	No Action (e.g., handles well in heavy snow)	No Action (e.g., few luxury options)

ent traditions: conjoint measurement or tradeoff analysis, advertising concept testing, and simulated test marketing.

By combining these different methodologies into one measurement model, it is possible to test many different message strategies and to forecast likely real-world behavior and sales for each strategy. And unlike advertising concept testing, the company can do this testing for thousands of different strategies. Moreover, the computer will search to find the best combination of discrete attributes and benefits—the combination that maximizes sales response.

How is this third step actually performed? First, we expose approximately 300 consumers—all decision makers in a product category—to an advertising concept that captures the distilled essence of the company's *current* advertising strategy. We show the concept in a competitive context with names, product visuals, and, often, price. We design this advertising concept to combine product benefits and attributes; a single concept may include up to ten different benefits and attributes.

Here, for example, is a hypothetical message strategy for the Mazda Miata:

> This is the new Mazda Miata.
> It is an automobile of both classic form and visionary technology.
> It is designed not only to perform right but also to feel right.
> The Miata is a true rear-wheel-drive, two-seat convertible roadster, powered by a 16-valve, fuel-injected engine.
> Miata's ride is based on a racing-inspired four-wheel double-wishbone suspension system.
> Four-wheel disc brakes and a driver's-side air bag supplemental restraint system are standard.
> For less than what you might expect, you can drive one of your own.
> The Mazda Miata. It not only gives you a glimpse of the '90s ... it takes you back, as well.

In this example, the key benefit, a car that recalls the sporty roadsters of the past, is supported by five specific attributes or features: two seats, fuel-injected engine, suspension, safety features, and low price.

We can describe the concept using the evocative, persuasive language of advertising, or we can prepare a concept colorlessly, using only a few words or phrases to capture each benefit and attribute. Either a copywriter or a researcher, in other words, could write the concept, but whoever does so must carefully control the number of ideas, words, and writing style in all the different concepts to maintain the study's integrity. If some concepts sound dramatically better than others because of the copywriter's skill, obviously this bias will color the findings.

Following exposure to the advertising concept planted among descriptions of three to eight competitive automobiles, consumers rate the concept on the eleven-point purchase probability scale and on the twelve seven-point affective and cognitive scales we have described on pages 128 to 133.

This rating data coupled with Miata's marketing plan—the current strategy—result in a forecast of real world awareness through sales. The forecast, calibrated against real world results, helps to "tune" the model so that later forecasts are grounded in real world Miata experience. But companies typically want to know more. They would like to test thousands, perhaps millions of alternative message possibilities to find the most effective few.

To address this need, the same interview just discussed includes a full profile tradeoff section, which, in the case of an automobile, might involve nine key message decisions:

- Basic positioning
- Styling type
- Creature comforts
- Safety features
- Intellitech options (e.g., talking computer)
- Performance characteristics
- Resale value
- Engine options
- Warranty issues

Imagine that each of the nine messages offers two (and only two) choices: for example, one positioning message communicates automotive intelligence, and the other, sex appeal. That's 512 possible combinations (2 to the ninth power). To address this problem, we use an experimental design that selects a subset of message strategies to be tested. These designs usually measure main effects, all two-way interactions and some higher order interactions as well. And again, we measure purchase probability (assuming awareness, availability, and the decision to buy a new car) on the eleven-point scale for each concept.

But suppose each message has *five* choices for each of the nine factors—a not unreasonable supposition. Under "Styling," a car might be described five different ways (e.g., "Aerodynamic," "Classic form," "Test track born and bred," "Youthful," or "Soft and willowy"). Take five to the ninth power, and the number of message possibilities soars to 1,953,125. Now what?

One way to handle this problem is to take the 300 respondents through the same additional questioning discussed in chapter 6 that permits us to estimate the sales response for each attribute and benefit without fatiguing the respondent. The answers to these questions will result in tables such as the following that show the effects of offering (or not offering) different benefits and attributes.

ESTIMATED PURCHASE PROBABILITY FOR AUTOMOBILE ATTRIBUTES AND BENEFITS (A REDUCED LIST OF MESSAGES FOR ILLUSTRATIVE PURPOSES)

Messages	Attribute or benefit	Estimated purchase probability
Basic positioning message	Aggressomobile	-6.6
	Love magnet	-2.0
	Intellitech	8.6
Styling messages	Aerodynamic	-8.5
	Classic form	-2.3
	Test track born and bred	1.2
	Youthful	3.2
	Soft and willowy	6.4
Creature comfort messages	16 seat adjustments	-3.2
	Lumbar support	3.2
	Leather seats	0.0
Warranty messages	None	-8.9
	Some	3.1
	All	5.8
Intellitech messages	Living room stereo	-10.7
	Built-in radar detector	-8.0
	Talking safety computer	2.4
	Automatically closing door	4.1
	Four-wheel drive	5.7
	Fuel efficiency monitor	6.5

The numbers in the third column represent each attribute and benefit's forecasted effect on purchase. For the basic positioning message, an "Intellitech" story is much stronger than either positioning the car as an Aggressomobile (powerful, fast, and low slung) or as a Love Magnet.

Indeed, communicating an Intellitech story raises the purchase probability by 8.6 percent over the average of all messages tested. The Aggresso-mobile story *reduces* purchase probability 6.6 percent below the average.

A more important question, however, is how to combine attributes and benefits into an overall advertising message. Traditional tradeoff analysis has a simple answer: just add up the effects. The winning concept or message is the one with the highest value.

Indeed many marketers take this approach. They take the same twenty or thirty attributes or benefits they've always had, test them to see which the advertising should include and how many the ads should contain. The following data shows that as the company moves from one message—that is, one attribute or one benefit—to twenty, consumer "would-buy" scores increase from 26 percent to 91 percent.

One marketing director looking at this table decided that the eight-

---

THE RELATIONSHIP BETWEEN THE NUMBER OF ATTRIBUTES AND BENEFITS AND PURCHASE INTENTION

Number of attributes and benefits	Percent "would buy"
One	26%
Two	39%
Three	55%
Five	73%
Eight	80%
Twelve	86%
Twenty	91%

---

message strategy was the most efficient and went with it. Eight messages, 80 percent "would buy": it has a nice ring. This kind of thinking turns up in much direct mail solicitation. There are so many messages, so many attributes and benefits, so many features, they stumble over one another. This is not advertising; it's a list of goodies produced in the hope that, if someone reads it, he or she will find something appealing. Clearly, it helps to know each attribute and benefit's main effects, but there's more to effective advertising than simply adding them up to find the highest value.

Consider the two interesting, but conflicting, relationships in Figure 8.5. The left side of the exhibit indicates that forecasted demand rises as the number of messages within a concept increases. This occurs in every

Figure 8.5 *Two Conflicing Relationships*

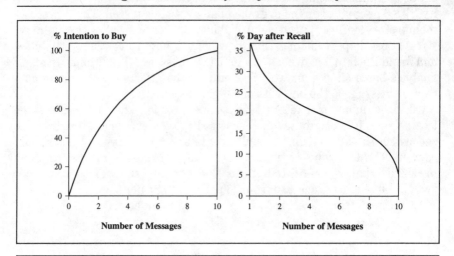

tradeoff study, and it's the same phenomenon we saw when we were originally designing the product. Not surprisingly, the more a company promises, the better the numbers.

But the chart on the right shows an equally interesting relationship. Real-world data suggest that the more messages a company packs into an advertisement, the lower the expected recall of any one message and, in some cases, the advertisement as a whole. Simple-minded stories, in other words, may not be the most persuasive, but they are the best remembered.

These curves, by the way, exhibit different shapes for print advertising and television commercials, and different shapes for low- versus high-involvement decisions. Print campaigns and high-involvement decisions permit more memorable messages per advertisement than television advertising or low-involvement decisions.

A message engineering model not only calculates the main and interactive effects for all combinations of attributes and benefits—seeing how they work alone and how they work together—but also takes into account the effects that different numbers of messages will have on advertising recall as well (see Fig. 8.6). In other words, for each survey respondent, the computer calculates what effect the number of messages will have on estimated dollar demand for each combination—that is, for all the various mixtures of attributes and benefits.

Depending on the situation, demand may peak with three messages,

Figure 8.6 *The Relationship between Number of Messages and Demand Corrected for Memory Effects*

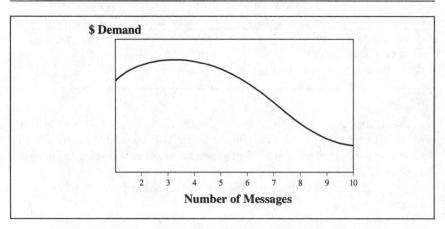

but each company has to draw its own curves. These vary significantly depending on the main and interactive appeal of each message, the choice of media, and the consumer's level of involvement. For an automobile decision, three messages are probably always too few, while as many as ten may maximize demand because consumers want a great deal of information. For a beer decision, three messages may be enough because consumers do not need much information about a beer.

The model searches through all possible message strategies—in this case, all 1,953,125 of them—to find the one forecast to yield the maximum level of market response. For Mazda, this could well have turned out to be to position the Miata as

> An automobile of both classic form and visionary technology ... a convertible ... a two-seater ... a true rear-wheel-drive roadster ... with a 16-valve, fuel-injected engine; short throw, five-speed transmission; racing-inspired 4-wheel double-wishbone suspension system; and 4 wheel disc brakes ... driver's side air bag ... designed to not only perform right, but also feel right.

In other words, a thirteen-message strategy (3 benefits, 10 attributes).

As a final step, we forecast awareness through sales. In almost all cases, the model's strategy beats the one submitted by the marketing manager. Here's the difference in forecasted results in one application:

FORECASTED PERFORMANCE (12 MONTHS FROM LAUNCH)			
	Management's message strategy	*Model message strategy*	*Degree of improvement*
Awareness	26.0%	30.0%	15.4%
Dealer visits	9.0	10.5	8.6
$ penetration	4.8	5.2	4.3

The computer model's recommendation leads to an awareness forecast 15.4 percent higher than the strategy the company started with, dealer visits forecast to be up 8.6 percent, and forecasted sales to increase 4.3 percent.

What this means is that a company can now improve its advertising through

- Knowing precisely the effect of communicating (or not communicating) each benefit or attribute (or both) on consumer demand or profitability (or both).
- Gaining insight into how benefits and attributes can be "engineered"—that is, combined—into motivating messages.
- Identifying those messages forecasted to yield the greatest sales response.
- Forecasting awareness through trial and sales for the winning message strategy and comparing the winner to the message strategy selected by company management.

In fact, since the model is available on a personal computer floppy disk, it is possible for marketing managers to play out their own message strategies. For any configuration the manager chooses, the model will estimate awareness, purchase probability (given awareness and availability), trial (that is, penetration), unit and dollar sales, and market share.

But once a company has developed the most effective advertising message, what kind of execution should be developed? What should the ad look like?

≡ The More People Like the Advertising, the Better It Works

After a marketer has selected its message strategy, the advertising agency's task is to find a way to execute it in a memorable, persuasive, and sales-producing way. At least, that's what agencies would say. The facts are that most advertising today is neither memorable nor persuasive, and there's no more evidence that most campaigns produce a sales return-on-the-advertising investment than that Judge Crater, Amelia Earhart, and Jimmy Hoffa are enjoying old age as shell divers in Jamaica.

Discoveries are unfolding, however, that provide insights about what does make advertising effective. These discoveries could have a major impact on the industry. The first discovery can be traced back to 1980 when the Advertising Research Foundation decided to set up a committee to investigate copy testing procedures. Professors Kevin Clancy and Russell Haley were selected as co-chairmen of its methodological subcommittee.

The following year, the subcommittee surveyed 125 advertisers to determine how frequently two or more advertising executions were copy tested and later evaluated in the real world to see which one had the biggest effect on sales. The logic here was simple: Find the types of copy tests (technique or measures) that are most predictive of real-world sales performance.

Initially, eighty-one advertisers produced 183 such cases. But after years of discussion and analysis, the committee found only five pairs of commercials that met the criteria. After years of work, only five instances were found where two different commercials were copy tested and later demonstrated differential sales effectiveness.

During the next few years, the ARF committee designed an experiment in which these five pairs of packaged goods commercials were tested using a variety of copy evaluation tools and measures. Its specific objectives were to determine the effectiveness of

- Copy tests, as presently conducted, to identify known sales "winners,"
- Individual measures,
- Types of measures (e.g., persuasion or recall),
- On-air and off-air designs,
- Pre/post and post-only designs,
- Single-exposure and multiple-exposure (reexposure) designs, and
- Any one copy testing *system* over the others.

When Russell Haley reported the results of this analysis for the first time in January 1990, industry excitement was high. People wanted to know what the study would show and what new discoveries would emerge.

Basically the study found, to everyone's surprise, that *the single best predictors of sales effectiveness were attitudes toward the commercials.* The more people liked them, the better they worked. The particular scale used ranged from, "I liked it very much" (a 5) to "I disliked it very much" (a 1).

Two diagnostic items (the commercial "Tells me a lot about how the product works" and "This advertising is funny or clever") were also highly predictive of sales response.

The conventional recall and persuasion scores that are widely regarded today as *the* criteria for evaluating advertising copy were, on average, poor performers. Taken as a whole they were not significantly related to sales at all.

Several particular recall and persuasion measures, however, performed quite well. Overall brand rating (a five-point "poor" to "excellent" scale), a persuasion measure, did very well and recall of brand name (without any cues) did even better.

The study suggested, in essence, that an exclusive focus on recall *or* persuasion measures for evaluating ad copy is misguided; both merely play a role. On the other hand, people's attitudes toward advertising and their reaction to it—an unheralded set of measures—are critically important and should not be ignored.

≣ Simulated Living Rooms Produce Better Results

At the same time that the ARF was working hard to find the best predictors of advertising sales performance, Television Audience Assessment engaged us to study the relationship between people's involvement in television programs and advertising response. We designed an experiment in which people would watch a television program that contained eight different commercials in two different types of viewing environments—a "traditional forced exposure viewing situation" and what we called a "simulated-natural environment situation."

Those assigned to the traditional forced exposure viewing environment were led, in groups of twelve to fifteen respondents, into an undecorated room with folding chairs arranged in a semicircle in front of a video monitor. After completing a preexposure questionnaire, they were instructed to turn their attention to the monitor *only* and refrain from conversing with one another.

In the simulated-natural viewing condition, on the other hand, smaller groups were brought into a room that *simulated a living room atmosphere*. The carpeted room was furnished with comfortable chairs, sofas, and all other amenities found in the "typical" in-home viewing environment. Newspapers, magazines, and snacks were placed on a coffee table in the center of the room, while coffee and other beverages were made available on a buffet-style table at the rear of the room. A television set was placed in one corner of the room, easily viewed from all sitting locations. After completing the same preexposure questionnaire, respondents in this latter treatment condition were *not instructed* to view the program. They could watch, read, eat, converse, write a letter, or do as they wished.

What we found was that simulated-natural testing provided higher levels of discrimination and validity. By the nature of the more naturalistic viewing conditions, the simulated natural test environment led to *lower*, more "realistic" advertising response scores than the forced exposure environment where respondents exhibited, in effect, an artificially high level of attention to the only stimuli available. Interestingly, the simulated-natural testing environment resulted in enhanced discrimination among commercials by respondents. This discovery is important to copy research since the respondents' ability to discriminate between commercial executions is the key to separating "effective" from "ineffective" ads.

The table shows the average ad response scores for the test commercials. Only the purchase interest measure shows no *statistically* significant evidence of an attenuated response due to exposure environment.

ADVERTISING RESPONSE FOR FOUR TEST COMMERCIALS (BY VIEWING ENVIRONMENT)

	Forced exposure	*Simulated natural exposure*
Unaided recall	26.8%	18.3%
Aided recall	68.0	45.0
Copy point credibility	44.0	31.0
Purchase interest	16.5	15.6
Pre- and post-behavior change	11.3	6.2

Next, to further examine the comparative levels of response discrimination in the two test environments, coefficients of variation were calculated for each measure in each environment. We discovered that variation is noticeably greater for all commercials in the simulated-natural environment. This suggests a higher level of discrimination inherent in simulated-natural environment copy testing. Since this testing approach is not used in the marketing and advertising industry, we hope that the promise it has shown in our work, coupled with the ARF study findings, will lead ultimately to copy testing tools that are highly predictive of marketplace performance.

≣ Don't Buy Media to Increase the Clutter

A report from the media trenches: Roddy Freeman, vice president and group media director of the W. B. Doner & Co. advertising agency, wrote in the September 1990 *Marketing & Media Decisions*, "A few months back, a [media] planner stopped in my office after speaking to a client. We had developed a plan consisting of magazines that were highly likely to be read by the brand's heavy users. The client had rejected the plan, said the planner, because the magazines' readers already used the brand. She wanted to reach people who did not use it."

From our perspective, both the planner and the client were mistaken. We don't believe a company should select magazines on the basis of heavy users, any more than it should select heavy users as a target audience. But a company should not select media on the basis of nonusers either.

Typically, however—and this is a sweeping generalization—companies (or their advertising agencies) select media to reach as many eighteen- to forty-nine-year-old women as they can afford (the television strategy) or to reach as many heavy users as possible (the print strategy). These two approaches mean that companies waste from hundreds of thousands to millions of dollars a year putting their messages where they cannot possibly have any effect—except, perhaps, to increase consumer irritation at the advertising clutter.

The 1980s saw two massive and complex media trends—fragmentation and measurement. These will almost certainly continue through the 1990s. *Fragmentation* means that American consumers simply have more media options than ever. These options include the traditional media: television (network, independent, cable), magazines (more special interest publications), newspapers, radio, books, and movies. But these media choices include options like video cassette tapes, laser discs, the Prodigy interactive computer service, home computers, and video games. Since time is finite and since every new medium tends to supplement rather than replace older media, audiences fragment.

Not only do consumers have a greater variety of media from which to choose; they also are being exposed to more advertisements than ever before. They are seeing commercials in doctor's waiting rooms; in school classrooms; on supermarket shopping carts and on the Checkout Channel; in stadiums, ball parks, and race tracks. There are ads on video monitors in subways, bus stations, and airports; on nine-screen video walls located in the center of shopping malls; on television monitors in health clubs and in video arcades.

At the same time, marketers will have more and better tools to measure the various audiences that these advertising media attract. A. C. Nielsen, Information Resources, Arbitron, and other companies are

The Check Is in the Mail ... 191

developing mechanisms—such as passive people meters and bar code scanners—by which they will be able to tell exactly who watched what commercials and what they later bought at the supermarket.

≣Program Involvement: Help or Hinder?

What is the effect of the television program involvement on advertising response?* In other words, will the same commercial placed in two different programs that have the same viewership and the same audience profiles generate the same advertising response or a different response depending on viewer involvement with the program?

Since the 1960s two fundamentally opposed theories have evolved: the *negative effects hypothesis* and the *positive effects hypothesis* of viewer involvement. According to the first theory, the more involved viewers are in a television program—the more they like it, are held by it, are tuned in to it—the weaker their response to the commercials. A strong program, this view holds, has a "video vampire effect"; it sucks the life out of the commercial messages.

The positive effects hypothesis takes the opposite position. It says that involving programs produce engaged respondents who ultimately demonstrate more favorable responses to commercial messages carried by the program. The more involving the program, the more positive the ad response.

Over the last thirty-five years, more than thirty research studies explicitly testing media environment effects turned up evidence for both positions. When we investigated those studies, however, we found that the methodologies used were very different. Negative effects findings, for example, were almost invariably based on forced exposure—artificial environment studies, undertaken among small, nonprojectable samples, often students. These researchers regarded high versus low involvement as a characteristic of the program, not the individuals watching it.

Involvement, you will recall, has to do with individuals, not the buying decision, advertising, or medium. Is *Monday Night Football* a high-involvement program? It is if you care about football; if you don't, it's not.

The positive effects hypothesis, on the other hand, tends to be supported by natural, real-world environment studies based on far larger and more representative samples. In almost all these studies, the researchers regarded involvement as a state of mind of the people watching the pro-

*The authors acknowledge with thanks the contribution of David W. Lloyd, Ph.D., of Yankelovich Clancy Shulman, to this discussion of the effects of television program involvement.

gram and measured it using standard rating scales: for example, a five-point "favorite program" scale could range from a "poor program" to "my favorite program." Unfortunately, most of these studies measured recall only, not a full range of advertising response indicators.

We decided to design a study that would overcome all these drawbacks. We began with five simple hypotheses:

- One can measure "program involvement" in a reliable, valid manner.
- Involvement is positively related to advertising response: the higher the level of involvement in a program, the stronger the effects of advertising shown in that program.
- Involvement does vary by program and varies considerably by viewer within a given program audience. Programs ranked in terms of involvement and exposure are not the same thing. If you rank programs by involvement levels, you get a different order than if you rank them by exposure.
- The cost per thousand people "involved" or "impacted" is different from cost per thousand people *exposed* to advertising.
- Finally, since cost-per-thousand (CPM) ratings are different from cost-per-thousand-impacted (CPMI) ratings, media planners would make different decisions depending on which they used.

The details of the study methodology are not important here (they are available, however, to anyone interested). We did attempt to expose the 470 randomly selected female heads of households to programs and commercials in conditions that mirrored normal in-home viewing conditions as closely as possible.

Our first task was to construct a program involvement measure. We selected thirty items to explore cognitive, emotionally based, behavioral, and mood-altering reactions to different programs. The most important and significant factor we labeled "entertainment value." This factor included items such as these:

- This program was a cut above the average TV show. It was thought-provoking as well as entertaining.
- There were parts in this show that really touched my feelings.
- This show had the ability to make me feel some of the same things that the characters were feeling at times.
- I was really involved in the program. By the end I wished it had lasted longer.

We asked respondents to report how strongly they agreed or disagreed with each item using a forced-choice scale, and we added the scores for each respondent across all items in a factor.

While we measured many variables, the five key variables were unaided recall, aided copy point recall, credibility for each message recalled, purchase interest using the industry's favorite five-point rating scale, and pre- and post-changes in buying intentions on a constant sum scale.

The first key thing we found was that under simulated-natural environment conditions, "program involvement" exhibits a significant positive effect on all measures of ad response. Here are the figures:

ADVERTISING RESPONSE FOR FOUR KEY COMMERCIALS (BY PROGRAM INVOLVEMENT)

	Program involvement		
	Low	*Moderate*	*High*
Unaided recall	18.4%	21.0%	22.2%
Aided recall	34.0	48.0	54.0
Copy point credibility	24.0	37.0	41.0
Purchase interest	13.2	15.7	17.0
Pre- and post-behavioral change	6.4	12.6	14.4

The figures indicate that, as program involvement goes up, all five commercial or advertising measures also go up. The bottom row of figures, for example, measure the pre- and post-change in behavior. Among people low in program involvement, the average change was 6.4 percent. Among people high in involvement, the figure was more than twice as large, 14.4 percent.

But what are the media implications? If program involvement enhances advertising response, and if involvement means more than simple viewership, then cost per thousand people *involved* or *impacted* should replace cost per thousand *exposed* as the tool of choice for media selection decisions. Although marketers have purchased media based on costs per thousands of people exposed, known in the industry as *CPMs* for decades, we say it's a myth that this approach has been, or will continue to be, helpful.

The fact is that we now have evidence that media vehicles do differ considerably in terms of involvement or impact—even holding audience size or rating constant. Clearly, if media impact determines ad response, knowing this can aid or impede a campaign's success.

The key question is whether the cost per thousand and the cost per thousand impacted are closely related for the same set of programs. Would a company buy the same or different media if the decision were based on impacted viewers rather than the total number?

We were able to estimate "advertising effectiveness" scores for forty different prime-time and news or current events programs. Below you can see the comparison between the cost per thousand and cost per thousand impacted for the ten programs in the top quartile—that is, those that rated highest in both cost per thousand and cost per thousand impacted.

CPM/CPMI COMPARISON FOR THE 10 TOP PROGRAMS

Programs in top quartile	CPM	Index value	CPMI	Index value
1	$10.92	.96	$8.17	1.67
2	12.07	1.08	9.29	1.39
3	12.43	.67	9.80	1.53
4	12.78	1.08	11.18	1.08
5	12.91	1.39	11.60	1.47
6	13.19	.99	11.81	1.40
7	13.51	.67	11.84	1.08
8	13.67	1.67	11.99	.96
9	14.08	.90	12.12	1.30
10	14.52	1.16	12.52	1.16

The average cost per thousand for these ten shows is $13.07; the average cost per thousand impacted, however, is $11.03, a significant 18.5 percent cost savings.

The table shows that in seven of the ten cases, the cost per thousand impacted index value is greater than the cost per thousand index value. In two cases the indexes are identical, and in only one case is the CPM index value greater than the CPMI index value.

Cost per thousand impacted figures therefore offer higher levels of predicted effectiveness as well as lower costs. But how to demonstrate their potential overall superiority over cost per thousand? One way, of course, is to demonstrate overall cost efficiency.

To do that, we divided the average predicted efficiency scores by their respective average cost per thousand for each approach. The resulting "efficiency ratio" for cost per thousand was 8.1; the ratio for cost per thousand impacted was 11.8—a 46 percent improvement.

This research finding indicates that television program involvement *does* appear to be positively, causally linked to advertising effectiveness. Since program involvement, attitudes, or "impact" seems to vary significantly by program, media decisions should take these differences into account.

And while we do not have the research to prove the case, we suspect a similar study of magazines would make the same point: people who are deeply involved in the editorial content are also interested in the advertising. People who read computer magazines are interested in computers; people who read an entertainment magazine may or may not be interested in computers.

The cost per thousand people and the cost per thousand people *impacted* are not the same. Our preliminary analyses suggest that they are potentially very different and that media decisions would be similarly different based on the proposed versus traditional approaches. Since the concept of cost per thousand impacted appears to offer what advertisers want and are willing to pay for, then advertising agency media planners need to take differential viewer involvement more directly and systematically into account.

≡ Media Scheduling Can Be Tested Prior to a Real-World Experience

Twenty years ago it was common for Procter & Gamble marketing executives to launch front-loaded campaigns for new and repositioned brands. By *front-loaded* we mean that the bulk of the media buy would occur early—often within three months after launch—so that the brand manager could be assured that brand awareness and trial (that is, penetration) would peak within the first six months.

Word of the value of front-loaded campaigns spread from industry to industry like an infectious disease. The result was the death of many advertising programs that might have survived with a different media schedule.

We have been using simulation technology for years to examine the relationship between type of media schedule (e.g., front-loaded, pulsed, or continuous), product (new or established), purchase cycle (once a week, once a month, six times a year, twice a year), and other factors. The results are fascinating. Front-loaded schedules always seem to work best for *fast turnover, new* products (one to four or more purchases per month). They invariably fail for *slow turnover* brands irrespective of whether they are new or established (those brands purchased only twice a year or less frequently). The reason is simple: a front-loaded campaign will fire up awareness when people are not yet ready to buy. It's like heating the furnace on a warm day. When people are ready to buy because they've used up the stock of whatever the new product is designed to replace, they've already forgotten the new brand exists. When fall turns to winter, the fuel burned in summer does nothing to warm a cold house.

These, of course, are just a few examples. The facts are that media schedules are often built without much science and are based on hunch, tradition, mythology, and experience gained at roulette tables. Yet simulation technology can be employed to provide insights into what kind of media schedule is best for a particular product in a specific market.

≣ Evaluating Your Ad Campaign Has Become an Imperative

The days of investing $20 million in an advertising campaign and not tracking its performance are over. An increasing number of CEOs will demand accountability for this investment. As we show in Chapter 11, a good tracking study can provide not only a scorecard on how the campaign is progressing but a blueprint for changes that can be used to improve the program.

Smart advertisers often start with a model such as the one shown in

Figure 8.7 *Model of How Advertising Works for a High-Involvement Durable*

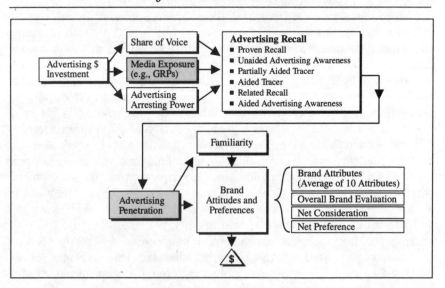

Figure 8.7, adopted from work we have done for a marketer of expensive, high-involvement consumer and industrial durable products. This marketer not only tracks each link in this chain for its own products, but it tracks competitive brands as well. As a result, the company is able to answer such questions as these:

- How much effectiveness am I getting for my advertising investment as compared to enemy products?
- What is the relative contribution of share-of-voice, absolute media exposure, and ad arresting power to ad recall and other measures of effectiveness?
- Which measures of recall work best?
- How do these different conventional measures combine into a single measure of true advertising recall, labeled *advertising penetration?*
- How does penetration lead to familiarity, brand attitudes, and preferences?
- How does everything tie to improved sales and, eventually, return on investment?

Advertising clearly needs help. Many people still believe the myths: that it does not matter whether people like your advertising or not, only how memorable and persuasive it is; that advertising works best in markets where a brand is doing poorly, markets where you have the greatest opportunity to impact sales; that every campaign should be front-loaded.

The way to help advertising, we believe, is to start with a clean slate, to take the steps necessary to come up with memorable, effective messages, and to place these messages where the target market will see them.

The steps are relatively easy to take, but they require time and effort. Obtain a list of all possible attributes and benefits. Screen the list to determine the strongest messages. Evaluate these messages alone and in combination in terms of forecasted sales. Then include the winning message in a large number of different executions to be tested using a methodology that takes into account new discoveries concerning measures that are predictive of sales response and the benefits of simulated-natural environment testing.

Once we have the strongest possible execution and message, we have to evaluate media not on the basis of total audience—on the basis of cost per thousand—but on the basis of the people our message actually impacts. Finally evaluate the best possible schedule using simulation technology.

But before we actually go into the market, we may want to test things first.

FOCAL POINTS FOR MAKING ADVERTISING MORE EFFECTIVE

- Start with a clear understanding of the marketing environment, a profit-producing marketing target, a strong positioning, and a carefully configured product and price.
- *Message:* Use message engineering technology to identify the most powerful message strategy possible.
- *Execution:* Select the most powerful execution from many alternative possibilities using criteria that predict sales.
- *Involvement:* Measure the viewers' involvement with the medium and the advertising and buy media based on costs per thousand people involved.
- *Media schedule:* Run the ads where and when they will have the greatest impact on the target audience.
- *Ad tracking:* Continuously track consumer advertising awareness and attitudes and buyer behavior through to sales and profitability. That way, the next time the CEO asks, "What is the return on our advertising investment?" there will be an answer.

9

IT'S BETTER TO
FLY A SIMULATOR
THAN CRASH
THE REAL THING

Assume we've methodically taken all the steps we've already described. We've carefully analyzed the environment, picked a target market, decided on a positioning, computer-designed our product, researched a price, and all the rest. Why not just launch the product and get the jump on the competition?

While there may be times when that's appropriate (and we'll spell those out in a moment), if big bucks are riding on the launch, we'll want to test the market first.

A simulated test market (STM), in which the computer program represents the national market, gives us answers quicker (three to five months versus twelve to eighteen) and less expensively ($100,000 versus $3 million) than a "real-world," in-market test.

A real world test, however, may still be necessary to establish trade acceptance and competitive response (although we can—and will—build assumptions about both into the simulated test market).

For any business, a test market's goal should be to introduce a product or service to the target audience, measure its response, by both trial and repeat purchases, and project that response to the full launch. We want to do a test in a condensed period of time (more on time to come) and at a reduced cost relative to a full-scale launch.

The common denominator for all businesses is that the research technology exists today to take simulated or small-scale test data and project this test data to a national launch with a high degree of accuracy and certainty.

The top executive who is reviewing the marketing plan must ask a number of questions about the product test:

THE BOTTOM LINE: WHAT A CEO WANTS TO KNOW

1) Before we invest millions of dollars introducing this marketing plan nationally, how sure are we of market success? After all, most new products fail to achieve sales and profit objectives.

2) Have we taken the product through all the targeting, positioning, product design, and the other exercises outlined earlier?

3) Have we done a simulated (or real-world) test market to save time and money and to minimize our risk?

4) Before we go into the simulated (or real-world) market test of this product, have we objectively set an action standard, market share goals, or sales volume hurdle? The death-wish marketer decides whether to launch the product after seeing the test results; marketing intelligence sets a standard before.

5) What have we done to ensure that simulated test market research provides us with more than a simple volume forecast—that it actually provides us with the insights needed to improve the program?

≣ Ways a Real-World Market Test Can Go Wrong ... and Right

How many ways can a market test get derailed? Companies discover new ones every day. Take Procter & Gamble and its soft 'n munchy Duncan Hines brand cookies as a cautionary example.

Frito-Lay, with Grandma's Rich 'n Chewy brand, was first into the test market, although P&G had been working on soft cookie technology for years. In the test, Grandma's quickly captured one-fifth of the Kansas City, Missouri, cookie market, far exceeding Frito-Lay's most sanguine expectations, not to mention its most optimistic projections, as reported by Stephen Kindel in *Financial World*.

What happened? A Frito-Lay competitor (not P&G), concerned about Grandma's threat, had sent a research company to Kansas City to learn why people would purchase the brand. Because interviewees had to experience the cookies to discuss them knowledgeably, the researchers bought cookies for the interviews. Lots of cookies. So many cookies, in fact, they pushed Grandma's share even higher. By chance, P&G followed Frito-Lay into Kansas City with its Duncan Hines soft cookie brand, where it achieved the same highly skewed results for many of the same reasons. Indeed, the results were so positive, P&G decided to take the product national.

Unfortunately, by the time the national roll-out started, says Kindel, the public had lost interest in packaged soft cookies because they were overprocessed and tasted it and had gone back to the old-fashioned kind. P&G ultimately had to write off soft cookie factories in Tennessee and Florida.

In another story, General Foods developed what amounted to a chocolate flavored Kool-Aid. The product developed tremendous momentum within the company even though the consumer response was not overwhelmingly positive for a watery chocolate drink. Discounting the research and hoping for the best, the company went ahead and introduced the product into three test markets.

Meanwhile, Nestlé, working independently, had developed its own watery chocolate drink and had beaten General Foods into market testing by a few months. When it saw the GF entry, the Nestlé management said, in effect, we must be on to something! General Foods wouldn't go into test market if they didn't think the product had promise. We'll cut our own test short, go national, and position ourselves as the market leader—always the best place to be in the consumer's mind.

Which is what Nestlé did, thereby managing to lose more money than they would have lost if they completed—and believed—their own research.

On the other hand, a fast food chain, which like all its competitors had focused on lunch and dinner, decided to increase profits through more efficient use of its facilities. That meant taking a hard, close look at breakfast. A study of social trends showed the time was right for a fast food breakfast: people with limited time for morning food preparation might respond to such an offering.

The company, however, needed to understand whether the breakfast customer would be similar to or different from the lunch and dinner customer, whether the company needed similar positioning or different positioning: all the issues we've already discussed.

The change meant a significant investment. To make people aware of the new breakfast offerings, the corporation would have to advertise heavily. It also would have to make a capital expenditure to design and create the operations systems that could produce breakfast products.

The fast food chain introduced breakfast in three representative towns in a regional marketing area. It monitored restaurant sales in a control group in an area closely comparable to the towns in which it was introducing breakfast. It then tested different advertising weights and different variations on the service and different product configurations. By testing the fast food market in this way, the chain minimized the risk and maximized the opportunities before the national launch. When the chain did roll out breakfast, it was a tremendous success.

One more example: An overnight courier service realized the fax machine was going to be cutting into its business. Top management decided to come out with a fax-like service that, while it would cut into the business somewhat, would also generate some new business.

The company picked an area, advertised the service, and monitored the results. While the initial response was positive, it found that after a year, consumer interest in the service dropped dramatically. The fax machine alternative was becoming even more appealing, and their fax-like service had no long-term future. The company scrapped the project.

Test markets are fraught with problems. Often the company selects a test market because it's easy to manage, not because it represents the markets the company actually wants to reach.

Even modest efforts by competitors can spoil the company's ability to read the test market results. Companies sometimes sabotage product tests by telling their sales people to pull the competitor's new products off store shelves, turn them sideways, or move them to other shelves where they won't be noticed.

Fortunately, what competitors can do in a test market to affect a brand's performance is not what they're likely to do in the national market. The national market is just too big and unmanageable.

≡ Why New Products Continue to Fail

Thoughtful executives, looking at trade reports, sometimes wonder why new product success rates have not improved during the past thirty years. About as many new products, as a proportion of all new products introduced, fail today as failed during the 1980s, the 1970s, and the 1960s. Given the sophistication we've seen of the new product research methods, models, databases, and research systems during the past few decades, you would think that new product survival rates would have improved. Success rates should be improving, rather than remaining the same or deteriorating. But they haven't.

Marketing observers offer several hypotheses. One suggestion is that as more sophisticated marketers employ increasingly sophisticated research systems, competitors quickly neutralize any advances. It's a zero-sum game played by firms with rising levels of expertise. Market share equilibrium results and constant new product failure rates are the norm.

Another hypothesis: Advertising today, in terms of media weight and copy, isn't strong enough to launch a new product successfully. For example, according to A. C. Nielsen Company figures, the time people spent viewing per television home per day has been relatively stable for ten years: it averaged 6 hours, 38 minutes in 1980; 6 hours, 55 minutes in 1990; and peaked at 7 hours, 10 minutes in 1986. Meanwhile, the cost of commercial time has continued to skyrocket, and the absolute number of commercial messages has increased as stations add commercial seconds and companies run two 15-second spots in the place of one 30-second spot. A company has to spend more money to reach the same number of prospects than it had to spend just five years ago, and, when it does spend the money, its message is lost in a cacophony of other ads.

A third hypothesis—and the one we're going to focus on—is that the marketing battlegrounds of the 1960s and 1970s were, as we've remarked before, very different from those of the late 1980s and 1990s. If the earlier period was the age of offensive strategy, we now live in an age of defensive strategy.

In the 1960s and 1970s, marketers using tools with admittedly weaker capabilities relied more on hunch, judgment, and creativity to launch the occasional new product. If a new product proved to be an early success, competitive response was often too little and too late. Following a "wait and see" period, competitors might follow up with a modest 35 percent increase in spending or promotion and, perhaps later in the year, new copy. It was a gentleman's game, fought by Marquess of Queensbury rules.

But if the 1960s and 1970s were the age of the good offense, the 1980s proved to be the age of the good defense. From the middle of the 1980s and into the foreseeable future, competitive response to new products and new campaigns has been and will continue to be swift and sure. Soon after a launch, the new brand (or new campaign if an established product) is hammered by the products it was designed to dislodge.

Since all three theories are plausible, which one is true?

≣ Don't Stop Introducing New Products

It's a trick question. They're all true. More sophisticated marketers *are* using more sophisticated new product development and testing tools. And, in a zero-sum game played by firms with increasing expertise, market share equilibrium *is* the result. Also, companies make success more difficult for themselves when they cut back on advertising and shift the money to promotion.

In our view, shared by some and argued by others, advertising works better than promotion to position and launch new products. Although promotion can be very efficient in generating new product trial, it fails to provide consumers with the buying rationale necessary to warrant repeat and sustained purchasing. So the shift to promotion has hurt new product efforts.

At the same time, marketers *are* increasingly defense-minded. One firm's offensive thrusts are countered by another's often massive levels of defensive activity—advertising, promotion, price cuts, trade deals, and more. They've seen this pressure in test markets, in regional roll-outs, and in national introductions. As the arsenal of defensive weapons becomes more powerful, it reduces the likelihood of a successful new product introduction. At the same time, however, the more powerful a marketing weapon is, the greater its destructive power, and the more difficult it is to implement it. Highly destructive weapons in marketing warfare, like military warfare, are both expensive and time-consuming to build and launch (see Fig. 9.1).

Take a recent experience we had with what we'll call "The Case of the Annihilated Brand." This food product had an advertising and promotion budget, projected nationally, of $70 million. The marketer assumed that competitive spending might increase as much as 80 percent over the base period. With this assumption as the input, the simulated test market research forecast a 3.6 percent share of market by the end of the first year.

Figure 9.1 *The Relationship between Destructive Power and Difficulty of Implementation*

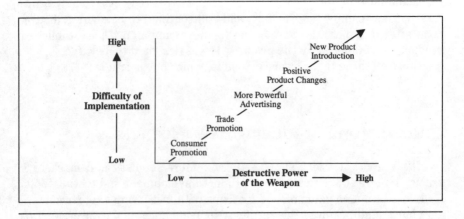

The actual share was 0.7 percent, and the product was a clear disaster. What happened? Poor research? Inadequate effort on the company's part? We were called in to perform an autopsy.

We found that the company's advertising and promotional spending for the new brand was in line with what it had planned. The competition's spending, however, had not increased 80 percent. It had increased *630 percent*—$1 billion worth of advertising and promotion, projected nationally. The new food product was simply annihilated.

As an aside, the competitors who increased their advertising and promotional spending 630 percent could not have sustained this level of spending, at least not for very long and not nationally. They were losing money. But this was not a national introduction, and the competition obviously felt it was worthwhile to lose money in the test market to prevent the new brand from establishing itself.

Companies deploy five kinds of weapons with increasing levels of destructive power to crush new brands:

- Consumer promotion (mainly coupons).
- Trade promotion (discounts, special displays, co-op advertising, etc).
- More powerful advertising (improved message strategy or execution or both).
- Positive product changes (formulation or packaging or both).
- A new product.

Each has a positive effect for the competitor who uses them and a clear negative effect on anybody else's new product (see Fig. 9.2). The

Figure 9.2 *The Relationship between Weapon Deployment and New Product Damage*

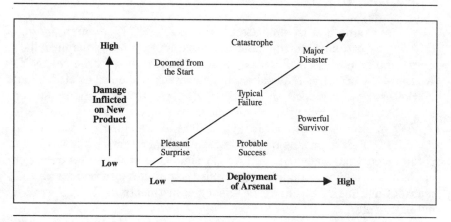

competitor who uses any of these today can inflict substantial damage on a new product, leading to the typical new product failure. A company that employs the entire arsenal can produce a major disaster for a competitor, and companies are using these weapons more and more. Our recent survey of marketing directors at *Fortune* 100 companies found three out of four saying that competitive defenses are tougher today than ten years ago.

Between the neutralization that takes place in the marketplace with rising sophistication levels, the marketing budget's shift to promotion, and the competition's defensive activity, it's no surprise that new product success rates have not improved. But does that mean companies should stop introducing new or repositioned products or services?

Hardly. It *does* mean that in the 1990s—as we have indicated throughout the earlier chapters—companies will have to plan even more carefully and employ all the marketing tools available. Companies need to rethink how they structure their marketing efforts—ensuring that marketing people obtain and use cost information, for example, to evaluate hundreds of thousands of alternatives on the basis of profitability.

But the question remains: what, if anything, can marketers do to improve the likelihood of new product success in this age of promotion and unprecedented levels of competitive response? How in the 1990s can companies anticipate defensive competitive response and develop and test offensive strategies designed to overwhelm those defenses? And how can companies do all this without costly, time-consuming test marketing?

≡ The Three Advantages of Simulated Test Marketing

They can do it with simulated test market (STM) research, by getting all the bad news in the laboratory, without spending major dollars only to be hammered in Pittsfield, Mass., Merion, Ind., Rochester, N.Y., Kansas City, Seattle, Milwaukee, or any other test market city. What marketers need is a decision-support system to help them choose among all of the plans a company might develop.

When a company commits major dollars to launching a new product, it wants to reduce risk as much as possible. When that risk is large, we recommend that management first do simulated test market research and adjust the marketing plan, then put the product into real-world test markets and make any more necessary adjustments, and finally roll it out nationally.

We believe simulated test marketing research is the best way a company can reduce risk when launching a new product (or restaging or repositioning an existing product), but test marketing—simulated *or* real world—is not always necessary.

Brian Shea, the manager of marketing research at Ore-Ida, tells us that they don't bother with simulated test market research when the cost of the STM is greater than the potential loss should consumers and the trade totally reject the new item. If, in other words, the risk to your overall brand franchise is fairly low and people will continue to buy the company's other products and think well of the firm no matter how the new (or restaged) product does, Shea would not see much need for STM.

On the other hand, we, like Ore-Ida, see three major advantages to doing simulated test marketing research:

1) It reduces risk. These risks include the marketing and sales dollars but also the capital risk—the expense of putting in production lines or building a new factory to manufacture the product. Since eight out of ten new products fail, why would a company want to spend $2 million or $3 million and wait a year and half to get the results of a failure when it can spend $100,000 or $150,000 and take three to six months to learn how to fix the problems?

2) It increases efficiency. If you had two or three new-product development projects underway, and one seemed to offer more volume and greater margins, you would move in that direction rather than another. The STM can indicate the project offering the greatest return. An STM can also improve the company's marketing efficiency in a project it does go ahead with—to see the effect, say, of shifting the budgeted $1 million from television advertising to a coupon, or vice versa.

3) It maintains security. As soon as you put a product into a real-world test market, the whole world knows about it, starting with your competitor's salespeople. And competitors can react either by trying to knock off your product or by smothering the baby at birth.

The issue is not STM *or* real-world test. We are *not* saying that, based on the STM, a company can go directly into national distribution. The STM offers advantages, but so does the real-world test. A real-world test gives you a much better feel for the trade acceptance of a new product. Ore-Ida once did a STM in which the company assumed 90 percent distribution. When it brought the product out, however, it obtained only 10 percent distribution. The retail grocery trade saw the item as a once-a-year loss leader and did not want to carry it year round. "We were trying to develop this category into a continuing business, and the retailers just wouldn't do it for whatever reasons they had," says Shea.

≣ The Importance of Time in Marketing

Yet another reason exists for a simulated test market: it can save the company time. The STM can give you results in three to five months where you may have to wait more than a year for the same results from an in-market test.

Time, as an element of competitive advantage, is only beginning to gain currency. But as a strategic weapon, time is the equivalent of money, productivity, quality, even innovation. George Stalk, Jr., a vice president of the Boston Consulting Group, wrote in the July–August 1988 *Harvard Business Review,*

> The ways leading companies manage time—in production, in new product development and introduction, in sales and distribution—represent the most powerful new sources of competitive advantage. While time is a basic performance variable, management seldom monitors its consumption explicitly—almost never with the same precision accorded sales and costs. Yet time is a more critical competitive yardstick than traditional financial measurements.

A company that builds its strategy on flexible manufacturing and rapid-response systems is a more powerful competitor than one with a traditional strategy based on low wages or manufacturing cost efficiencies. "These older, cost-based strategies require managers to do whatever is necessary to drive down costs," writes Stalk, "move production to or source from a low-wage country; build new facilities or consolidate old plants to gain economies of scale." These all do reduce costs but at the expense of responsiveness, and in the 1990s customers will be more interested in response than in price.

Western time-based competitors include Benetton, Federal Express (and all of its competitors, including the U.S. Postal Service), Domino's Pizza, Wilson Art, and McDonald's. Many such companies, however, are Japanese: Sony, Matsushita, Sharp, Toyota, Hitachi, NEC, Toshiba, Honda, Hino, and more. At these corporations, time is the measurement of performance. By reducing the consumption of time in every aspect of the business, these companies also reduce costs, improve quality, and stay close to their customers.

We're beginning to see examples large and small of this interest in, and use of, time as a strategic marketing tool. For the first time in 1990, H&R Block earned about $85.8 million (11 percent of revenues) by sending consumer federal income tax returns electronically to the IRS. The appeal to consumers? Taxpayers due refunds were promised a check in two to three weeks versus six weeks or more if they filed the old-fashioned way.

Citicorp's Mortgage Power Plus competes for the consumer's dollar by delivering a loan commitment in as little as 15 minutes, as opposed to the two weeks to a month banks traditionally take.

Nike, L. L. Bean, James River Traders, and other firms are working with Federal Express to speed deliveries. Nike guarantees that a retailer can offer any customer any size, style, and color by next-day air express; the retailer may pay the premium or pass it along to customers. L. L. Bean promises consumers delivery within two days for a small premium per order; MacWarehouse, a computer software and accessories distributor, offers next-day delivery at no extra charge.

On the manufacturing side, there's the growth of just-in-time inventory, but also the increase in the speed by which information moves around the globe. The Limited, for example, takes the latest fashion trend from Paris or New York, transmits it to factories in southern China, and delivers cheaper versions to its 3,200 stores weeks before the designers produce their originals for sale. The Limited has outgrown fax machines, replacing them with high-resolution computer images sent via private satellite transmission networks. "Within 60 minutes of a customer order, we can send a visual representation of the style, shown on the store's favorite model, to Hong Kong," Stephen R. Du Mont told the *New York Times* (May 13, 1990). Du Mont is the executive vice president of Mast Industries, the manufacturing subsidiary of The Limited. "It comes out on ink-jet printers with a quality similar to a lithograph you might frame and put on your wall. And we can do it in about 16 million colors." Mast strives to recognize and deliver a new style in 1,000 hours. That's about forty-one days between the buyer saying, "I need 10,000 of these," and the clothing delivered to the store.

As the ability to distribute information literally at the speed of light grows, more companies will take as their motto, "Provide the most value, for the lowest cost, in the least time."

Because today's highly fragmented markets consist of a large number of small opportunities, companies can no longer afford to spend equal time responding to every potential customer. Time-based marketing allows companies to serve key customer needs quickly, which in turn creates more value. In an era of time-based competition, a firm's competitive advantage is defined not by cost but by the total time required to produce a product or service. "Early adopters report that actions modeled on just-in-time—simplified flows, waste reduction, reduced setup times and batch sizes—can also dramatically reduce time in product development, engineering, and customer service," says Dr. Joseph Blackburn, associate dean of the Owen Graduate School of Management at Vanderbilt University. "Firms able to achieve faster response times have reported growth rates over three times the industry average and double the profitability. Thus the payoff is market dominance."

≣ Testing the Water without Getting Wet

Simulated test marketing research can be traced back to 1968 when Yankelovich, Skelly & White introduced the Laboratory Test Market. The system was pretty basic: YSW exposed a group of about 500 consumers to advertising for a new P & G product and its competitors; they were then invited into a test store and given an opportunity to buy the product. Several weeks later, YSW researchers contacted these people at home and asked if they'd like to reorder and asked their reaction to the product. YSW factored that data by norms it developed over time to estimate the new product's success or failure. The system, though primitive, worked fairly well and, over the first ten years of its history, proved accurate about 90 percent of the time in simply forecasting success or failure.

In 1977 Florence Skelly, one of the YSW principals, met Dr. Kevin Clancy, one of this book's authors. She knew Clancy was interested in mathematical models and knew that he had worked on the New Product Early Warning System at BBDO Advertising. Skelly asked him if he could combine the Laboratory Test Market technology databases with an established mathematical model to refine the forecasts. Clancy said he thought he could, and he and Professor Joseph Blackburn, then a management scientist at Vanderbilt University, spent the next year working on a model they eventually called Litmus™.

The first presentation of the model's results felt something like a showdown at high noon. At one end of the Yankelovich Skelly & White conference room table were Clancy and Blackburn; at the other end, were the Laboratory Test Market veterans led by Robert Goldberg, a new products guru, who had been doing it the YSW way for ten years or more and were reluctant to change.

Skelly and Goldberg had given Clancy and Blackburn twenty marketing plans—twenty cases for which YSW already knew the real-world results—and asked them to run a forecast through the Litmus model. Each group had twenty envelopes in front of them. Clancy's envelopes contained the forecast of what the product would do based on the marketing information and the model's calculations; the LTM veterans' envelopes held the product's actual results. The LTM veterans expected major differences between the forecast and the fact because they could not believe that a mathematical model could match all the intelligence and expertise of the group that had been doing these forecasts for years.

In fact, the Litmus model's forecasts were virtually identical to the actual results in seventeen of the twenty cases. The results were so close that Clancy and Blackburn decided to write up the results for publication. Over time, Litmus has become one of the most validated simulated test marketing models in the world. It is routinely employed for new packaged goods and increasingly used—with modifications—for consumer durables and services. Parts of the system have been applied for business-to-business cases as well.

Litmus, of course, is not the only simulated test marketing research system. Others include the following:

- Assessor, offered by M/A/R/C in Dallas, Texas, was first available in 1973. Virtually all of Assessor's 1,000-plus studies have been for packaged goods, and 22 percent of those have been food products.
- Bases, a recent spin-off of Burke in Cincinnati, Ohio, was first available in 1978. Bases has conducted over 3,000 studies, half of which have been for food products, 30 percent for health and beauty aids and household products, the remaining 20 percent for other products.
- ESP, offered by the NPD Group in Park Ridge, Illinois, and Port Washington, New York, was first available in 1972 as Panpro. ESP has conducted over 2,000 packaged goods studies, 65 percent of which were food products.

Other simulated test market methodologies in use include Comp offered by Elrick and Lavidge, Inc. (Chicago); News Planner by BBDO Worldwide (New York); Leo Burnett Model by Leo Burnett (Chicago); and Adopter by Data Development Corp. (New York).

≡ What an STM Needs for a Forecast

Although not every simulated test market research system requires the same information from the marketer, performs the research in the same way, or provides exactly the same forecasts, we are going to write about them in general as if they did, rather than focus on any one system.

The better systems today represent the offspring of a marriage between sophisticated mathematical models of the new product marketing mix and less sophisticated, but undeniably clever, simulated test market research systems. These better systems integrate marketing science modeling, automated intelligence technology, historical databases, and simulated test marketing research.

STMs today are generations away from the old five-component multiplication models of the 1960s and 1970s, some of which are still in widespread use. The old models' methodologies were based on taking a year-end awareness number (component 1) and multiplying it by an awareness-to-trial (2) and distribution estimate (3) to forecast penetration. The penetration figure, coupled with repeat purchase (4) and usage rate (5) data, helped the company forecast sales.

The problem with the five-component model stemmed from the

primitive manner in which marketers estimated or guessed at these five different parameters. Perhaps the best example of the problems endemic to such a procedure can be seen in component 1. Until the introduction of the Litmus model in 1978, the client marketing company and agency guesstimated an awareness figure. That is to say, the client and agency, without any model, without any historic databases, would conjecture the year-end awareness number, the percentage of the target audience that would be aware of the product. They were almost always wrong. They almost always overestimated the true awareness by a significant factor. Given that the awareness number drives everything else, the percentage by which marketers overstated awareness represented the extent to which they overstated the forecast.

In contrast, today's better STMs capture *every* important component in the marketing mix—from media weight and schedule through promotion, product, and positioning—and assess the effect of any plan on brand awareness through to market share and profitability (see Fig. 9.3).

But what does such a system actually do? Why would a manager use one? Basically, today's STMs test any plan the marketing manager wishes to consider—even a competitor's plan. The marketer simply enters the plan into the computer and the model forecasts consumer awareness, sales, profits, and much more, as we'll see in a moment.

Some systems can go beyond the volume forecast. For example, the Litmus system permits marketing management to ask "what if?" ques-

Figure 9.3 *Marketing Mix Model for a New Product*

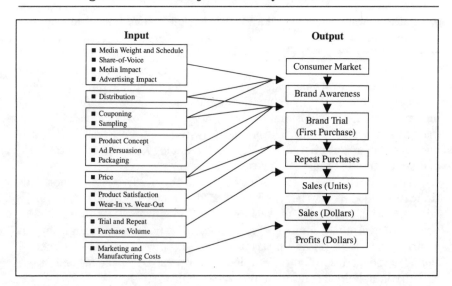

tions such as, "What would happen if I decreased media spending 25 percent?" or "What would happen if I increased consumer promotion 10 percent?" Litmus will actually recommend a plan, and we have not seen a case yet where the plan recommended by the STM doesn't beat the one submitted by product managers. Sometimes the margin is modest; other times it's overwhelming.

The level of sophistication of today's STMs can be illustrated by a submodel that allows them to forecast total brand awareness by month. The model provides estimates of the proportion of people who become aware of the product due to advertising, couponing, sampling, and distribution. By the end of the product's first month in the world, the STM forecasts sixteen different awareness states. By the end of the twelfth month, the problem has become far more complex, and the STM has to consider more than 30 billion awareness, trial, and repeat states.

To undertake an STM, a marketer must provide the consulting firm with a large number of inputs, most of which come right out of the marketing plan. Since the forecast grows out of these assumptions, the closer they are to reality, the closer the forecast will be. Companies have a tendency, we find, to hope for the best in their assumptions; it's a tendency we do our best to resist because small hopes can turn into large disasters.

The inputs from the company include

- The market's size (in buyers, units, and dollars)
- Copy testing results
- Advertising budget for the test product and competitors
- Media schedule, by month
- Consumer promotion, by month
- Trade promotion, by month
- Price
- Distribution build (the proportion of stores carrying the test product, by month)
- Expected marketing costs and margin contribution.

The consulting firm takes this information and designs a research study to *simulate* the likely trial and repeat purchase for the new (or restaged) brand. To do this also requires a supply of the test product and the competitive product (or products), advertising for the test product in finished, rough, or even concept board form, and competitive product advertising.

For a simulated test marketing study, we recruit approximately 600 consumers, scientifically selected and representative of the product category's buyers. We invite them to participate in a research study in a central testing facility in three or more different markets. We question these respondents about their product-related attitudes and purchase behaviors in the product category, and we then expose them to the advertising embedded in a television program for the new or restaged brand and for competitive brands.

Following this exposure, we ask the people to write down their comments about the program and the advertising. We then invite them into a simulated store (a small store stocking test brands, competitive brands, and related product categories) where they can buy anything they want at a significant discount—typically 25 percent. The proportion of consumers who buy the test brand, corrected for by product category norms, is taken as an estimate of the probability of trial (given consumer awareness and product distribution) in the real world.

Four to six weeks following these simulated purchasing experiences, we contact the consumers by telephone and give them the opportunity to reorder the new or restaged brand. For products with an expected wear-out effect, such as cold cereals, we undertake one or more follow-up reorder waves (sometimes called *sales waves*). We are able to use the reorder numbers, together with other attitudinal data, to estimate first and multiple repeat purchases for the new product. We then plug the trial data, repeat data, and all the information gathered earlier from the marketing plan into a very sophisticated mathematical model to generate a forecast, an example of which is shown in Figure 9.4.

With all this as background, how do new product forecasting systems capture the effects of competitive retaliation?

≣ STMs Can Measure Competitive Response

Until recently, pretest market simulation systems, with a few exceptions, didn't really capture competitive response at all. Litmus did include share-of-voice as a parameter, but most other measures of market response assumed "normal" levels of competitive activity, an assumption clearly out of sync with marketing reality.

Because of the rapidly changing nature of competitive response, however, researchers have begun to address this problem. We've learned, for example, that some of the "new" competitive promotional factors like featured pricing can be measured in the laboratory simulation during the experiment.

To understand how this is done, it might be helpful to understand more about the simulation experiment.

In a Litmus simulation study, people move through three stages: exposure to product advertising in a television program or other adver-

Figure 9.4 *Simulated Test Market Output*

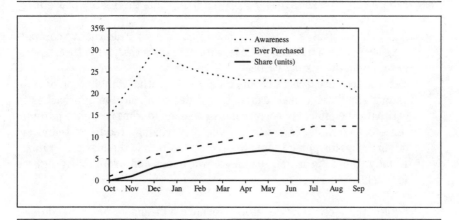

tising or promotion or both; opportunity to buy the product in a simulated store; and follow-up phone calls to measure repeat purchase. We
have discovered that we can measure the effects of competitive pricing
strategies in this experiment with an acceptable level of validity. The
procedure is very simple: vary the prices of competitors on the shelf in
the simulated store.

In a study for Hefty Steel Sack bags that led to the brand's successful national introduction, we tested three different price points for Hefty
and three different competitive price points to learn how Hefty would
perform under different competitive pricing scenarios.

Other competitive response factors require a combination of the
experiment and self-reported measures included in the interview, such
as competitive couponing. Most consumers don't use coupons for most
purchases. To measure the effect of consumer promotion, therefore, we
need to first estimate the probability that someone would use a coupon in
the real world and then observe that person's behavior in the laboratory
environment.

Finally, some competitive variables we wish to capture require a
judgment call based on real-world data, if it's available, and the marketing or research manager's surmise. Take for example shelf dominance.
Our clients tell us that they can estimate the share-of-facings they can
buy as a part of trade deals. What they don't know is how this share-of-
facings relates to sales. Since laboratory experimentation does not seem
to measure this variable very well, we have had to turn to judgmental
and historical relationships in our databases while continuing to test
alternative research methodologies.

Armed with the capability of roughly capturing competitive effects, researchers can forecast sales and profits using this three-step procedure:

- First, the company's marketing management creates alternative competitive scenarios: a most likely case, a more serious case, a life-threatening case, and a doomsday case.
- Second, the researchers use an STM model with a combination of laboratory simulation, measurement, and decision calculus approaches to estimate the effects of each scenario on each market response parameter—for example, increasing radio advertising, reducing television advertising, dropping the price—for every item in the marketing mix.
- Finally, the STM model forecasts awareness and profitability figures for each scenario.

The company can now develop alternative offensive plans to counter likely competitive response. Afterwards, the computer can generate awareness-to-profitability forecasts for each plan. Common strategies that companies take in trying to neutralize competitive response include

- Adjusting each component in the marketing plan up or down in terms of its budget.
- Evaluating different decisions for each component; for example, new advertising copy or pricing strategy.
- Modifying the introduction's schedule—deciding between the "big blast" and the "accretion" strategies.
- Finally, examining a "hold" versus "fold" position.

≡ When the STM Forecasts Failure

Even though a company's marketers may do their best to define the target market, position the product, maximize its profitability, and create effective advertising before the simulated test market research, STMs, by their nature, forecast failure more often than not. Failure is a forecast that may not please the client (although it usually beats failing in the marketplace).

New product efforts, as we've said before, gain a life of their own. Not long ago, we did a STM study for a company that was interested in introducing a cleverly positioned soft drink that had a unique bottle. To introduce this new drink, however, the company would have to build a new bottling plant to manufacture the product, and both the plant and the equipment to manufacturer it would cost many millions of dollars.

The study went on for a long time. It was very complicated, and, at every stage of the process, the marketing research director told us how important it was to come up with a good number because the number had to support the decision to build this plant. From our standpoint, the client was waving a red flag, one that said, "Don't come up with a number that gives us the go ahead because, if you do, we'll have to build this factory." The message the client *thought* he was sending was, "Make sure you do everything you can to tease out more sales so we can go ahead and build the factory." Companies don't hire consultants to lie necessarily, but they do want them to support their judgments.

We finally met with the client research director and presented the STM's preliminary forecast, which came down to: don't build the factory. The research director became furious: "I can't present this to my management! These numbers are impossible! I don't know how you could have ...!" And much, much more. Two days later, at 9:00 in the morning, he walked into our office unannounced. He had never been to our offices before, but he said he had to talk about the product. He stayed until noon, talking about the project, showing us data, going over old research reports. We went back over our work, but we could not make the forecast any better.

Two weeks later, we made the big presentation with the president of the division. We usually start with the forecast and then get into the nitty gritty detail supporting it. Five minutes after we began our presentation, the research director took issue with it and we took issue with him. After we argued back and forth for a few minutes, the division president said to his research director, "I don't know why you're arguing this point. I never thought this product had that much promise. All the results we've gotten at the other stages have been mediocre. We know there are a lot of problems associated with the product, so don't take it personally." And, at that point, the research director began to debate with his boss.

When the dust settled, the research director still had his job, but the company had decided to abandon the product. But we see over and over that people become emotionally involved in their products, which is probably a good thing, but not when it seriously clouds their judgment. We've been asked what would have happened to the research director and product manager if the company had built a multimillion dollar factory and *then* learned the product was a lemon?

They probably wouldn't have suffered. One survey we saw several years ago found that the average tenure of a product manager was eighteen months. The median was about twenty-four months, and hardly anyone was in the job as long as three years. The survey helped explain why so many new product introductions and so many new campaigns for established products are failures. The people who introduce the failures are rarely around to account for them at the end of the process.

≣ How Simulation Can Actually Improve Results

A sophisticated decision support system combines simulated test marketing with mathematical modeling of the marketing mix. Such a system goes beyond forecasting first-year volume potential to provide insights into improving the advertising, the concept, the product and packaging, and the marketing plan itself to increase sales and profits.

Marketers can ask the sensitivity analysis component in a model to evaluate every ingredient in the marketing plan in terms of their effects on sales or profits or both. The model will run hundreds—in some cases thousands—of simulations to identify those factors that contribute most to marketing success.

For example, we recently performed a sensitivity analysis on only a few variables for a new product. The model showed that by dropping the number of prime-time 30-second commercials by 20 percent, the company would save $870,000 and lose 345,000 sales units. At the same time, the model indicated that putting approximately the same amount of money—$877,000—into daytime television would increase this media vehicle's usage 40 percent and increase sales 549,000 units. In other words, a switch from prime-time to daytime 30-second commercials is forecast to increase sales by 204,000 units at an incremental cost of only $7,000 (see Fig. 9.5).

Marketers can use the same sensitivity component to model competitive response. First experience and past history can help to estimate a competitor's plans to stop the new product. Then the model can help to determine which offensive strategy will overcome the most likely defense.

Figure 9.5 *Example of a Sensitivity Analysis for Selected Marketing Components*

	-40%	-30%	-20%	-10%	+10%	+20%	+30%	+40%
Prime 15 Second								
Change in Sales (000's of Units)	-97	-71	-44	-27	+27	+44	+71	+88
Cost (000's of $)	-295	-222	-148	-74	+74	+148	+222	+295
Prime 30 Second								
Change in Sales (000's of Units)	-725	-531	-345	-168	+168	+327	+476	+628
Cost (000's of $)	-1741	-1305	-870	-435	+435	+870	+1305	+1741
Day 15 Second								
Change in Sales (000's of Units)	-44	-35	-27	-9	+97	+27	+35	+44
Cost (000's of $)	-75	-56	-38	-19	+19	+38	+56	+75
Day 30 Second								
Change in Sales (000's of Units)	-610	-451	-301	-150	+142	+284	+416	+549
Cost (000's of $)	-877	-658	-439	-219	+219	+439	+658	+877

Another example of how simulated test marketing can improve a marketing plan is through critical attribute analysis. Critical attribute analysis enables a marketer to assess the attributes and benefits that affect a buyer's purchasing decision most highly. It provides insights into the factors that contribute to or inhibit product trial. And it permits a company to evaluate how well a product or service fulfills the buyer's prepurchase expectations.

Critical attribute analysis, unlike traditional research and analysis, goes beyond the buyer's self-reported behavior to estimate the true impact of features on brand preferences and purchasing behavior and related brand perceptions with behavior. By taking a multidimensional approach, linking motivating power of features with brand perceptions, the analysis identifies product strengths, weaknesses, and opportunities. Once a company has this information, of course, it can build on the product's strengths, work to minimize its weaknesses, and take advantage of any opportunities.

See, as an illustration, the data shown in Figures 9.6 and 9.7. Figure 9.6 shows the ratings of the new product among people who purchased it in the simulated test market laboratory. The points on the graph show eleven different attributes and benefits rated in terms of motivating power (using an approach similar to that described in Chapter 5) and perceived advantage versus disadvantage for the new product compared to the brand the consumer uses most often. Note that "low in calories," "nutrition," and "quality ingredients" are all high in motivating power and high in perceived comparative advantage.

Figure 9.6 *Critical Attributes Analysis*
New Brand versus Brand Most Often Purchased

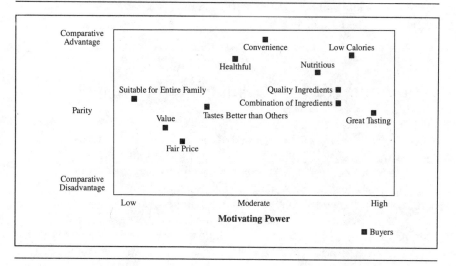

Figure 9.7 *Critical Attributes Analysis*
New Brand versus Brand Most Often Purchased

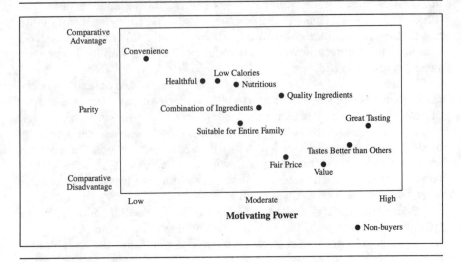

Now take a look at Figure 9.7. There are the same attributes as rated by people who *did not* buy the new product. Note that "low calories," "nutrition," and "quality" are less motivating for these people while "great tasting," a highly motivating characteristic, is perceived as negative (i.e., the new brand is at a competitive disadvantage).

What this suggests is that the number of new product buyers could be increased *if* the new brand corrected its weakness on the perceived taste dimension and/or heightened the importance to consumers of its low cal, nutrition, quality ingredients promises.

≣ Computer-Aided Design of Marketing Plans

The ultimate test of simulation technology comes when the system is called on to identify and describe a financially optimal marketing plan. Just as we discussed computer-aided design of products and services in Chapter 6 and computer-aided design of advertising message strategies in Chapter 8, new developments in marketing science now enable us to employ computer-aided design of marketing programs.

Once a forecast is provided to a client of awareness through profitability and all the diagnostic details described earlier (e.g., sensitivity analysis, critical attribute analysis, etc.) are analyzed, an optimization

Figure 9.8 *Forecasted Performance of Machine versus Manager Plans*

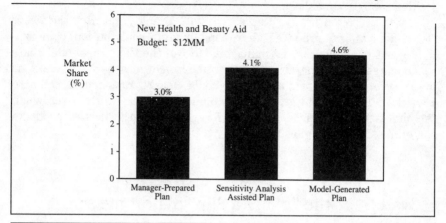

assignment can start. We can briefly describe how the Litmus model addresses this problem. The model begins its analysis with five levels of advertising spending, five levels of promotion, five levels of distribution, and five levels of sampling—the levels ranging from very low to very high. For example, a client might say that it would never spend less than $1 million dollars to support a new brand or more than $50 million. The model would then pick three levels in between, for five levels in total.

Litmus then runs 625 simulated test markets (5 x 5 x 5 x 5 = 625) and uses this database to analyze the relationship between each of the four marketing factors (advertising, promotion, distribution, and sampling) and both sales and profits. Equations are then constructed in order to solve an optimization problem *for this particular product.* The model literally searches through billions of possible plans in order to find the one plan that—subject to management constraints—maximizes brand profitability over a multiyear period.

Comparisons of plans prepared by managers with plans prepared by managers after they have been assisted by simulated test market insights, such as sensitivity analysis, reveal that the use of simulation technology always helps—it helps make the plans more profitable. But optimization technology—what we like to call *model generated plans*—results in marketing programs that are vastly superior to those provided by marketing managers.

Figure 9.8 shows one recent case of a new health and beauty aid supported by a fixed budget of $12 million dollars (i.e., the client wanted to spend no more, no less). The client's marketing department produced a plan that yielded a 3 percent share; help provided by sensitivity analysis improved share to 4.1 percent. But the model-generated "optimal" plan yielded a 4.6 percent share.

Is optimization always this successful? Frankly, no. But the *worst* the model can do is produce a share (and/or profit contribution) comparable to that of the marketing manager. Most of the time, the model beats the manager by 15 percent or more and sometimes by 35 percent or more. Differences of this magnitude could clearly transform a mediocre plan and a failed brand into a better plan and a success. But even when the simulated test market research forecasts product success, products sometimes fail. What goes wrong?

≣ Watch for the "Many a Slip" Syndrome

Perhaps the biggest failures come about because the assumptions on which the model made its forecast were flawed. Brian Shea at Ore-Ida tells us that the volume forecasts from all the STMs they use have been very accurate when the input assumptions are correct. Problems arise when the required input assumptions turn out to be mistaken. For example, if the company estimated a distribution level of 90 percent and obtained only 80 percent, the volume forecast would be off substantially because, in that industry, distribution has almost a one-to-one correspondence to volume.

Not only may the assumptions be mistaken, the dynamics of the market may change between the STM and the actual test market. The company may have a new competitor, one it did not know about when it began the simulated test market research. "If somebody gets out and beats you to the punch," Shea points out, "things change and you're not going to necessarily get the same volume you had when you ran the model. But I have found that the model itself is pretty valid and reliable."

We find with other clients that the company's own commitment changes between the STM and the market test. Or, to put it another way, in most simulated test markets, companies seem to assume an adequate level of marketing support, support that may disappear by the time they begin the product's national introduction. It's very easy to say in a simulated test market study that you're going to put $24 million in advertising behind the brand because no one has to write a check. It's quite another thing to execute against such a plan.

Discrepancies arise between the simulated test market performance and the actual test market because the real world is messier than an STM. Discrepancies also arise between the test market and the real world, or national, performance. Over and over, companies obtain distribution levels in the test market, that are much higher than they ever see again. Why is that? Because the sales force is tuned into the fact that this new product is coming out, and they work harder than ever. This hypersensitivity to the product's success brings results the company never sees again.

Suppose the real world test results are significantly worse than the simulated test market research results. We automatically say to the client, "Tell us what's happening in the test market. ... Tell us what the shelf facings are ... the distribution ... what's going on in terms of trade activity ... consumer promotion ... what the competition is doing ... your share of voice." With these new inputs, the STM can virtually always match what's going on in the market.

At that point, we can ask different questions: "Given what's going on in the marketplace, is there anything that we can do, anything that we can learn from the simulation that would produce a better plan? Given that the competition has increased its advertising and promotional spending in the test market 630 percent, can we add test markets until it becomes just too expensive for him to continue?"

The main objective of simulated test marketing research today is not to obtain a volume forecast. The objective today is to provide diagnostic insight designed to help improve the likelihood of success. Simply telling marketers that they're going to obtain a 5 percent share or a 10 percent share doesn't make them happy. They want insight from the study that will help them build an even better plan—one with an even lower risk of failure.

≣ Sex After Death—Using STMs to Restage Products

While simulated test marketing research works best with new products, you can also use it for restaging (or repositioning) an established product and for extending a line. As we've said before, every three or four years, as top management notices product sales sliding slowly towards oblivion, someone says, "Why don't you turn around this dying brand?" While it's possible to use STM for a restaging effort, it's much more difficult than introducing a new product for at least two reasons:

- The restaged product has a history; it exists; people have bought it in the past. So, the trick is to measure the difference in sales between the restaged product and what sales would have been without the restaging.
- The second and related reason is that often the incremental sales are so small they're very hard to measure. You don't know whether you're

measuring random noise or an actual change. So, to do an STM for restaging an existing product usually takes a much larger sample size than for a new product, and it takes much more sensitivity in the research measurement to pick up true differences.

Most firms doing a restaging, however, make a mistake. They change only one or two elements in the marketing mix. They change the label and maybe tweak the advertising ... and watch the product continue its slide. Consider that if the average, established brand in the average product category is declining by 0.3 percent of a share point every year, and if there are a dozen ingredients in the marketing mix, and if you change one of them, how much effect will it have? How much absolute change of sales could possibly be due to any one of the twelve ingredients in the mix? How much would be due to, say, advertising weight alone, or to positioning alone? The answer is: very, very little, perhaps too small to be measurable.

On the other hand, the more elements the company changes, the greater the likelihood that the restaged product will perform like a new product. We like to call this the "big think, big bang approach." If you change the product formulation, the packaging, the advertising, the pricing strategy, the promotion strategy, the distribution, even the name, by calling it *new and improved*, you've produced sex after death—the restaged product begins to behave like a new product, and simulated test market research can be more helpful.

Line extensions share many of the same problems of restagings. The product already exists in another form, and you're trying to measure the difference between the extension and the existing product(s). This problem is further complicated by the extension's propensity to cannibalize the existing product. The challenge is to measure net incremental sales, which can be anywhere from difficult to impossible.

Because the use of test market simulation methodologies similar to that discussed here enables a marketing executive to evaluate hundreds, perhaps thousands, of alternative plans prior to an actual test market, we believe that serious marketers have little choice but to experiment with this kind of technology, to build and test and validate models that simulate real world introduction. The costs of real world introductions are too high and the likelihood of failure too great to continue with traditional approaches.

The choice we feel is between what Professor Len Lodish of the Wharton School has recently described as being "vaguely right" or "precisely wrong." The common approach of not evaluating plans before real world introduction is precisely wrong. This is particularly true for consumer durables companies, service marketers, and business-to-business marketers who rarely attempt to simulate marketing programs. The alternative, the kind of multi-step process we've described, may not be 100 percent perfect. It may be vaguely right, but it is the only viable option. Evaluating marketing plans, and competitive responses to these plans, prior to expensive, risky real-world introductions has become an imperative.

THE KEY DOS AND DON'TS OF SIMULATED TEST MARKETING

- Be a champion for your new (or re-staged) product, but don't be a blind champion. Maintain a healthy skepticism about the product's likely performance, and remain objective throughout any test, simulated or otherwise, concerning marketing plan inputs, competitive activity, and forecasted results.

- Choose the proper sample to test. Randomly select product decision makers in markets that are representative of the nation.

- Expose people to your product and its advertising in a way that best simulates or reflects the real world. The closer the research environment mirrors the real world environment, the more valid the forecast.

- Use research technology proven to be successful in forecasting marketplace behavior and sales.

- Don't provide a level of support in a real-world test market or estimate a level of support in a simulated market that you would not maintain nationally.

- Prepare for competitive response. In a simulated test market you have to calculate different competitive response levels.

- Be very careful in estimating all marketing input factors—the more you overstate or guess incorrectly, the less accurate will be the forecast.

10

YOU DON'T NEED TO DELIVER PERFECT PRODUCTS AND PERFECT SERVICE

Not long ago, a Yonkers woman wrote The Company Store, a mail-order down quilt retailer in La Crosse, Wisconsin. She was dissatisfied with two pillows she had bought five months earlier for $46. The cotton batting had become matted and flat. What, if anything, would The Company Store do about it?

A correspondence manager wrote back: "Thank you for your letter. I am sorry you are not happy with the merchandise. We do feel we have good quality merchandise, and if a customer gets something she feels is not good quality, we do want to know about it. This is the only way we can make the necessary adjustments to our merchandise." The letter invited the customer to return the pillows for either an exchange or credit.

Two months later the customer finally got around to returning the pillows and ordering one replacement. When the replacement arrived, a printed note said, in part, "your continued satisfaction means everything to us."

Were the pillows defective? Probably not. Did the customer take advantage of The Company Store? From one point of view, she did. Cotton stuffed pillows are not fine goose down, and they are priced accordingly. So, why should a retailer take back merchandise that is not defective, that is exactly as described in its catalog—six months after the sale?

From the customer's perspective, however, mistake or responsibility is not the issue. The pillows did not match her expectations. If the retailer had returned a polite brush-off—"You used them, you keep them"—or not responded at all, the woman would have been stuck. Her only recourse would have been to never order from The Company Store again. This would have been a small decision for her and, by one measure, a trivial one to the company.

Instead, The Company Store made a decision that, theoretically at least, pleased the customer and won her loyalty and positive word-of-mouth advertising.

In our view, virtually every business has so many competitors it can not afford to lose a significant portion of its customer base. Yet not every company has embraced the idea of retaining most, if not all, of their customers unequivocally. And, for companies that don't believe customer service is a major issue, customer service and satisfaction as primary goals are difficult ideas to implement. The CEO may know it's no longer enough to promote the right product in the right place at the right price. However, at the level where the company touches the customer, customer retention may still only mean "business as usual" with the usual horror stories about poor service and satisfaction.

We are convinced that in the 1990s, the companies that thrive and grow will provide not only excellent customer service; they will be monitoring that service *and* customer satisfaction. Management will know what customers want and feel, and it will make whatever adjustments are necessary to satisfy them. The intelligent CEO will be asking questions like these:

THE BOTTOM LINE: WHAT A CEO WANTS TO KNOW

1) How satisfied are our customers with product quality and service, especially on those critical factors that drive our business?

2) Do we have performance evaluation systems in place for tracking customer satisfaction generally and service satisfaction in particular?

3) How are we performing in terms of customer service and satisfaction compared to our competitors?

4) How many customers do we lose each year (or every quarter) because of poor product or service?

5) What would it cost to keep these unhappy customers, and how does this cost compare to the cost of finding new customers?

6) Does a commitment to customer service and satisfaction mean that we must offer "zero defect" products and "exceptional" service?

☰ A Quality Product Is Just the Beginning

Today *every* business must pay special attention to satisfying customers. Customers expect quality products—that's a given—but in addition they want personal service, prompt response to their complaints, and a strong sense that the company they're buying from values their patronage.

Few companies meet these customer criteria better than L. L. Bean in Freeport, Maine. Not long ago a customer in Atlanta called L. L. Bean to order three sleeping bags. The customer wanted them immediately. He could not wait the three days an express delivery would take. The company was able to locate a L. L. Bean employee who was traveling to Atlanta on company business. She carried the sleeping bags with her and delivered them to the customer at the airport the same day.

In another story illustrating extraordinary customer service, a movie studio called L. L. Bean to say they were in the midst of filming and one of the actors was wearing a Bean shirt. The studio needed an exact duplicate—in a particular size—for the stunt man to wear when he was on camera. Unfortunately, L. L. Bean had discontinued the shirt at least a year earlier and the company had none left. However, Bean had sold the last few shirts it had had in stock to a liquidator in Nevada. A Bean customer service representative called the liquidator, who had a few of the shirts left and one in the right size, and arranged to have it delivered to the stunt man.

A colleague told us a wonderful story about a similar experience with Ralph Lauren. For their first wedding anniversary, John wanted to treat his wife to a very special evening. Since she loved opera, John purchased (by pulling a few strings) second row seats to the New York Metropolitan Opera's opening night production of *Salome.* The day before, on business in Boston, he spied "the perfect" basic black dress at a Ralph Lauren retail outlet. Though he knew his wife's size, he knew the dress would have to be altered and that could take up to two weeks. He described his dilemma to the store manager, who called the alterations department at the Ralph Lauren shop on Madison Avenue in New York. The answer: "Have your wife drop by the New York store by 3:00 P.M. tomorrow, and we'll have the dress altered in two hours. Someone will bring it to your hotel by 5:15 P.M." The dress was perfect. His wife looked beautiful. The night at the opera will be remembered for years. And Ralph Lauren won two loyal customers.

All this is fine if you are L. L. Bean or Ralph Lauren, but what if your relationships with customers are indirect? Most manufacturers have an intermediary between the company and the ultimate consumer. In the liquor business, your customer is really the wholesaler. Seagram's has marketing programs for wholesalers as well as for consumers. Airlines and hotels reach prospects through travel agents. Apparel manufacturers may advertise in fashion magazines, but without retail buyers they can't reach the people in the stores.

In the past, manufacturers regarded these intermediaries merely as a channel, or sometimes an albatross. Feed them, take them golfing, keep them docile. But we see intermediaries not just as a channel or a distribution problem, but as a marketing target, a market different from the consumer market. We find that manufacturers are beginning to realize that they have to understand the intermediaries' needs, tailor programs to them, and design products that reflect their needs.

Du Pont, in developing its StainMaster fiber, which is sold to the mills that weave it into carpet, appointed a six-member committee of marketing, R&D, and financial people to find an answer to this question: "How does what we're doing affect the customer?" The committee spent three years consulting with retailers and mill operators, asking for suggestions about how to price StainMaster and to publicize its benefits. Du Pont launched StainMaster with the company's largest new product advertising campaign ever. The fiber revived carpet sales industrywide and produced over $2 billion in revenues for Du Pont. Says Tom McAndrews, director of Du Pont's flooring systems division, "The key is, we looked at our customer as the entire distribution chain. You can't simply meet the needs of the end user."

Holly Farms introduced a fully cooked chicken that was popular with consumers, but grocers complained that the package sale expiration date came too soon after the chicken was delivered and they refused to stock it. Holly Farms improved the packaging, which permitted them to extend the expiration date, and sales doubled. Having learned a lesson, the company is making friends with meat department managers by visiting stores more often and sending them a quarterly newsletter, *Fresh News from Holly Farms.*

The distribution channel is not just a vehicle for delivering your product but can be an important customer or client as well. The media buyer at the advertising agency is not just a buyer, but a reader of your publication. The travel agent is not just a travel agent, but somebody who stays in your hotel. The business long-distance telephone customer is not just a business buyer, but a heavy at-home consumer.

≣ Perception Is the Only Reality

A basic truth in managing customer satisfaction is that perception is the only reality. In other words, it doesn't matter how good you are, but only how good your customers perceive you to be.

To manage these perceptions requires a company to look into its customers' minds. Depending on what it finds, the company may then have to restructure basic sales and service policies, painful though that may be. The change is worth suffering because, as we have found in our work, raising the percentage of repeat business is usually far more valuable to a company than shaving production costs another penny per unit.

Compaq Computer is an interesting example of a company that spends literally millions of dollars every year to monitor and better understand customer perceptions about service.* It has several interesting challenges that grow out of the founders' original decisions. When Joseph R. "Rod" Canion, current president and CEO, William Murto, and James Harris, current SVP engineering, incorporated the company in February 1982, they made two far-reaching and, for the time, radical decisions. They decided to make their personal computers perfectly compatible with IBM's PC, which had been introduced in August 1981, and they decided Compaq would sell exclusively through independent dealers.

At the time, this distribution decision was radical because virtually the entire computer industry had always sold its products directly to the end-users. The IBM salesperson sold IBM; the DEC salesperson sold DEC; the Prime salesperson sold Prime; and an organization tended to buy only IBM or DEC or Prime. And, if there was a problem, they could call the factory representative for help.

Compaq's founders, who had come out of Texas Instruments, believed that customers wanted broad selection in hardware and software and availability, and no manufacturer could offer selection and availability—not even IBM—except through a dealer channel, says Doug Johns, Compaq's vice president, corporate marketing. And Compaq believed that, by foreclosing all other sales options from the beginning, while risky, the policy could generate dealer loyalty since Compaq would be (and is) the only personal computer manufacturer that did not sell directly against its dealers.

The idea provoked some debate within the company. Manufacturers—and their executives—entering the personal computer market at that time had, for the most part, already been in the mainframe and the minicomputer market, which has a completely different structure. They were not comfortable relying exclusively on independent dealers.

As it turned out, of course, Compaq's decision proved correct. Sales shot from $111 million in 1983, to $503 million in 1985, to $1.2 billion in 1987, to almost $3.9 billion in 1990. It was the first company in history to exceed $2 billion in sales within five years of its first product introduction.

*The authors want to acknowledge with thanks the contributions of Doug Johns, Compaq's vice president, corporate marketing, and Andrea Morgan, manager, product/advertising research, to this description of Compaq's operations.

Compaq's founders realized that, given the pricing personal computers carry (low relative to minicomputers and mainframes), and given the kind of support the end-users need, dealers would provide the best local sales and service. Most dealers understood and therefore sold effectively only a few product lines; because Compaq wasn't competing with them over key accounts or other direct sales, the dealers pushed Compaq products.

Compaq's decision, however, meant that, unlike a company selling directly to the ultimate consumer, it had two sets of customers to consider: its dealers and the dealer's customers, the end-users. As a result, customer service and customer satisfaction became far more complex than for a company selling directly to a single end-user. If the dealers were happy and the end-users were not, Compaq would be in trouble; similarly if the end-users were satisfied and the dealers aggravated, Compaq would also suffer.

To satisfy both dealers and end-users, Compaq must consider *both* in its marketing plans. Because dealers are the company's only source of distribution and therefore only source of revenue, Compaq must look at the way the dealers do business and try to create programs that serve the dealer and positively affect the dealer's profitability. In late 1990, for example, Compaq raised its warranty labor reimbursement rate 60 percent; it was the first to offer to cross-ship parts to a dealership overnight.

On the other hand, if Compaq's products don't have enough customer appeal, the right functionality, and the right price, even though the dealers may feel positive about Compaq and, say, its warranty reimbursement policy, they're not going to promote its products, because ultimately they are interested in revenue. Therefore, the company puts all its product concepts through rigorous concept testing and positioning research to be sure it has the right product for the right market and that the positioning is correct. The company offers more than 350 product options, such as monitors, memory boards, and fixed disk drives; it introduced about 110 product options during 1989 alone. According to Andrea Morgan, manager of product and advertising research, Compaq may invest heavily to develop a new product only to learn from customer research that the product does not meet the customer's needs. In that case, the company has to return to the drawing board to redesign the device or, occasionally, if it's beyond redesign, to kill it. While Compaq introduced a portable computer eighteen months ahead of IBM and was the first to market a computer based on Intel's 386 chip, it delayed introduction of its laptop until it could satisfactorily develop the prototype's display and battery technologies. Although Compaq's machine appeared approximately a year later than other laptops, Compaq's STL/286 captured 40 percent of U.S. laptop sales through computer dealers in 1989.

≣ Customer Satisfaction: Not the Same as Customer Service

Compaq, like other intelligent marketers, makes the key distinction between customer service and customer satisfaction. Customer service covers those tangible activities the company can do to affect different situations positively. Sometimes the situation is literally service: the product is broken and needs to be fixed. Other times the need is product availability. Customer service covers delivery schedules, service spares, service training, warranty reimbursement, co-op advertising, and much more. These are logistic, sometimes mechanical issues, and they offer different problems or opportunities for the company.

They are also issues a firm may take for granted, and any one of them is a small bother if neglected. However, what may be a minor irritation to the manufacturer can be a huge problem to the dealer. Efficient dealers watch every nickel. They care, for example, about Compaq's service loaner computers: when Compaq sends them, when Compaq takes them back, how much credit they get, and how quickly Compaq reimburses them.

End-users care about things like product reliability, appearance, functionality, price, and more. Does it feel like a quality product? Does it do what the user wants it to do? Does it do what it was advertised to do, and does it do it reliably? If it breaks, how does the dealer fix it? Is it fixed quickly and effectively at a reasonable cost? The answers to these questions fall under customer service; their sum, measured against the dealer's or the end-user's expectations, would be customer satisfaction.

The customer's expectation plays a key role. Compaq's Doug Johns draws an analogy from another industry. If a consumer knows enough about cameras to know exactly what he wants to buy, he will be interested in only two things: price and availability. He can call a direct sales company and talk to a brusque clerk who wants him to spit out the camera model and his credit card numbers because she has thirty other lights blinking on her switchboard. A week later the camera arrives in a dingy cardboard box, but wrapped securely so it works. The customer knows how to operate it and can read the manual if he doesn't. Despite the clerk and lack of sales help, this customer's satisfaction with the organization is fairly high.

If, however, a consumer does not know much about cameras and needs help, he can go to a camera shop to learn about different models, features, F-stops, and lens settings. If the salesperson is brusque and the chosen camera not available for a week, the customer will be dissatisfied, even if the price is the same as the mail-order firm's. The buying experience does not match the customer's expectation.

Many American companies have introduced customer satisfaction and service systems during the past decade. Fueled, in part, by Tom Peters' and Robert Waterman's *In Search of Excellence,* satisfaction and service tracking measurement has become big business. Some of the work on measurement is good. Much, however, is problematic. Among the more common problems are these:

• *Using mailed questionnaires.* These yield a selective sample that is not representative of a firm's customer base. Americans like to cheer and complain. Mailed satisfaction studies produce disproportionate numbers of both cheerleaders and gripers. The middle range of reasonably contented or mildly displeased customers fail to cooperate and are therefore not included in the resultant database.

• *Conducting research through the sales force.* Some firms, including major companies who should know better, employ sales force down time to contact and interview customers. The sales force cannot be expected to conduct unbiased research. This is the proverbial case of putting the fox in charge of the chicken coop. And, to mix metaphors, this is not research, it is fishing for compliments.

• *Talking expectations, measuring something else.* There has been a surge of interest among satisfaction researchers in measuring customer *expectations.* Books have been written on this topic, and hundreds of academic articles published. Consultants scour the country in search of companies who will use their latest expectation measurement models. Unfortunately, we haven't seen very many examples of expectations measured well. Asking customers about expectations directly in a survey doesn't easily work; the topic is too complicated and doing it indirectly, via importance ratings, involves the kind of primitive technology we discussed in Chapter 5.

• *Measuring company service and satisfaction in a vacuum.* Every firm needs to evaluate its service and overall satisfaction performance compared to its competitors. Today, most customers have experience with multiple competing firms in the same industry. Customers have used at least two different computers, owned two or more makes of car, flown two or more airlines, etc. Therefore, such comparisons must be built into all service and satisfaction research.

• *Ignoring customers' needs.* A surprising number of studies are done in which customers are asked to rate markets and competitors on a variety of dimensions without recognizing (and measuring) that these dimensions may motivate individual customers differently. Some people may be price-conscious, others quality-conscious, still others service-oriented. All dimensions of evaluation, in other words, are not created equal, and it does not take very sophisticated technology to figure out which ones are more important than others.

• *Conducting death-wish research.* Death-wish research includes all of the flaky research tools discussed earlier when we talked about positioning and advertising. You don't measure customer satisfaction and service quality through the use of focus groups, shopping mall samples, user conferences, importance ratings, gap analyses, and the like, unless *you want to reach the wrong conclusions and make the wrong decisions.*

How should satisfaction research be carried out? Clearly, it should be performed by a professional organization independent of the marketer, and it should use measurement tools developed jointly by the client and the researchers. For efficiency reasons, in most cases, the research should be done by phone using professional interviewers reasonably proficient in the vocabulary of the industry. The sample should be representative of a firm's customers and large enough to ensure the data's stability.

The questioning procedure should tap into customer evaluations in terms of twenty to forty tangible and intangible attributes and benefits discovered by pilot testing to be related to the firm's critical success factors. And the research should look at the client firm and at least two competitors. Moreover, the motivating power of each attribute and benefit should be measured for each respondent to create the strategic cube and blueprint for strategies discussed in Chapter 5.

Satisfaction research has to be systematic; a company should do it regularly. Companies make a mistake when they do research only when they think they've got a problem. Compaq does a user satisfaction study among 1,700 end-users twice a year. The large sample is the minimum size necessary to capture all the major issues–products, price, service, distribution. Compaq has found that when it does research on one topic, the dealers or the end-users often talk about something else that is very important to them. Without regular studies, it might miss the new development.

However, the bottom line of all user satisfaction research is how the company can improve its performance and its customers' satisfaction.

≡ The Case of the Sick DIY Chain

A chain of do-it-yourself home centers was facing declining sales despite overall growth in the DIY market. Its customers were fleeing, particularly in markets where a major new competitor was opening new stores. Among the customers who remained, average spending per customer was declining.

This chain asked us to do some satisfaction research, research that would

- Identify exactly what factors drive customer satisfaction.
- Find out how well the chain was perceived as delivering on these factors.
- Evaluate the competition on the same critical factors.
- Use this information to develop a strategy for out-delivering the competition on all the factors that matter most in driving consumer satisfaction.

We call this a blueprint for action, and we illustrate one on page 115 in Chapter 5.

We interviewed 600 do-it-yourself customers in the chain's key markets. The interviews measured consumer behaviors such as frequency of DIY visits, spending or other involvements; the number and size of do-it-yourself projects; how much consumers spent by different types of product categories at DIY and other building supply stores; and how knowledgeable and competent these consumers were.

We also wanted to learn customer expectations of DIY outlets. We asked them to tell us the relative desirability to them of more than thirty different characteristics, attributes, and benefits of DIY centers. The list included tangible and functional characteristics such as service, the amount of sales help, quality of merchandise, breadth of selection, and prices. The list also included many intangible factors we felt contributed to the choice of a DIY outlet: the level of confidence in the store, the pleasures and lack of frustrations shopping there, and the respect paid to customers.

Once we'd found the relative desirability of all these characteristics, we asked consumers to evaluate competitors based on how well they delivered these characteristics. We also identified consumers' relative propensity to shop at each of the competitive outlets. We wanted to understand how the chain stacked up relative to the competition on the things consumers want most.

What we hoped to find was some area of high consumer motivation in which the chain was superior—that is, something in the upper left box of the "blueprint for action" chart on page 115.

However, we discovered an uncomfortable truth: Consumers perceived no significant advantages for this DIY chain on any of the most highly motivating characteristics.

On the other hand, customers perceived the chain to be significantly weaker in the breadth and depth of merchandise. Also, customers considered the employees poorly trained. These key weaknesses were competitive strengths for the new stores entering the markets and were obviously associated with some of the customer loss.

The surprise came when we shared this finding with management. Management was indignant; it believed that the merchandise consumers wanted was always available, that it was *not* out of stock.

A gap obviously yawned between the management and the consumer perceptions. So we set about to understand this gap, given that it was motivating customers to switch to the competition.

Talking to customers at the stores, we discovered that the stores were not efficiently laid out, that their sheer size obscured exactly what the customer was looking for. We also learned that employees were unaware of much of the store's stock, especially items available in the back room warehouse.

In response to these problems, the store management initiated several customer information programs:

- Store entry maps with indexes for major product groups.
- Floor signs corresponding to the maps.
- Computerized touch-screen stands for customer questions.
- Customer service information training programs for employees.

What happened? Over the next year, the competitive disadvantage on merchandise availability declined. Customers were happier and recognized the larger merchandise availability at the company's mega-outlets. These customer perceptions resulted in increased transactions, higher customer loyalty, and improved profits.

Obviously, for all these good things to occur, several things had to happen first:

- Management had to recognize that customers were bailing out and that there had to be a reason that these defections were occurring.
- Management had to be willing to compare the company's performance to the competition's.
- Management had to accept marketing research as a tool to help understand customer perceptions.
- Management had to treat customer perceptions as real no matter how much they differed from reality.
- Finally, management had to change policies in response to consumer perceptions by implementing new programs and managing customer impressions through these programs.

≣ Current Customers Are Worth Five Times More Than New Ones

In our experience, most companies don't know what a loyal customer is worth in dollars and cents. They spend most of their marketing budget and attention on obtaining new customers, relatively less on satisfying and retaining old ones. This is a mistake. We have found that, for most of our consulting clients, whether we are talking about packaged goods, retail apparel, or heavy tractors, current customers are generally worth five times more than new customers.

Professor Philip Kotler recently reported the same experience and the same numbers. Quoted in the *Marketing Science Institute Review* (Spring 1991) Kotler said, "Many markets have settled into maturity. There are not many new customers entering the product category, and the costs of attracting new customers are rising and competition is increasing. In these markets it costs about five times as much to attract a new customer as to maintain the goodwill of an existing number."

Fortune magazine recently put a dollar figure on exactly how much repeat business can be worth. MBNA Corporation, formerly the credit card operation of Baltimore-based MNC Financial (which was, in turn, a division of Maryland National Bank), reported that it cost $100 on average to acquire a new credit card customer. By contrast, a customer MBNA has had for five years represents about $100 a year in profits; a customer the firm has had for ten years represents, on average, $300 a year. Stew Leonard, the head of the phenomenal Norwalk, Connecticut, dairy and food retail business, estimates that a loyal customer is worth $50,000 in sales over a ten-year period.

Surprisingly, there seems to be a sense in marketing that finding and closing new customers (acquisition programs) are more exciting than holding on to current customers (retention programs) or increasing business volume among current customers (expansion programs). As an illustration, in our marketing consulting practice, we estimate that for every ten clients of our firm, seven ask us how to build trial (increase the number of first time customers), two or three ask about repeat purchase (retention), and one is concerned about increasing usage level (expansion).

This myopic view is hardly restricted to packaged goods marketing. It is a contagious disease that has spread across industries.

We have an upscale women's apparel retailer client who recently did a study among their "best" (defined by the client as *heaviest*) customers—women who spent approximately $800 or more last year in their stores. It turned out that this client was receiving only 22 percent of the dollars these women spent on clothing overall. What is worse, 12 percent of them had defected altogether during the past year (charges gone to zero). Why was this happening? The client had been spending enormous sums of money on direct marketing trying to find new customers and was, in our view, ignoring the current customer potential for enhanced revenues and profits.

We also work with several automobile clients whose current customer efforts are weaker than their new customer programs. Yet what could be more important to an automobile manufacturer than reselling first-time buyers? Retention rates for domestic automobile companies are, in general, weak and need serious attention.

This cross-industry phenomenon we have labeled the *death-wish paradox*. Companies put more intellectual and financial capital into programs of less value and, even if these programs are successful, the ultimate cost is high.

THE DEATH-WISH PARADOX			
Customer type	Marketing effort	Value to marketers	Cost of programs
New customers (Acquisition programs)	High	Low	High
Current customers (retention programs)	Moderate	High	Moderate
Current customers (expansion programs)	Low	Moderate	Low

An exception to this paradox is the case of new buyers recently entering a product category. It makes good sense, for example, for Nissan Motors to offer a leasing program to recent college graduates without credit histories to bring them into the Nissan family. It also makes good sense for American Express to invest heavily in programs for young professionals like recent MBAs. The reasoning is simple: new buyers just entering a market can, through buying their first car or acquiring their first credit card, bring significant lifetime benefit to the acquiring firm. "Get them early and they'll stay long!" is the rallying cry for this kind of sensible thinking.

But spending vast sums on acquisition programs for experienced buyers is another example of death-wish marketing, a story that has already been told in Chapter 4 on targeting.

≣ Is It Really So Easy to Retain Customers?

Is it possible to retain customers? More possible than most managers believe. For example, MBNA's president set up a card retention department in which sixty-eight telephone service representatives call customers who want to close their accounts to ask them to stay. These representatives may do whatever is necessary within reason to keep them: some of the possibilities we could imagine include changing the billing cycle, requiring a smaller monthly minimum payment, or waiving annual fees. According to *Fortune*, these representatives typically rescue half the defecting accounts.

Almost all companies in our experience can develop and implement programs to hold on to current customers or increase their share of the customers' business or both. One of our business-to-business service clients recently faced this retention problem when they decided to take a significant price increase. Historical data showed that when the firm had raised prices, it had lost as much as 12 percent of its customers. Frightened by the prospect of repeating the past, this marketer undertook a tradeoff study (discussed in Chapter 6) to determine what they could do, and at what cost, to minimize customer attrition. Following the implementation of an attrition management program based on the research on the price increase, the firm experienced only a 3 percent loss in customers and a significant overall gain in profitability.

Why aren't more companies implementing programs designed to keep current customers and increase their usage or purchase frequency? We don't know. But we do know that in the 1990s the death-wish paradox will and must experience a death of its own.

≣ "Perfect" Products and "Perfect" Service Are Not What You Need

One conclusion that we hope you won't draw from this chapter is that companies need to provide customers with "perfect" products and "perfect" service. Indeed, during the past few years, we have witnessed a 180-degree turn by some American companies that are now fixated on how to guarantee the highest level of product quality or the highest level of customer service or both. Today "zero defect" products and "maximum delivery" service have become boardroom goals and corporate watchwords for consumer and industrial firms from coast to coast. The underlying theory—and myth—is that offering "perfect" products and "perfect" service will lead, naturally, to maximum profitability.

Across a broad range of categories, however, our research reveals a counterintuitive discovery. Customer satisfaction with product and service does increase profits to a point (it's never good to produce shoddy merchandise), but beyond that point profit declines. The reason is that extremely high levels of product and service quality are often unnecessary; they represent overkill, and the cost of delivering them is exorbitant. If bank customers, for example, will tolerate waiting in line for as long as five minutes, why add enough tellers to reduce the wait to 30 seconds? The cost will not bring another dollar into the bank.

Buyers of consumer and industrial products often fail to discriminate between "perfect" and just "very good" products and service. Yet the cost of moving from "excellent" to "perfect" can be high (see Fig. 10.1).

For these reasons, a marketing investment in "perfect" quality products and service is unlikely to be the best investment a firm can make. Rather, corporations should seek to find a financially optimal balance between customer needs and expectations and the firm's resources, capabilities, and the associated costs of implementation.

To achieve this balance requires a firm grasp of customer service and customer satisfaction issues—two parallel roads to Eldorado.

Figure 10.1 *The Relationship between Customer Satisfaction and Market Program Profitability*

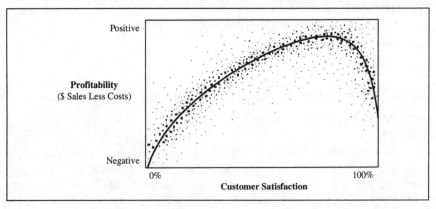

ROAD SIGNS TO ELDORADO

- Routinely assess company performance compared to competitors in terms of customer service and satisfaction, *two different* but related success factors.
- Avoid all the common problems of service and satisfaction research.

1) Don't do the research by mail and don't use your sales force as interviewers.
2) Be skeptical of "buyer expectations" models that have little to do with either buyer needs or expectations.
3) Measure service and satisfaction over time and compared to competitors.
4) Don't ignore customer needs; discover their hot buttons before you evaluate your performance.
5) Overcome the many temptations to do death-wish research. There is no shortcut to Eldorado.

- Find out how much your current customers are worth and the cost of keeping them rather than acquiring new customers.
- Beware the death-wish paradox—putting the lion's share of your investment in an acquisitions strategy when retention and expansion strategies will surely make the most money and the most sense.
- Remember the counterintuitive discovery that "perfect" products and "perfect" service may lead to ruin. It's not necessary to be better than excellent.

11

TRACKING SHOULD NOT ONLY TELL YOU HOW YOU'RE DOING BUT WHAT TO DO

If marketers have done their homework and done it well, they have researched and made decisions in at least ten critical areas:

1) The environmental analysis.
2) Market segmentation and target selection.
3) Positioning.
4) Product design.
5) Pricing.
6) Mass media advertising.
7) Direct marketing.
8) Promotion.
9) Distribution channels.
10) Sales force allocation.

We're now ready for a prelaunch countdown. A smart manager might ask how confident he or she is that each issue has been thoroughly researched and the correct decisions made. Confidence could be expressed as an eleven-point scale, ranging from 0 (no confidence at all) to 10 (100 percent confident). Giving pricing a 2, for example, would be saying the manager is 20 percent confident in the decision. Summing across all ten decisions the manager would have a "marketing plan confidence factor" ranging from 0 to 100. Clearly any plan with a *confidence factor* less than 70 should be reconsidered if not scrapped altogether.

Assuming that the manager is reasonably confident of success, all systems are "go." After months of work, the marketing plan is finally ready to be implemented; the new or repositioned product or service campaign is launched. What happens next? All too often, in our experience, management sits back like nineteenth-century military strategists waiting for reports from distant battlefields. Sometimes the reports don't arrive for months; oftentimes a conclusion concerning the program's relative success isn't reached for a year or more. All too often, as we have repeatedly argued, when the conclusion is reached, it is that the campaign failed to achieve its objectives.

How many managers would invest a significant chunk of their personal fortunes and wait a year to find out how the investment is doing? How many managers, investing as individuals, would take a chance if they thought the risk of failure was high? How many, even if they thought the risk was modest, would fail to monitor the investment's performance? Unfortunately, these lapses in critical thinking seem to happen when naturally risk-averse individuals hold positions of responsibility in corporations. They begin to behave in ways that might suggest a belief that corporate bank accounts can afford major losses. We say this because corporations routinely launch million-dollar, 20 million-dollar, even 100 million-dollar marketing programs before putting systems in place to carefully track, evaluate, and help improve campaign performance. CEOs of the 1990s won't tolerate such a slipshod approach to sizable corporate investments. There are many things they will want to know:

THE BOTTOM LINE: WHAT A CEO WANTS TO KNOW

1) We know the ROI on our pension and investment portfolio. What's the expected ROI on our marketing dollars?
2) How confident are we of marketing success, that the program will achieve its goals and objectives?
3) Do we have a marketing performance evaluation system in place?
   Such a system would *track*

- Campaign penetration.
- Marketplace attitudes and behavior.
- Customer satisfaction.
- Brand equity.
- Sales.
- Profits.

4) Does our evaluation system provide us with regular reports that measure our marketing performance compared to competitors' performance on a timely basis?

5) Does our system go beyond mere scorekeeping? Does it provide us with marketing intelligence—a blueprint for action?

6) What are we doing differently today compared with a year ago as a result of the system?

≡ If You Don't Know the Product's Sick, You Can't Seek a Cure

As we've remarked several times, most new consumer packaged goods products, most new campaigns for established products, and most service campaigns are failures. They succumb for the reasons we've outlined—the wrong target, positioning, message, pricing, and all the rest. Often, tragically, they die because management did not know they were sick until it was too late to help. They might have been saved with evaluation research, often called *tracking research.*

Tracking research has a reputation for being dull, repetitive, and unenlightened, undertaken by dull, repetitive, and unenlightened researchers. A derogatory euphemism for it is "bean counting," and people who do it are "bean counters." Some companies do not budget for tracking research because they do not understand or believe the effort can improve their marketing; some do not believe it's worth the money. "If the marketing program works, it works, and we'll know it. If it doesn't, it doesn't, and we'll know that too. So why waste another penny on research?"

But tracking research can be the marketing department's DEW (distant early warning) line. Take, for example, the following case from our experience, one we call "The Death of the High Roller Credit Card." The case is real, but we have changed the details to disguise the company.

The story began when a major credit card company decided to launch a premium credit card designed for affluent Americans, people earning more than $75,000 a year. For an annual fee of $300, the card would be accepted at restaurants and hotels around the world. Of great interest to the affluent, however, the card would open the doors to private golf, tennis, and social clubs from New York to Tokyo, provide access to a $30,000 line of credit, and personal valet services in every major market. The marketer hired a well-known research company (not us) to do an elaborate and sophisticated concept test, which suggested that 15 percent of all prospects would sign up for the service.

The manufacturer's top management would have been delighted with a 10 percent share. Even with a 5 percent share, the new service would break even in the first year. But a 15 percent share would be the success story of the decade. Euphoric about the possibilities, the marketer put the delivery system into place, hired an advertising agency, developed a direct mail campaign, and launched the service. The total effort cost about $10 million.

Within six months management knew it had launched a debacle. Fifteen percent of the prospects did not sign up. Neither did 10 percent or 5 percent. In fact, the actual number was closer to 0.5 percent.

Management's initial reaction to the disaster was, "Market research did it again. Bad research overstated the concept appeal." Indeed, that seemed to be the situation; the research had overstated consumer interest by almost 30 to 1.

At that point, in an unusual step—since most companies bury their mistakes with as little notice as possible—this financial services company called us in to discover what really went wrong—*to do an autopsy*.

The first thing we did was a one-wave tracking study, in which we traced the various input-output relationships—like the number of brochures the company mailed, the number of people who recalled receiving the brochure, and other factors—to identify the cause of death. We found only 60 percent of the target group claiming to have received the mailing for the company's new service. Somewhat less than half of those who actually recalled receiving the mailing, or 28 percent of all prospects, said they read most or all of it.

Of those who read the mailing, 71 percent were aware of the new service. To obtain the awareness measure, take 71 percent of the prospects who received and read the mailing (or 71 percent of 28 percent) for an answer of 20 percent—that is, the percentage of all prospects who were aware of the service.

It seemed to us the direct mail piece was very confusing. Even after reading it twice, the new service's unique attributes and benefits were not clear. We found it difficult to describe this new service's advantages compared to similar services with which we were already familiar. We were not alone in this opinion, because when we measured consumer comprehension of what the new service offered, only a quarter of the aware prospects had really understood the offering. Twenty-five percent of the 20 percent aware prospects is a 5 percent comprehension level.

Finally, when the research focused on the people who were both aware of the new service *and* understood what was offered, 16 percent had already signed up for it and more were about to. Sixteen percent of 5 percent is less than 1 percent of all prospects. The monitoring study and the direct mail campaign results, in other words, showed essentially the same thing. Researchers call this *convergent validity*.

But look at the table. The figures in the right column are those the marketer must have assumed if management was expecting a one-to-one correspondence between the concept test results and real-world performance.

AFFLUENT CREDIT CARD TRACKING RESEARCH		
	Achieved	*Assumed*
Received mailing	*60%*	*100%*
Read material	*28*	*100*
Awareness	*20*	*100*
Comprehension	*5*	*100*
Conversion to purchase	*16*	*15*[a]
Sales	*0.5*	*15*
[a] The rate estimated from the concept test.		

In the highly artificial, forced exposure environment of a concept test interview, there is 100 percent reception, 100 percent reading, 100 percent awareness, and usually 100 percent comprehension. Multiplying the 15 percent share-of-purchase estimate (which actually turned out to be fairly accurate) by 100 percent gave the marketer the misleading sales estimate on which he based the national launch.

The preliminary diagnosis might have been "death due to research overstatement," but the true cause of death was a poor marketing plan, one that failed to generate sufficient awareness and comprehension. But the company would not have known this without the tracking study. It would have known only that its auspicious new service had died.

≡ Learn Whether the Product Is Thriving or Dying

Knowing the cause of death is better than nothing, but a tracking study can—and should—do more. It can tell a company whether its product or service is alive and well, alive but not so well, or sick and dying. A good study can even help raise a product from the dead. To have a successful performance evaluation program, a company must take four steps:

1) The company must make the campaign's goals and objectives explicit. Everyone in business tosses around the words *goals* and *objectives* but, as we'll see in a moment, one executive's idea of what constitutes a goal or an objective may be very different from another's, and they both may be useless.

2) The company must make its implicit conceptual model of the input-output process explicit. The model should define what's involved in moving from marketing investment to sales and profits. Consumer packaged goods marketers need to think of moving from brand awareness, to trial, repeat, and market share. Financial services marketers must consider awareness, attitudes and perceptions, overall evaluation, buyer behavior, and market share.

3) The company must undertake a tracking study to estimate the parameters of the conceptual model soon after launching the product or service into the real-world test, either a test market or a regional or national introduction.

4) Finally, the company must connect all the steps together in a mathematical model to link planned input with forecasted output. The model should help forecast one end of the chain—say, sales—that results from an earlier step, say, advertising investment.

What is an example of a proper objective? For the affluent credit card, the objective might be to increase the number of card holders 30 percent within four months. For the Nissan Infiniti, an objective might be to bring 15,000 prospects into dealer showrooms within six months of launch.

An objective must be realistic, specific, and measurable. An objective cannot be fuzzy, ethereal, or soft such as, "Our objective is to increase the number of people who feel good about our company and its new product" or worse, the all-time most popular objective: "Our plan is to build awareness." A bank's objective might be, "A 10 percent increase in the percentage of customers who open an IRA by April 15th." A bro-

---

EXAMPLES OF MARKETING CAMPAIGN OBJECTIVES

	Objective
Packaged good	8% average market share (in dollars) for introductory year
Savings bank	20% increase in the percent of customers who open an IRA by April 15, 1992
Brokerage firm	800 new leads for sales calls within 90 days in New York State
Computer company	Increase of 15% in number of MIS managers who select brand by year end.

---

kerage firm's objective might be, "800 new leads for sales calls within ninety days in New York State." All are realistic, specific, and measurable, but in our work we regularly see marketing objectives that are not specific or measurable or realistic, and sometimes, not any of these.

But what are the steps or stages to achieve the objective? The affluent credit card had five: (1) reaching the prospects; (2) getting them to read the direct mail piece; (3) building awareness; (4) ensuring comprehension; and (5) conversion to sale.

The marketer should diagram this process and set a goal for each stage. Without such a model and goals, the company will have no idea how or why a particular campaign performs the way it does because a marketing program can achieve or lose the same objective in the marketplace for different reasons.

For example, here's a simple, low-involvement model and the goals and objective set by the marketing manager for a new consumer durable. The model goes from awareness through consideration to purchase. Note below that the campaign's objective is to increase purchases by 10 percent—from the current 20 percent to 22 percent.

AWARENESS → CONSIDERATION → PURCHASE → $ SALES

	Current level	Planned level
Awareness	60%	70% (a goal)
Consideration	40	45 (a goal)
Purchase	20	22 (the objective)

Once the company has a model, it requires research at each step in the process. A typical study is based on telephone interviews among 300 to 500 prospects for the product or service. One survey before the campaign (a prewave survey) followed by two to four during the marketing effort's first year (the postwave surveys) are common. The tracking criteria capture the goals and objectives of the company's model and its campaign.

As we suggested earlier, a company may do this kind of study for many different reasons—not just to find out why a new product died. A far better reason is to provide an early, actionable forecast of where the product is headed, to diagnose the flu before it becomes pneumonia. For example, based on a few data points collected early in a campaign, the company can forecast how the campaign will perform by year end with a reasonable level of accuracy.

The graph in Figure 11.1 forecasts campaign penetration. That is, the line measures the proportion of prospects who were aware of something unique about a new service. During the first thirteen weeks after the company launched the campaign, we collected three data points and forecast what would happen later in the year. The solid line reflects the actual data, the dotted line the forecast. Since in this case the forecasted numbers were considerably lower than the goal, this chart set off alarm bells at the company's headquarters.

To make such a forecast requires a mathematical model that connects marketing input variables to market response measures. These inputs include the company's detailed marketing plan with

- Basic category information
- Media flow charts
- Direct mail flow chart
- Copy test reports
- Public relations plans

- Distribution plans by month
- Sales force allocation plan
- Marketing and manufacturing costs

Plus research-based estimates of

- Awareness-to-trial conversion based on advertising, sales calls, public relations, and direct mail
- Multiple (that is, repeat) purchase
- Trial and purchase volume for different positioning, product, and pricing options

Figure 11.1 *Year-End Forecast Based on Three Data Points*

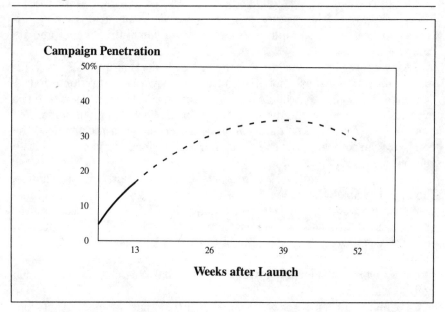

This is the model we described as step 4 on page 247. By gathering such data and building a model, the company can make forecasts for each step in its conceptual model and compare them to the year-end goals and objective. For example:

END-OF-YEAR PERFORMANCE

	Performance forecasted after 13 weeks	Goals and objectives
Awareness	37%	53%
Purchase consideration	15%	22%
Share of buyers	3.2%	4.7%
Share of dollars	1.6%	2.4%

In this case, after thirteen weeks, the marketer had forecast that only 67 percent of the dollar share objective would be achieved (1.6 percent versus 2.4 percent). This discrepancy resulted from the advertising campaign's weaknesses at the awareness stage. The goal was 53 percent awareness by year end; the research forecast was that, on the current course, it would be only 37 percent. If the company could correct this problem, it would improve the likelihood of achieving its objectives considerably.

When management receives such a forecast, it must become a diagnostician and evaluate all the reasons for the breakdown at the awareness stage. These reasons could include an inefficient media buy; advertising that is not attention-getting or memorable; inadequate point-of-sale material in the channels of distribution; or weak performance by the direct mail program. In this case, the marketer diagnosed weak advertising as the problem; the agency developed a new campaign, launched it later in the year, and turned around an ailing product.

One of our favorite examples of tracking research used wisely goes back twenty years. Coca Cola at the time dominated the soft drink market and Pepsi was a distant second. Both Coke and Pepsi had developed new advertising campaigns and, by accident, launched them within a week of one another. Coke's campaign was "It's the real thing" (remember the music?) while Pepsi advertised "You've got a lot to live and Pepsi's got a lot to give." More emotional, more physical, and more intimate than any of its previous campaigns, Pepsi's Live/Give campaign explored the images and settings of a maturing Pepsi Generation. The conscious emphasis was still on the young user, but the modernistic, technological dimension of mobile, active youth was downplayed in favor of warm, tactile, physically active youth. No talking whatsoever occurred so that the entire message was delivered in the highly orchestrated, vocally dramatic jingle.*

---

*Louis, J. C., and Harvey Yazijian, *The Cola Wars* (New York: Everest House Publishers, 1980), p. 246.

Within six weeks after launch, Pepsi enjoyed an insurmountable lead in terms of campaign penetration (the portion of soft drink consumers who remembered something about the advertising), 30 percent to 18 percent, despite the fact that Coke was spending more money on its campaign. After six months many people in the industry believed that Coke had made a mistake; it should never have dropped the "Things go better with Coke" in favor of "It's the real thing" as Pepsi's penetration numbers continued to leave Coke far behind. Forecasts done off the tracking study data suggested that Pepsi's campaign was so successful that Pepsi would soon overtake Coke in sales in food stores, the only place where consumers are faced with a choice between the two cola giants. And for a time, the forecasts were right as Pepsi toppled Coke in terms of recall of its advertising and consumer behavior in the marketplace.

≣ Life after Death: Using Tracking to Improve Marketing Programs

Marketers can also use tracking research effectively to measure performance relative to competition in terms of each stage of the company's model. Take the example of awareness. Since we know that awareness builds exponentially with each marketing dollar invested, a company can use tracking study data to plot a product or service's performance compared to the competition's. The important question is not to ask how is Visa doing compared to MasterCard, or Coke to Pepsi, or Ford to Chrysler, but to ask, how are Visa and MasterCard, Coke and Pepsi, Ford and Chrysler doing relative to the size of their marketing investment?

Figure 11.2 illustrates a point; we cannot, unfortunately, show actual data for proprietary reasons. But assume for the moment the figures are real. As companies invest marketing dollars, consumer awareness increases—just as one would hope. The computer calculates the best solution to all the data points and draws a line representing this solution—the curve on the chart. A company located right on the line would be perfectly average; companies above the line enjoy greater consumer awareness than expected (given their marketing investment) and those below less than expected. This hypothetical chart says that while American Express spends the most money, Visa has greater consumer awareness per dollar spent. MasterCard, which has spent almost as much as Visa in this hypothetical example, is not doing as well. If this were

Figure 11.2 *Credit Card Case*

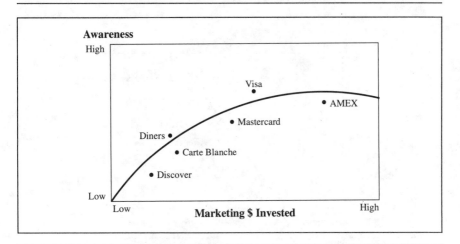

true, MasterCard might want to develop and test alternative advertising strategies, or executions, or both.

In the same way, the company measures every link in the hypothesized model of how marketing works in a particular product category. For example, the relationship between awareness and purchase consideration tends to be linear; as awareness increases so does purchase consideration. In most service categories there must be some awareness before the company sees any purchase consideration at all. With an impulse item, awareness may not be as important.

Figure 11.3, with disguised data from the insurance industry, illustrates these points; the linear relationship and the considerable level of awareness required before the consumer considers purchasing at all. In this case, Northwest Mutual seems to enjoy more purchase consideration than its awareness suggests it deserves, while John Hancock is getting less. The greater the distance above the line, the greater the competitive advantage the company enjoys. The more a company is below the line, the weaker its competitive posture.

The next step in the chain might be the conversion of purchase consideration to actual buying behavior, measured in terms of share of customer (Fig. 11.4). Again, it is possible to take this data, plot it on a graph, draw a line between the points to show average performance, and see instantly which companies convert a larger share of prospects into customers and which convert a smaller share.

Figure 11.3 *Insurance Case*

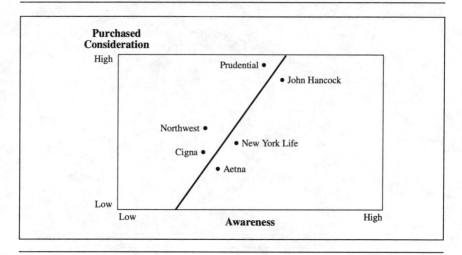

Finally, there's the link between share-of-buyers and share-of-dollars (Fig. 11.5). If the relationship were perfect, this would be a 45-degree line and all firms would sit right on it; as a company's share of buyers rose, its share of dollars would rise equally. The relationship is not perfect, however, because some firms have larger volumes than others. Firms above the line generate more dollars per customer than firms below the line.

Figure 11.4 *Brokerage Case*

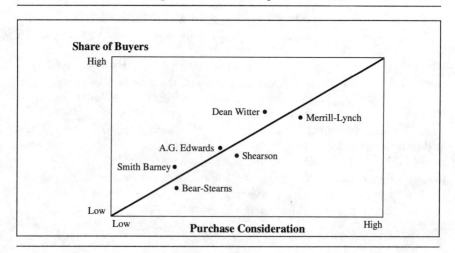

Figure 11.5 *Package Delivery Case*

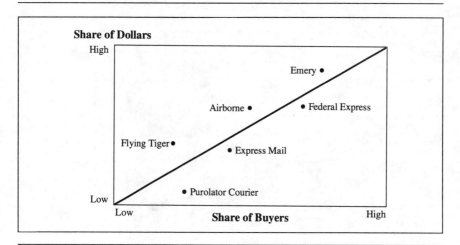

Observing where the company falls vis-à-vis the competition on this line, and for all other stages in the company's marketing models, provides management with insights into the strengths and weaknesses of its marketing programs. Sometimes this intelligence can be used to resuscitate a dying brand or even resurrect a dead one.

≡ Media Effectiveness Can Be Tracked

One tracking question comes up frequently: Can you figure out the contribution of different media vehicles? Does print, for example, work better than television, or network work better than cable? Sophisticated tracking and analytical methodologies can answer such questions.

We recommend that the market tracking questionnaires contain measures of media exposure for each major medium the program employs. Then, later, at the analytical stage the company can examine advertising effects for each vehicle separately. Figure 11.6, for example, shows that for a major marketer of copying machines, among both business buyers and upscale consumers, an investment made in magazines, particularly business and news publications, had much more effect than either network or cable television. Advertising awareness increased 63 percent among business buyers heavily exposed to business publications and 11 percent among business buyers who were lightly exposed. In contrast, little difference was observed between business buyers heavily exposed versus lightly exposed to network television.

Figure 11.6 *The Effects of Media Exposure on Advertising Penetration for Copying Machines*

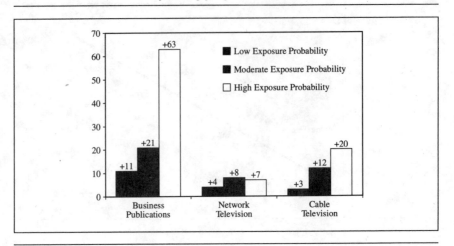

By contrast, in a study for a new soft drink, network television demonstrated tremendous increases in brand awareness and trial while print performed at a mediocre level.

Our point here is not to argue for the superiority of one medium over another, but rather to show that media effectiveness can be tracked and diagnoses made to improve campaign performance.

≡ From Scorecard to Blueprint

In summary, performance tracking, done well provides a marketer with not just a scorecard but a blueprint for future direction. The scorecard gives the basic numbers: how the firm is performing over time relative to its competitors in terms of key indicators of success. This information is essential but insufficient to the marketing manager. Marketing intelligence, as we keep referring to it, is required for insight into how the marketing program can be improved to produce an even greater return-on-investment. Good tracking research, well analyzed, can do this. It can answer questions such as these:

- Are we achieving our goals and objectives?
- Are we spending the right amount of money on advertising promotion and the other components of the marketing mix?
- How are our mass media and public relations efforts performing

compared to competitive activity? What can we do to enhance them?
- Which media vehicles are working best? Which least?
- Are we moving the needles in terms of buyer perceptions, attitudes, and performance? If not, why not? If so, what can we do even better?
- Ultimately, is our marketing program producing a strong return on investment, or would we be better off writing a check to our favorite mutual fund? If it's not producing a good return, how do we improve it?

☰ The Marketing Audit: A Comprehensive Annual Review

Performance tracking also provides an invaluable database for the annual marketing audit, something all firms should undertake.

The marketing audit does to the marketing department what a financial audit does to the accounting department. It is a comprehensive review of a company's marketing environment (which the environmental scan we described in Chapter 3 has already covered), the company's marketing objectives, strategies, and activities. The audit identifies operational strengths and weaknesses and recommends changes to the company's marketing plans and programs (one reason that marketing people tend to oppose such an audit). A well-designed marketing audit examines the marketing organization's effectiveness, marketing's productivity, and all functional relationships within the marketing organization.

Because a marketing audit is so comprehensive, the firm must conduct it as systematically as possible. Before the auditors examine the first document, before they interview one employee, customer, or supplier, the company prepares a detailed structure for the audit. This structure includes the significant points to be examined, the questions to be asked, and the type of information sought. Ten central issues should be addressed by every audit:

1) An assessment of key factors that impacted the business for good or for bad during the past year. This assessment should emphasize an evaluation of marketing "surprises"—the unanticipated competitive actions or changes in the marketing climate that affected the performance of the marketing programs.
2) An assessment of customer satisfaction based on research undertaken among key target groups.
3) An assessment of distributor, vendor, or intermediary satisfaction undertaken among key stakeholders.
4) An assessment of marketing knowledge, attitudes, and satisfac-

tion of all executives involved in the marketing function.

5) An assessment of the extent to which the marketing program was marketed internally and bought into by top management, marketing, and nonmarketing executives.

6) An assessment of the extent to which each decision in the marketing mix—e.g., targeting, positioning, pricing, advertising, etc.—was made correctly after evaluating many alternatives in terms of profit-related criteria.

7) An assessment of the performance of advertising, promotion, sales force, and marketing research programs with an emphasis on return-on-investment issues.

8) Very important, an overall assessment of whether the marketing plan achieved its stated financial and nonfinancial goals and objectives.

9) An autopsy of all aspects of the plan that failed to meet objectives with specific recommendations for improving next year's performance.

10) An assessment of the current value of brand equity for each brand in the product portfolio.

Other questions would cover target markets (Has the company identified and measured major market segments?), competitors (Who are the principal competitors, how are they positioned, where are they headed?), pricing (What is current pricing strategy?), marketing channels (What are the trends in distribution?), sales administration (Are sales costs planned and controlled?), advertising (How does the company measure media effectiveness?), and sales promotion (Does the promotion effort support a marketing objective?). Companies conduct specialized audits to measure specific functions. Two popular areas that specialized audits investigate are product management and marketing communications.

For the same reason the company hires an independent accounting firm to audit its books, an individual or organization independent of the marketing department should audit the marketing. An independent audit may not always be possible because outsiders may not have the necessary qualifications; then the company will have to use in-house talent to prepare the audit. Although top management cannot expect company employees to be totally disinterested, we have seen instances where a task force within the firm performed an audit professionally and evenhandedly.

We believe a company should schedule regular marketing audits, generally once a year. If a company conducts regular audits, it should find few nasty surprises uncovered by the report, and it should be able to correct problems before they develop into a crisis. If the firm waits for a crisis before initiating a marketing audit, the number of unhappy surprises may be more than management can handle.

The marketing audit is a planning tool that goes beyond the day-to-day controlling activities of management. In addition to looking at how well the firm does what it's doing, the audit considers whether the firm is doing what it should be doing at all. The results sometimes perturb top management, especially the first time a company conducts an audit. We have seen audits that uncovered substantial differences between reality and what company management believed to be true about its marketing effort. But it is better to learn about the company's shortcomings from an impartial auditor than from an angry customer or, worse, from an aggressive competitor.

The marketing revolution taking place means that companies recognize changes in the marketplace and aggressively change the way they do business as a result. They monitor their marketing effort, and they audit the marketing process. They obtain the information they need to correct small problems before they become serious crises. Companies move from death-wish marketing to marketing intelligence.

EVALUATING MARKETING PROGRAM PERFORMANCE

- Do a "confidence factor" analysis for each of ten success factors well before the marketing program is launched.
- Set specific, realistic, and measurable marketing goals and objectives.
- Put in place a sophisticated tracking system to monitor performance over time against goals and objectives.
- Ensure that this tracking system provides insight into your program's performance compared to your competitor's.
- Design the system so that it does more than bean counting. You don't simply want a scorecard. You want marketing intelligence to make the program better.
- Equally important, undertake an annual marketing audit—with all the effort and seriousness of purpose that goes into the annual financial audit.
- At the end of the year, answer this question: Is your marketing investment generating a reasonable return on investment?

12

TAKING MICROMARKETING SERIOUSLY: MANY MARKETS OF ONE

One-on-one marketing is the logical extension of targeting. In our targeting efforts, we look for those people who will be most interested in our product or service. Up to this point, we've been identifying groups that are likely prospects.

Given access to publicly available information about customers and prospects, marketing to individuals is becoming cost-efficient. Marketing to individuals may be considered a form of direct marketing, but traditional direct marketing, although an increasingly common tool, is losing efficiency. The number of contacts is growing while the response per offering is declining. As a result, the direct mail industry is beginning to express concerns that "catalogue saturation" will turn people off rather than turn them on.

Our view is that direct marketing can be improved considerably with a more efficient use of targeting methodologies and databases. The latest developments enable a marketer to obtain the names and addresses of the company's best prospective customers and more.

This new ability makes obsolete conventional geodemographic coding models in which the marketer identifies ZIP codes or census blocks with a high percentage of prospects. The ultimate application of the new technology is to go beyond targeting to create and implement individualized marketing programs in the way that the movie *Wargames* portrayed global warfare carried out by computers.

In preparation for this revolution in target marketing, the CEO must ask some key questions about the company's current direct marketing efforts:

THE BOTTOM LINE: WHAT A CEO WANTS TO KNOW

1) How are our direct marketing programs performing? Are they showing gains, or, like most programs, are they losing efficiency?

2) Are our customer and prospect selection systems state-of-the-art or are we using conventional approaches such as other companies' mailing lists or off-the-shelf geodemographic systems?

3) Does our customer and prospect selection system reflect the latest developments in marketing science technology?

4) Can our customer and prospect selection system produce a list of the specific names and addresses of people that we know want our product or service?

5) Have we ever thought about developing a system that uses automated intelligence to go beyond list generation to implement a direct marketing program?

≡ What One-on-One Marketing Might Read Like

The day is not far off when you can receive a letter like the following from the best department store in town:

Dear Mr. Gilfeather:

I would like to remind you that your wife Maureen's birthday is coming up in two weeks on February 27, and we have the perfect gift for her in stock.

As you know, she loves Escada clothing, and we have an absolutely beautiful new suit in red, her favorite color, in a seven, her size, priced below typical retail value of $1,500 at $1,250.

If you like, I can gift wrap the suit at no extra charge and mail it to you next week so that you will have it in plenty of time for her birthday, or, if you would like, I can put it aside so that you can come in to pick it up. Please give me a call within the next 48 hours to let me know which you'd prefer.

In any event, I appreciate your business and hope to hear from you soon.

Sincerely yours,
Kathy Lester
Store Manager

As we have been saying all along, markets are breaking up, media is fragmenting, and products continue to proliferate. What is a mass market product today? Coca-Cola? Possibly, but with Coke, Coke Classic, Cherry Coke, Diet Coke, Caffeine-free Coke, Caffeine-free Coke Classic, Caffeine-free Diet Coke, each available in 12-ounce cans, 1-liter bottles, 2-liter bottles, perhaps not.

Louis W. Stern, a professor of marketing at Northwestern University's J. L. Kellogg Graduate School of Management, has said, "Marketing warfare in the 1990s will be a fierce, down-and-dirty struggle fought neighborhood by neighborhood." And Joel D. Weiner, senior vice president for marketing services at Kraft USA, says, "The mythological homogeneous America is gone. We are a mosaic of minorities. All companies will have to do more stratified or tailored or niche marketing."

More examples: Waldenbooks, through its Preferred Reader Program, is able to send personal letters to its very best customers offering books tailored to their interest at a discount; at the Four Seasons Hotel chain, the staff greets guests by name and remembers everyone's individual requirements; and Merrill Lynch recently introduced a new investment product by sending its customers a personalized analysis of their portfolios that showed what their returns would be if they were to invest in the new product.

≡ Companies Reorganize Themselves

But the trend toward one-on-one marketing extends beyond the ways companies reach prospects to the companies themselves.

Herbert M. Baum, the president of Campbell USA, says that top management realized in the mid-1980s that the United States was no longer a mass market for consumer goods but a series of regional markets. In response, Campbell divided its sales force among twenty-one mostly autonomous regional operations, each accountable for local market planning and spending. The company pushed responsibility down the hierarchy to the sales people in the field, renaming them *brand sales managers*. While these people had little marketing experience, they found themselves in charge of spending the marketing budget. And while Campbell ran into problems with the changes and Baum had to spend weeks on the road explaining them—"I appeared on panels, which included our customers, just to talk about the benefits of regionalization"—revenues, unit sales, and profits all rose. "We really feel it has worked; our sales have never been stronger," says Baum.

In 1988 General Foods, after a test in Denver, divided the country into regions and set up groups to market directly to individual retail outlets. GF managers, using the retailer's computerized data that identifies buying preferences, can determine which products and how many of each product should be placed in each store.

It is easy to understand and adjust for regional food preferences: Campbell sells more chili in the Southwest than in New England. And it is easy to understand that managers in the local market should have the authority and the means to react to competitive moves or to take advantage of local opportunities.

But it is not quite as easy to understand and know how to react when traditional mass markets shrink or break apart. Mass marketing grew because it was more efficient than traditional marketing. The supermarket is more efficient than the old-fashioned general store because the retailer shifts so many functions to others. Where a clerk once bagged and packed flour, sugar, crackers, coffee, and other bulk staples, the manufacturers assumed (and mechanized) that function. Where a clerk once plucked each item from the shelf, customers now make their own selections. The supermarket is becoming even more efficient as more of the sophisticated chains adopt the concept of *aisle managers*. That is, they make a manager responsible for maintaining profits in a single aisle (think of an aisle in your local supermarket as simply a collection of related products) in a single store.

Mass media—first magazines, then radio, then television—grew because advertisers could reach audiences more and more efficiently. Aside from the inherent differences of each medium, which may or may not improve advertising effectiveness (radio permitted sound and music; television added motion and color), the cost of reaching an individual prospect dropped with each new medium. There may have been waste ("I know that half my advertising is wasted," John Wanamaker is reputed to have said, "but I don't know which half"), but on a per person basis, the advertising was so cheap, no one really cared. However, now, as markets fragment, waste and therefore cost grow.

Perhaps network television advertising is a bargain when only half the people watching are prospects. It may be a bargain when only a quarter of the viewers are prospects. It may still be a bargain when only 10 percent of the viewers are prospects. But nevertheless, as the viewing (or listening or reading) audience contains fewer and fewer prospects, the medium becomes less efficient, and, at some point, the thoughtful marketer considers an alternative.

Obviously, reaching and motivating fewer people is more expensive on a per person basis than reaching a mass audience. Yet, as we (and everyone else) have pointed out, traditional mass audiences no longer exist. Not only have the audiences shrunk; they have fragmented. New competitors, products, brands, and line-extensions mean, like the Coca-Cola example, there is hardly a product category in which marketers are not contending for dominance in relatively small markets.

In response, advertisers and marketers are turning to database modeling and micromarketing as a way to reach their target audiences more efficiently and effectively.

≣ Databases Are Nothing More Than Electronic File Cabinets

We'll describe the idea behind the electronic file cabinet in a moment, but first we need a couple of definitions. A database is simply an accumulation of information. The Rolodex on a secretary's desk is a database. The telephone book is a database. A filing cabinet bulging with sales records is a database.

The computer has meant two things: All that information can be stored electronically; and it's possible to search through the data automatically for all the items that are characterized by certain criteria. For example, one could use the Manhattan telephone book to find all the people with listed phones who live on West 79th Street. It would take a while, looking at every address, but one could do it. If the Manhattan telephone book were available on, say, a Compaq computer, however, the machine could identify everyone who lives on West 79th Street in moments.

Database modeling takes individual consumer characteristics like age, income, interests, home ownership—hundreds in all—and assigns each a mathematical weight. These weighted scores, manipulated in a formula, can tell a company something important. For example, credit companies, using similar, if much simpler, scoring systems, can estimate the likelihood that a particular individual will default on a loan. They assign a mathematical value to a person's income, length of employment, type of and amounts of credit outstanding, home ownership, occupation, bank accounts, past payment patterns, and more. They create a formula, and, matched against past experience in the credit business, the answer predicts the statistical probability that the individual will, or will not, pay off a loan satisfactorily.

As we have said, a company cannot know a priori what will motivate a prospect to buy a product. But if the company knows enough about its customers, and if it could find other people in the population similar to these people in the characteristics that motivate them to buy the company's product, it would have found the best prospects. Individuals who are most likely to buy should be identifiable. New linkages to information technology bring the hope and promise of database modeling to reality to effectively counter consumer diversity.

Information technology, in and of itself, however, is an opportunity rather than a solution. To make it all work, a firm must combine new data-gathering systems, extensive individual and household databases, and sophisticated reporting systems. Right now, information technology remains primarily a business searching for market needs and applications it can serve.

One such opportunity is the marketer's need to identify hot prospects among noncustomers efficiently. Since the percentage of likely buyers in the general population for many products and services is usually small (often less than 1 percent), and the American population is large, this is the familiar "finding the needle in the haystack" dilemma.

Take a prototypical and very simple example. Given a potential market of 50 million people with relatively small market penetration (also known as a lot of noncustomers), a cost of acquisition of $49, and an average lifetime value per customer of $225, who are the best prospects to reach, and how does the marketer reach them most efficiently?

Ideally, we want to find those people who are likely to buy our product and know *how* likely they are to buy it. Are they *very* likely to buy or not so likely? Are they, in other words, 0.9s (almost certain to buy) or 0.1s? The statistics work like this: Bring ten people with an 0.9 probability of buying a given product into a store and nine of them will buy it; only one will walk out empty handed. There is no way to know which nine will buy, only that nine of the ten will. Similarly, if we bring ten people with a 0.1 probability into the store, only one will buy. Again, it is impossible to tell ahead of time who will actually buy, but clearly marketers (not to mention retailers) prefer to fill a store with 0.9s.

So assume a market size of 50 million. And assume an overall response rate of 1 percent—500,000 buyers—and an average lifetime value of $225 for each person. If the cost of goods is $171 per person, these buyers represent $27 million in net revenues (sales less cost of goods). Assuming advertising costs (acquisition and retention) are, on average, $49 per person, then the firm's net profit on these buyers is $2,500,000.

But remember that although the *average* response rate is 1 percent, it costs more to acquire some of these customers than others. Think of acquiring customers as a continuum. At one end, prospects respond immediately to the company's offer; at the other, prospects require a great deal of advertising and selling to convince.

For the sake of this example, we'll assume it costs only $46 to reach and retain the most responsive prospects—three-quarters of the total—$3 less per prospect than the $49 to reach them all. Correspondingly, it costs $58 to reach the least responsive quarter of the prospects. Suppose it were possible to put all 500,000 buyers into rank order, the 375,000 who are most responsive at the top, the 125,000 who are less responsive at the bottom.

A company that knew this information would promote to the most responsive consumers first and stop when it reached 375,000 buyers. The company would actually make more money from 75 percent of the market than if it reached and sold the entire market. Since the marketing cost per individual in the last 25 percent of the market rises above $54, these people cost the company more than it earns in incremental revenue.

A company does not need as many customers if it can find and sell its prospects more efficiently. *Indeed, it can actually make much more money by reaching fewer prospects more efficiently.* The trick, of course, is to find and reach those prospects.

And that's where one-on-one marketing comes in. It is now possible for a marketer to obtain the specific names and addresses of those consumers who are the most likely prospects for a product or service. Porsche, for example, could send a video cassette tape to just those people who are the most likely to buy a Porsche. Panasonic could send a brochure to just those people who are most likely to buy a forty-one-inch television set.

But such database modeling is not limited to expensive products with small markets. Packaged goods marketers can also use the system. For example, it is sometimes difficult to generate trial of a new detergent, shampoo, toothpaste, or cigarette, but once a target prospect has actually tried the product, he or she becomes a loyal consumer. Unless the company knows whom to target in the first place, however, sampling can be extravagantly expensive. The challenge is to find those people who, once they try the product, will stay with it forever. Using database modeling, a company can find these consumers and deliver a sample to them cost effectively.

≣ We Would Like to Find the Needle in the Haystack But We're Lost on the Way to the Farm

What patterns do marketers follow to find the needle effectively and efficiently?* Although we discussed targeting in Chapter 4, we want to

*We want to acknowledge with thanks the contribution of Dr. Thomas S. Lix, for both his contribution to the development of TargetBase, a YCS proprietary system, and for this discussion.

take a brief look at the subject from a different angle here to put the new technology into a context.

While companies and industries vary, they tend to use one of four targeting approaches:

1) *Systematic "trial and error."* The direct mail industry typically uses this approach. In this approach, the company tests and compares different combinations of positioning, price, package, and mailing list, mailing to a sample to see which combination obtains the highest response. By testing various combinations, the company attempts to find the package that generates the highest response to roll out to the entire list. Because such testing can quickly get out of hand—two positionings, three prices, three packages, and four lists mean seventy-two combinations—management seldom bothers to test them all, but instead selects the exact combinations to test based on experience and subjective opinion (or, if they have the expertise, reduce the number of combinations needed for testing by an experimental design).

But aside from the time and expense of testing various combinations, another problem exists. Suppose the company finds that the *Fortune* list works the best compared to the *Forbes, Business Week,* and the *Wall Street Journal* lists. But when the company has exhausted the *Fortune* list, then what? The company has to go through the whole testing exercise again because it cannot assume that the winning combination among *Fortune* subscribers will be the same for the *Wall Street Journal* subscribers. There is no way to extend the findings from one list to another. A company will know which combination works best with a given list, but it will not know why, which means that it cannot translate the experience to another list. To avoid this problem, direct marketers try to find other lists that overlap the first; but, of course, purging the people who have already seen the package reduces the new lists considerably.

2) *The "best customer" modeling approach.* This approach uses in-house data to predict response rates for targeted marketing to current customers only. In this approach, the company establishes a customer database and identifies the "best customers." The company then creates a model of the characteristics of the best customers. It applies the model to the full database and puts the entire database in rank order in terms of forecasted response.

There is nothing wrong with this method except (a) the list is limited and (b) *it could be that the current customers are the worst prospects for a new product* because of the company's distribution system, because of its advertising, because of the way it has communicated the product, or because of almost any element in the marketing mix. This is an important point. One of the most prevalent marketing myths is that a company's best prospects for a product or service must be people who "look" very much like current customers. This belief is shared by both industrial and consumer marketers, and it's wrong!

We have found companies taking the hard way to obtain a less-than-optimal group of customers. For example, a company could have its existing customers because it began to sell its product primarily through upscale retailers. The people who bought the product are the affluent consumers who shop in those stores. But if the company had chosen a different distribution system in the beginning, it might have found its market five times as large and half as expensive to reach. Indeed, if the company were to start over again, the current customers might not be the best group to target, let alone the best target for a new product or service.

3) *The geodemographic clustering systems.* These systems subscribe to the "birds of a feather flock together" principle that rich people tend to live in neighborhoods with other rich people and ethnics tend to live near people with similar backgrounds—that there is a certain amount of homogeneity to a neighborhood. Geodemographics combine information about people in geographic units—ZIP codes, census tracts, block groups, and the like—with what we know about their common demographic characteristics. In the most simple terms, clustering systems like Prizm, Vision, and Cluster Plus follow this pattern.

Take any one of the 46,000-plus ZIP codes in the country, and we can learn, for example, that the average age is thirty-four, the average household income is $37,000, and the average home value is $182,000. The U.S. Census data will also tell us things like race, gender distribution, average education, and typical occupations for the people who live in a ZIP. This information is interesting and often useful, if we know how to apply it.

The limits of geodemographic information—and the limits of most clustering systems, even when the supplier adds psychographic information to the geodemographic units—is that the results are always expressed in terms of aggregate units—census tracts, ZIP codes, even block groups with averages.

Here's the problem with aggregates. Suppose we do a psychographic cross-tabulation of our customers and discover that they are mostly achievers, one of the VALS groups. We then obtain a list of all 46,000-odd ZIP codes ranked in terms of achievers. The ZIPs with the most achievers become our prime target, while we can ignore the ZIPs with the fewest achievers. (Note that the cross-tab does not have to be a psychographic tabulation of achievers; we could be talking about people with money, with large families, or any other characteristic.)

But considering ZIPs with the most achievers is very inefficient because within each area there are many achievers, but there are lots of people who are not achievers—and therefore not targets for our product or service. So why would we want to deal with the aggregates if we could deal with individual people?

Another example. We are working in the automobile industry and we ask R. L. Polk in Detroit to provide us with a list of the names and addresses of a random sample of 3,000 people who have bought BMWs in the last year. Since we have the ZIP codes for the individuals chosen, we ask our researcher to pull out the demographic profile of each ZIP—not each individual, but each ZIP. We then develop an equation predicting the BMW buyer from ZIP code characteristics.

Having found that BMW buyers tend to be predominant in bicoastal ZIPS, upscale ZIPs, single-headed household ZIPs, under forty-five years of age ZIPs, and whatever, we then run a program to find ZIP codes that have those kinds of people in them. Now we're back to the original problem. BMW buyers may represent only 0.5 percent of the auto buying population, and even in the best ZIP codes, they may represent only 7 percent. So with 90 percent of the people buying something else, targeting the entire ZIP code is an inefficient way to reach BMW buyers. This method might be okay if we were trying to find a location for a BMW dealership, but if we want to target for mailings, for example, we'd like to do better than mail to nine out of ten people who are not prospects.

4) *The prime prospect identification survey approach.* Here, marketers attempt to add a layer of quantitative marketing research and scientific method to their targeting process. The researchers conduct a sample survey to identify characteristics of consumers interested in the product or service. This survey may include psychographic segments, attribute and benefit segments, people scoring high on a given trend or dimension, or people scoring high on behavioral intention. It is entirely possible, as we said in Chapter 4, to identify the best prospects within the population.

But sooner or later the company has to take prospect information to a media company and say, "I want to reach these people." At this point, all the carefully defined individual consumer data and profile prospect characteristics become reduced to some standard media selection criteria: "men, thirty-four to forty-five, college-educated, income greater than $50,000"; or, worse, "women, eighteen to forty-nine." The company has lost all the value of the individual because, to buy advertising, it has to select media on the basis of the closest available criteria, which is not very close. The sample survey process breaks down as it moves from individual level survey data to aggregate level target marketing and media selection criteria.

All four approaches have clear weaknesses. Both the systematic "trial and error" and the sample survey approaches, while projectable to non-customers, do not draw on a large pool of potential prospects nor do they provide individual level rating models that allow a score for each person.

"Best customer" modeling *does* provide individual level rating models but does not draw on a large pool of potential prospects, nor can the company project the model to noncustomers.

Geodemographic clustering draws on a large pool of potential prospects and is projectable to noncustomers but does not provide an individual level rating model. With advances in computer technology, however, and dramatic reductions in data processing costs, it is now possible to design a system that overcomes all of these weaknesses. Where we were once lost on the way to the farm, it is now possible to find the most efficient route to get there.

≡ Use of Space Age Technology to Find the Needle

We start with the consumer databases commercially available through a number of suppliers. These suppliers continually add information on everything from credit cards and automobile registrations to mail-order purchases, lifestyles, and activities—to name just a few possibilities. The databases contain encyclopedic and relatively accurate information on more than 170 million individual American consumers and almost all U.S. households. Direct marketers have been using a lot of this information for years. Access is relatively simple. Most suppliers are not tied to any sort of proprietary analytic technologies; they're basic database compilers.

Using such a database, we know where people live, who they are, and a great many other facts about each one of them. We know this information not just because they live in a certain neighborhood or because they're projected to be in a certain psychographic cluster, but because the actual information is available for the individual or the household or both. But how can a company use this information to find its target market?

Let's say a company markets fax machines, a product applicable to the general population but with a relatively small volume and penetration. Fortunately, the company does not have to sell many machines to make money, but clearly if it uses mass marketing techniques—network television, for example—the costs are likely to be exorbitant.

As the last step in the product and marketing plan development process for the new fax machine, the company undertakes a product design study like the one we described in Chapter 6. It samples more than the typical 400 to 500 people—1,000 is more than enough (and keeps this example simple). The company interviews these qualified prospects face to face, door to door, from coast to coast, shows them a description of the new fax machine along with descriptions of competitive machines, and probes their attitudes with a behavior prediction battery that looks at three dimensions of attitude—the affective, the cognitive, and the behavioral. As discussed in Chapter 6, this information can then be used to forecast the probability of purchase for the product for each respondent in the survey.

At this point, the company knows exactly who is primed to buy its product. It knows the reasons why, and it understands quite a bit about the customers as well. After all, the company had these prospects for at least an hour in the interview environment and learned as much as it could. If the company stopped right now, it would be exceptionally well informed. It has profiles of who would buy the product, information to feed the models that tells just how many fax machines it can sell, and, in some cases, it has the information it needs to fine-tune an advertising campaign or adjust the marketing plan. But let's take this example a step further.

Starting with the people forecast to buy the product based on the research, we have a wealth of information about them, so we pass our small data set (the source data) from the test exercise through the much larger U.S. consumer database. We match the records and extract any additional information that the consumer database has on our sample. The key is to supplement our existing data with information available not only on the purchaser group, but also on the other 170 million people in the consumer database. We build our bridge from a small sample of purchasers and nonpurchasers to the entire American consumer market (Fig. 12.1).

Note that we are not talking about something as simple or as naive as using demographics—especially aggregate level census demographics—as predictive variables for something like purchase behavior. This procedure uses individual characteristics. We used our research sample and behavior prediction battery to learn who would actually buy, why they would buy, and how they might be classified. We then used the U.S. consumer database and the individual level it provides to give us the necessary raw materials for the modeling process.

We *do* use demographics, but on the individual consumer level, not as an aggregate. We use demographics as an important indicator or part of the link between individual respondents in the research and the likely behavior of individual consumers in the market. To supplement and increase the power of this link, a company can merge data it already has in its main frame. Sometimes, this supplementation is as simple as knowing from earlier studies that subscribers to a particular magazine or owners of specific cars are likely targets. Sometimes, it's possible to develop complex multivariant statistical models by merging diverse information

Figure 12.1 *Append Readily Available Data to Source Data (on an individual basis)*

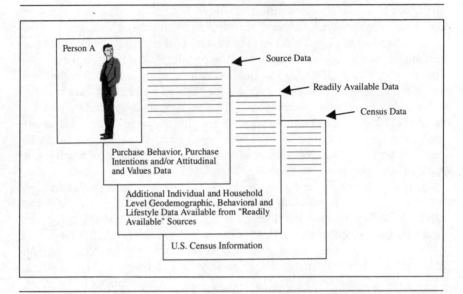

in a company's database, models that can estimate the simultaneous effects of numerous variables on a dependent variable such as purchase interest or brand loyalty. We have found that companies often have an enormous amount of data already available that can be made useful. Computer technology, with ever expanding capabilities and steadily decreasing cost, has brought the data within economic reach.

Basically we're talking about direct market list enhancement, which is hardly a revolutionary new concept since direct mail marketers have done this for years. We *are* carrying the concept into a much, much bigger universe.

The research we've just described can tell a company who, exactly, will buy the new fax machine. Not just that 2.7 percent will buy in the first year (assuming awareness and availability) or that they tend to have incomes greater than $30,000 or that they are mostly college graduates—but who exactly. If we have built the bridge from the test to the market properly, the computer will print out the names and addresses of approximately 4,680,000 very reachable people (see Fig. 12.2). This is not an inflated total of both people likely and not likely to buy. These are the specific people you'd *expect* to buy if we make them aware of the product and have the proper distribution.

So for this particular high-end consumer product, we're not talking about enough prospects for a national launch with network television

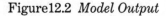

Figure12.2 *Model Output*

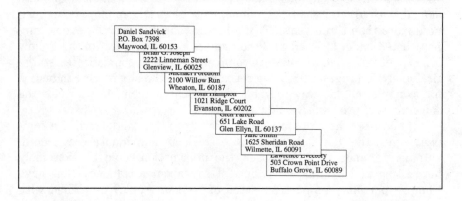

advertising and coupons in free-standing inserts. But for a new fax machine and a great many other products, more than enough prospects exist to launch a successful direct marketing campaign or a more traditional campaign with a direct marketing component.

Once the computer spits out the individual names and addresses, a company can generate specific and targeted information for everything from sample or coupon distribution to additional coded respondents for supplemental research, validation, or tracking programs. Management can ask a computer mapping program to draw attractive color-coded maps that it can use for roll-out strategies, test market selection, retail site analysis, regional media planning, and more.

≡ Doing the Same Thing in Business-to-Business Marketing

Why not do the same sort of thing in business-to-business marketing? Many companies selling to businesses know a great deal about their customers—a firm's age, size, sales, number of employees, growth trend, purchase cycle, purchase behavior, decision-makers, media consumption, and much more. It should be possible to create a model that would search for similar firms.

One could, except that databases containing the same kind of information about businesses as about consumers do not yet exist. But some business databases do exist. And companies are taking what's available, projecting to fill in the missing information, and selling the results.

Banks and others, for example, are able to obtain the names and addresses of, say, clothing manufacturers located in Manhattan with annual sales greater than $50 million, more than 200 employees, in business more than three years. That's better than approaching every company listed under "Clothing—Wholesale & Manufacturers" in the Yellow Pages, but not much. A software company selling its sophisticated statistical analysis program to media researchers in the advertising industry, for example, has no way to know that research chemists who face the same kinds of problems would be a market.

If one knew how to track the kinds of products and services a company buys, the way it is possible to track an individual's credit card, automotive, and other purchases, the information could be extremely interesting and helpful. What does it say about a company that buys Compaq personal computers instead of IBM or Apple? Combined with other information, it might say something about the company's philosophy: what it values, what it finds important, what risks it will take.

The marketing revolution is moving marketers to fill these information gaps. Today, companies are collecting data about businesses. Just as companies began assembling databases containing consumer information, so companies are beginning to combine business databases. Given the cost of a sales call, even the cost of telemarketing, there is as great an incentive to improve business-to-business marketing as to improve consumer marketing. Consider the difference it would make if a company knew, not that it had 5,000 prospects, but 5,000 prospects ranked by sales potential and propensity to buy. It would be invaluable to know, for example, that we make the most money selling to the first 1,362 companies on such a list.

STIMULATING SALES AUTOMATICALLY: 2010 TECHNOLOGY, TODAY

Plus Business Systems is another approach to selling consumers one at a time. It's a system we have been working on with a Yankelovich client. PBS is currently designed for affluent-market retailers. Since retail margins are being squeezed by rising costs and competition, the solution is to increase sales faster than costs, since a business's variable costs never rise as fast as sales (or if they do, the business soon disappears). The problem is to match customer needs and desires with store inventory.

This marketing software is designed to increase a retailer's sales and profits. The system employs automated intelligence technology combining the best of a "perfect salesman" with a "perfect advertising agency," to computer design and implement highly motivating, individualized, one-on-one marketing programs.

When customer needs and store inventory match, the store has a sales opportunity it can communicate to prospects. This, of course, is Retailing 101. But while virtually every retailer knows its inventory, few truly know their customers. What makes this system special is a customer profile with which the computer can automatically match the inventory to the customer and generate a personal letter—not a form letter, but a letter similar to the one at the beginning of this chapter that alerts the customer to special opportunities.

The customer profile includes

- Name, home address, and telephone number.
- Demographics, such as gender, date of birth, education, income (personal and family), financial situation, home ownership, and home value.
- Psychographic characteristics, such as shopping attitudes, hobbies, interests, and activities.
- Sociographics, such as shopping role, socioeconomic status, occupational status, marital status, spouse's name, and date of birth.
- Personal secrets, such as face and body shape, measurements, coloring, style and manufacturer preferences, sizes, and color preferences.
- Important dates, including the birthdays of children and parents; anniversaries; upcoming graduations, confirmations, and the like; moves in progress.
- Apparel needs, perceptions, and preferences, such as shopping behavior; dollar expenditures in total and by store; store and style preferences; store perceptions; and key purchases during the next six months.

Customers who respond to store cards, who join a preferred customer program, or who buy from the store will participate in the program. A retailer can offer a variety of incentives to participate: advance notice of sales, advance notice of new merchandise, special discounts or special treatment at selected times, a night at the opera, rewards for various purchasing levels.

Table 12.1 shows the key differences between conventional direct response marketing approach and this one-on-one approach in targeting, mailings, and customization.

- In the conventional approach being used by most retailers, the targets are all store credit card holders. In the new system, the targets are all customers (credit and noncredit) and all family members age sixteen and older.

- A conventional system usually holds little to no information about the

Table 12.1 *Key Differences between Conventional Direct Response and the Plus Business Systems Approach*

	1990 direct response	Plus Business robotic system
	Targeting	
Targets	All store credit card holders	All customers (credit and noncredit) and all family members age 16 and older
Information about target to assist in developing program	None to negligible	Substantial; everything from merchandise needs to psycho-, demo- and socio-graphics of customer and family
	Mailings	
Materials	Standard catalog 4–12 times a year	Monthly mailings to customers of customized letters and offerings
Triggering mechanism	Management decisions driven by seasonal factors and management desire to move specific merchandise	Robotic decisions driven by customer needs, key dates/occasions for customer and family, recent purchases of particular merchandise, inventory issues and management's desire to move specific merchandise
Product offering	Same merchandise offered to everyone	Different merchandise offered to different people

targets that can assist in developing a program. The new system has substantial information, everything from merchandise needs to the psychographics, demographics, and sociographics of the customer and her family.

• A conventional system mails a standard catalog two to four times a year. The new system sends customized letters and offerings to customers monthly. In a conventional system, management's decisions are

	Customization	
Mailing	None; same mailings to everyone	High; very different mailings to different customers
Tie-in with merchandise purchased by customer in the past	None	Substantial; mailings are driven in large part by this knowledge
Tie-in with knowledge about customer needs	Negligible	Substantial; needs of each customer are known
Tie-in with knowledge of customer's family	None	Substantial; needs of customer's family are known
Ability to talk to one family member about the needs of another	None	Substantial; a critical objective to this system
	Results	
Performance	Incremental profits less than 10%	20% + incremental sales and profits

driven by seasonal factors, and its desire to move specific merchandise triggers a mailing. In the new system, the decision is automatically driven by customer needs, key dates or occasions for the customer or her family, recent purchases of particular merchandise, inventory issues, and management's desire to move specific merchandise.

• A conventional system offers the same merchandise to everyone. The new system offers different merchandise to different people. Indeed, if a store has 50,000 customers, chances are that the PBS system would mail out 50,000 different individualized letters. That is, no two letters would talk about the same merchandise in the same way.

• There is, in other words, an extremely high level of customization—a different letter to every customer. Moreover, a conventional system cannot tie in with merchandise purchased by the customer in the past, while in the new system mailings are driven in large part by this knowledge. The conventional system's tie-in with knowledge about customer needs is negligible, while in the new system the needs of each customer are known. Likewise, the conventional system knows virtually nothing about the customer's family, while the new system knows a great deal about the customer's family.

• Finally, the conventional system has no ability to talk to one family member about the needs of another, while this is a critical objective of the new system. The letter at the beginning of this chapter on pages 261–262 is the kind of communication the system can generate. Addressed to the customer's husband, the letter is tied to the wife's birthday. Because the store knows the woman's size, her preferences in clothing and color, and the family's approximate income, it can suggest an appropriate gift.

The goal of this one-on-one marketing system is to increase the retailer's sales and profits among selected customers, increase the number of transactions per customer, increase the average size of the transactions, help identify merchandise desired by customers, motivate other members of the customer's household to become loyal customers, and help optimize inventory turnover and eliminate leftover stock.

In addition, the new system smooths out sales over varying time periods, days of the week, and months, which helps improve personnel utilization. It will increase the retailer's share of the consumer's purchases; and it will create reports that provide the retailer with information on product sales, customer profile, and customer satisfaction, and be an integral part of the retailer's point of sale system.

As more and more organizations capture and store information about individuals—their credit card usage, shopping habits, media consumption, demographics, interests and hobbies, even the movies they watch (through the video tapes they rent) or the books they read (as libraries automate the circulation function)—it becomes possible to create a detailed profile about the individual consumer. And with such a profile, it becomes possible to forecast the probability that an individual will purchase a given product or service.

A company will never know, of course, whether an individual consumer will or will not actually buy. But if it makes an offer to 10,000 people, each of whom have a 0.9 probability of purchase, it knows that it will sell about 9,000 products. That's a lot better than making the offer to 10,000 people and having no idea whether 9,000 products or 900 will sell.

The marketing revolution means, if nothing else, that companies will be more efficient in what they sell and to whom they sell. Advertising is a distraction when you have no need for or interest in the product. A catalog is junk mail when you don't want the products.

Advertising can be valuable information when you are in the market for the product. Have you ever noticed how, when you are in the market for a product—golf clubs, a car, a boat, a suit, a camcorder, a local area network, or whatever—you suddenly are seeing ads for the item everywhere? The ads have always been around, but you have been filtering them out.

As marketers, we want to reach those people who do need and want our product or service. We don't really want to fill the air with commercials people immediately zap or fill mail boxes with brochures people toss without opening. With our ability to obtain, manage, and analyze more information about more and more people cost efficiently, we are rapidly reaching a time when we reach only our best prospects—and leave everyone else alone.

WHAT ONE-ON-ONE MARKETING IS ALL ABOUT

- Direct marketing plays an important role in the marketing mix for many products and services. Yet the cost efficiency of direct marketing is in decline.
- Conventional approaches to targeting are among the reasons for this inefficiency. Heavily based on aggregate level characteristics (e.g., ZIP codes or census blocks), they direct more mail to nontargets that to targets.
- One-on-one marketing is the logical extension of targeting.
- Given more and more available information about customers and prospects, it is becoming cost-efficient to market to individuals.
- New technologies enable a marketer to obtain a list of the names and addresses of specific people primed to buy.
- A state-of-the-art application of micromarketing is a new software system that directs individualized messages to individual people. No two people would receive the same letter or catalog.
- Meanwhile, 2010 technology is being readied today to employ automated intelligence technology to create *and implement* individualized programs—computer-aided marketing warfare.

13

WITH ENOUGH COMPUTING POWER, YOU'VE GOT A MARKETING DEPARTMENT IN A BOX

In the past twenty years, marketers and researchers focused on collecting more and more information to the point of overload, at which point data becomes a form of intellectual pollution.

But just as smart bombs, cruise missiles, and Stealth bombers revolutionized warfare in the Persian Gulf War, new "star wars" technology will revolutionize marketing throughout the 1990s.

Using automated intelligence (AI) technology, sophisticated research modeling, and database systems, computers will do everything from write research reports to design ads, media schedules, and products and services—and ultimately implement entire marketing programs. That's why it's a myth to say that artificial intelligence shows little short-term promise in marketing and advertising. Machines will be built before the year 2010 that can replace marketing and advertising managers. Already we see precursors of these machines as computer programs are being introduced to deal with the fragmenting media and the torrent of marketing information.

A CEO therefore must ask the marketing director questions about these developments:

THE BOTTOM LINE: WHAT A CEO WANTS TO KNOW

1) What do we know about applications of artificial and automated intelligence in fields such as medicine, geological exploration, and manufacturing?

2) We are now overwhelmed by meaningless marketing data. Wouldn't an artificial intelligence or automated intelligence system that teases marketing intelligence out of that data be useful?

3) Have we considered "capturing" in an expert system the genius and experience of marketing experts to improve the efficiency and return on investment of our marketing effort for (a) more media impact, (b) more cost efficiency, and (c) less labor and time?

4) Have we considered systems that supplement, if not replace, marketing managers?

It's commonplace to say that the world is changing faster than most of us can grasp. The point of this chapter is to suggest how the world of marketing is changing and the changes we see in the very near future.

≣ What an Expert System Actually Does in Marketing

Not long ago Litmus™ recommended *against* an advertising agency's $11 million spot television buy as part of a new product launch.

Litmus, as we discussed in Chapter 9, is a sophisticated computer program, an evolving expert system that employs simulated test marketing technology and sophisticated mathematical modeling to help evaluate and develop marketing plans for new products. The advertising agency is one of the world's largest and is staffed with some of North America's best and brightest advertising and research brains. These people were more than a little perturbed at the recommendation. Perhaps "totally freaked" describes the agency's reaction better.

Both the agency's experts and the electronic expert were thinking about the same problem. The agency suggested the spot buys, but Litmus had discovered the following:

- There was no difference between spot and nonspot markets in terms of advertising response as measured by simulated test market research.
- Product usage in spot markets was 30 percent higher than in nonspot markets, but the cost of spot television was 40 percent more per gross rating point than network TV.

Therefore, Litmus sensibly recommended against the spot schedule and recommended a national network buy instead. The agency and the client looked at the data again and again and again.

And they finally agreed with the machine.

≣ In the 1990s, Marketing Technology Makes the Difference

While Litmus is, by today's standards, a fairly sophisticated system, it is, we know, primitive compared to what marketers will be using routinely by the turn of the century.

We expect that, during the 1990s, many companies will implement the technologies and approaches we've talked about in the earlier chapters. They will evaluate hundreds of thousands of targets in terms of profitability; they will position in terms of unique appeal; they will create advertising message strategies for maximum effect. Using the computer to find the optimal combination of appeal and profit, companies will engineer new products through computer-aided design.

And we expect that companies using these technologies will be more successful than their less-sophisticated, less technology-oriented competitors. We therefore see a growing concentration of marketing power in fewer companies as we approach the year 2010. Just as technology changed the nature of combat between the Vietnam War and the Persian Gulf War, technology will change the nature of marketing as we move through the 1990s.

Marketers today are beginning to look at the relationships between individual media exposure, couponing, and buyer behavior. We see a time coming when research companies—notably Nielsen Market Research and Information Resources Inc. (IRI)—will register this information not for an unrepresentative set of markets, the case today, but nationally. Marketing executives will be able look at these interrelationships to ask questions like,

- What would happen if we raised our price from $1.79 to $2.09?

- What would happen if we ran a thousand GRPs in a television campaign?
- What would happen if we increased a coupon's face value from 25 cents to 75 cents?
- What would happen if we increased our share of shelf-facings from 20 percent to 35 percent?

Marketers answer these "what if" questions today in only the most cumbersome and primitive ways. By the end of the decade, they will be able to answer them routinely—and more definitively—for every market in the country.

But we see computer technology finding the answers to even more basic questions. Today most marketers believe in the power of advertising, particularly for established products, in the same way that many people believe in a personal God or in a capitalistic economy. They take it on faith alone that advertising works, and yet we don't truly know whether it works or not. There's no compelling evidence that advertising for a product—any kind of product—produces a return on investment. Tools sensitive enough to measure advertising's effect do not yet exist. Yet by the end of the 1990s, through data-collection technologies that will become routine, we will have the evidence.

We see three broad, dramatic trends that affect marketing continuing, even spreading, in the 1990s: (1) new or transformed media (television, magazines, newspapers, and more); (2) new or improved methods to collect raw marketing data; and (3) new ways—expert systems—to channel the flood of data and turn it into information power.

≣ In Media, More Power to the Individual

We see no end to media fragmentation. Indeed, we see new media developing like Prodigy, the Sears/IBM computer information service. While media fragmentation means the marketer's task of reaching consumers is more complex, it also means that consumers are more absorbed in the medium.

One example: Where is the best place to advertise golf clubs? In *Golf* magazine and during the PGA telecast or in *Newsweek* and during the evening network news? The newsweekly and the news show have larger audiences and may, in fact, reach more golfers than the special interest publication and PGA show. But a golfer reading *Golf* or watching the PGA is thinking golf, and the advertiser does not have to divert his attention from, say, national affairs to golf.

As media fragments, the task of reaching consumers with sales messages becomes more complex. The MIT Media Lab of the Massachusetts Institute of Technology is dedicated to finding new ways to use computers to make mass media (television, print, movies) respond to individual tastes. According to Gordon Link, worldwide media director of McCann-Erickson and the MIT lab's only advertising agency sponsor, the laboratory's guiding philosophy is that all media are poised for redefinition, and the lab's purpose is to enhance the quality of life in an electronic age.

One way to enhance the quality of life is to reduce commercial and advertising clutter. Because media are critical to marketing, marketers must anticipate media changes. We, Backer Spielvogel Bates, and McCann-Erickson, see the following occurring during the next few years.

HIGH-DEFINITION TELEVISION

High-definition television has the clarity and richness of movie film. HDTV pictures have 1,000 to 1,200 horizontal scanning lines and scan fifty to sixty frames per second as opposed to conventional television's 525 horizontal scanning lines and thirty frames per second. This means a forty-two-inch TV picture seems just as crisp as a nine-inch. The HDTV signals typically carry four times as much information as conventional signals and deliver a compact-disk quality digital sound, which provides audio simply not possible on present TV sets.

HDTV has its problems. A high-definition signal requires 50 to 100 percent more band width than a conventional signal, and broadcasters are afraid there won't be enough room to accommodate high-definition stations. But engineers are currently working on two solutions—new amplifiers and signal compression—and the Backer Spielvogel Bates Media Department, in *BSB Projections 2000*, envisages an abundance of higher band width options by the turn of the century that will pave the way for HDTV and more channel capacity for the cable industry as well. Of course, additional channel capacity means more narrowly targeted cable networks, creating still more viewing options for consumers.

More cable networks imply more advertising outlets. These more narrowly targeted networks will offer marketers environments that will reach specific audiences more effectively than they can be reached today. Cable networks will become as targeted as radio and magazines, while advertising copy will become less generic and more directed to a specific audience.

But while the broadcast engineers are working to improve picture quality and increase band width capacity, video cassette recorder engineers are working on technology to automatically delete commercials. In Japan, one manufacturer has been selling a VCR that stops recording a movie at a commercial break and resumes when it starts again. The system will not work in the United States because the broadcast technology is different (the Japanese VCR recognizes a special signal stations broadcast before a commercial), but it seems to be only a matter of time until the technology is available and inexpensive enough for a consumer product. Indeed, if the technology were available (and legal), manufacturers could build a system into television sets that would automatically eliminate commercials before they could be seen.

At the beginning of January 1991, the Federal Communications Commission proposed making a special broadcast frequency available for ordering goods and services through television sets. Home shopping programs, for example, could supplement their programming by transmitting catalogues of products through a television set and amend them each day with new promotions. Colleges would be able to test students through broadcasts, and local pizza shops could advertise daily specials that viewers could order by using a small box attached to the television set.

The idea of interactive television, of course, has been around for years. The Qube cable service in Columbus, Ohio, in the late 1970s foundered on unwieldy technology and high cost. But with better technology and lower prices, the ability to interact with what one watches is on its way. The Lintas: USA advertising agency forecasts that 40 percent of U.S. households will have interactive TV by the year 2000.

The *Economist* observed in 1989 that the biggest threat to advertising-supported television may be pay-per-view cable television, for which around 10 million American homes currently have converters. Pay-per-view offers "whatever you want, whenever you want it, television." At some point, cable subscribers may be able to call up the movie—or old TV show, documentary, performance, or whatever—they want, when they want it, from a central "library" of CD/ROM and fiber optics, much the way a hotel guest picks a movie today. The snag right now is that technology cannot cope with more than a few hundred homes at a time wanting to view the same thing.

Cable television networks are not alone in investigating these possibilities; telephone companies want to sell programming through fiber optic lines. It seems only a matter of time before Americans have as much control over their television viewing as they have over their magazine reading.

RADIO

ABC Radio and CBS Radio have announced joint development and implementation of a new satellite-distribution system, designed to enhance the audio quality and expand the programming capabilities of existing systems. The new system will provide three CD-quality 20 KHZ channels in a band that currently allows for one KHZ channel. Backer Spielvogel Bates observes that the expanded distribution capability, plus the addition of the next generation of digital audio, will benefit radio stations, providing expanded services conveniently and economically.

But radio signals, like television signals, do not have to come through the air, and after two years of test marketing, Digital Music Express, Digital Planet, and Digital Cable Radio are now searching for subscribers willing to pay a monthly fee for commercial-free and, in some cases, disk jockey-free programs. Digital Cable Radio offers HBO, VH-1, and other pay simulcasts. Music Express's tuner comes with a digital display of the names of song, artist, album, label, and catalog number. Digital Planet plans to deliver actual radio stations from around the world.

MAGAZINES

Backer Spielvogel Bates speculates that one day magazines may be delivered via personal computer, a development that may be promoted by several factors:

• With increased postage rates, publishers are looking at alternative distribution methods, and computers provide relatively inexpensive data transmission. But even with the traditional magazine, publishers are looking at alternatives to the Postal Service and the newsstand. Meredith Corporation has distributed 400,000 issues of its magazines directly to readers' homes via a private contractor, while *People* magazine is also testing alternate distribution channels. These alternatives have marketing implications. Since the publishers pack the magazine in a plastic bag, it is possible to include product samples, coupons, booklets, and other material postal regulations do not currently permit.

• Environmentalists and the general public are increasingly concerned about paper scarcity and trash abundance. Since magazine publishers contribute significantly to both, and since more people are concerned about the planet's future, magazine publishers (and others—notably the Yellow Page publishers) may move away from paper as a way to disseminate information.

• On-line computer services, such as Prodigy, GEnie, CompuServe, and Knowledge Index, are making a variety of services available to consumers in their homes. Banking, grocery shopping, investment, travel arrangements, and games are readily available on computer today. As home computer penetration increases, consumers will demand more on-line data and have less time to read magazines (or watch television).

Eventually it may be possible to access only articles of interest and to create your own personal magazine on a computer terminal.

Simultaneously, publication printers are improving printing and binding technology so that it is easier and less expensive to insert an advertisement in a magazine or group of magazines delivered only to a selected subscriber list—those people, in other words, who most resemble the target market. Ink jet imaging allows advertisers to deliver personalized messages to individual subscribers inside the publication. The technology permits a marketer to personalize business reply cards, stimulate product trial through local price incentives (personalize coupons for example), enhance sweepstakes and contest offers, and accommodate co-op programs with local retailers. Packaged editions permit advertisers to target specific segments, such as recent movers, high-income seniors, or regular mail order, direct response customers. Publishers and advertisers can merge databases to create customized magazines for important audiences.

As markets become more segmented and selective binding technology improves, publishers will make many more packaged and customized editions available to advertisers. More customized editions targeted to specific niche markets will also affect the editorial product. For example, *Time* magazine may produce several different editorial editions, as opposed to the regional and demographic editions it currently produces, each addressing the needs of a different constituency.

THE ELECTRONIC NEWSPAPER

Newspaper delivery via fax machine has begun to appear. Both the *New York Times* and the *Los Angeles Times* send several-page summaries of the day's top stories to companies in Japan and Russia. Other newspapers are offering the service to local businesses. The *Wall Street Journal* has announced "Journal Fax," a one-page market and business news summary. As fax transmission speeds increase and as costs decline with improved plain-paper fax machines, this option may appeal to ordinary consumers.

Over 100 newspapers currently offer a telephone service that provides customers with daily information, from traffic reports to soap opera updates, and from crossword puzzle answers to advertised clothing purchase locations. The papers generally use 900 numbers, and the calls cost customers on average 75 cents a minute.

The MIT Media Lab has demonstrated a personalized computer newspaper called *Newspeek*, which contains news stories collected from news services and television broadcasts. McCann-Erickson describes *Newspeek*'s format as familiar to newspaper readers: the computer screen holds a front page with eight or nine articles, headlines in large type, photos in color, stories in columns. By moving a finger across an article, the reader can jump to the story's continuation, and then to related articles. The reader can obtain television news coverage, maps, photographs, and previous articles with a touch. Pausing on a word, such as *Coca-Cola* or *Bush*, causes that word to be highlighted in all other articles that include it. The computer remembers what it has been asked to show, and the following day will devote additional space to the subjects that most interested the reader. After time, if an individual always reads about the arts but never bothers with sports, sports items recede to a small box, while arts articles increase.

PLACE-BASED MEDIA

Some of the same technological developments currently transforming manufacturing and communications industries will spill over into store-based media by the late 1990s. By the turn of the century, satellite systems will deliver national, international, and local programming and advertising to video receiving screens—doubtless HDTV screens—at participating supermarkets.

Researchers estimated that in the 1980s, the average American was exposed to 150 advertisements a day based on four media: television, radio, magazines, and newspapers. With the growth of alternative media, that exposure may double even as consumers zip, zap, and otherwise avoid TV commercials, with nontraditional media making up a significant share of the increase.

The following examples of these alternative media all were available at this writing:

- Channel M, a four-screen video wall with top-40 music videos, advertising, and information in Aladdin's Castle Video Arcades. The target is twelve- to twenty-four-year-old males.
- Check-out Channel, a television screen at check-out counters with CNN and Headline News talent as anchors. The target is grocery store shoppers, predominantly female.
- Concierge, interactive kiosks in airports that take travel and entertainment reservations and gift orders. The target is adults, twenty-five to forty-nine, taking a dozen or more trips annually.
- Diamond Vision, signs in stadiums, ball parks, and race tracks. The target is sports fans, primarily male.
- Health Club TV, television monitors in health clubs that entertain and inform exercisers. The target is adults, eighteen to forty-nine, with an income of $36,000 or more.

- MallVision, a nine-screen video wall located at the center or middle court of a shopping mall. The target is shoppers of all ages, including teens.
- Metro Vision, high resolution video monitors in subways, bus stations, and airports, providing general interest subjects and travel information. The target is the working public; people fourteen to thirty-four, especially females.
- Patients Movie Network carries programming in hospitals edited for patients admitted for general procedures. The target is health-conscious adults.
- VideOcart, spun off as a separate company by Information Resources Inc., produces shopping carts with video screens. The screen presents advertisements to shoppers as they pass the appropriate shelf in the supermarket and displays other information such as store specials, new products, and the like.
- Whittle Communications is augmenting traditional media in doctors' and dentists' offices with news billboards carrying specialized advertising. The company is also introducing special television programs into professional offices and schools; the programs are tailored for the audiences and carry commercials.

TELEPHONES

AT&T developed 900 numbers in response to requests by television networks for a way to conduct instant polls of viewers. NBC used the first 900 number during the 1980 presidential debate. Two years later NASA asked AT&T for a 900 number so that reporters could hear conversations between mission control and astronauts on space shuttles, a number that NASA later promoted to the public. Until 1985, AT&T kept all money from the call—fifty cents for the first minute, thirty-five cents for each subsequent minute—but after April that year, the company began giving 900 providers up to five cents per call, depending on volume, to increase business. In 1987 AT&T permitted companies to charge up to $2 for the first minute of a call and keep $1.30; within months, firms bought up all available 900 numbers.

When consumers dial into 900 numbers, Automated Number Identification technology identifies their phone number, providing marketers a wealth of information without the customer knowing. By integrating phone number data with marketing databases, marketers know, for example, whether the caller is a good prospect for certain types of mail-order purchases.

Backer Spielvogel Bates projects that by the mid to late 1990s, technological developments of the Automated Number Identification system will permit marketers to merge a caller's phone number and home address with other databases, information above and beyond household size, number of children, marital status, household income, and car ownership. These numbers will then become a primary source for obtaining prospective client lists.

By the end of the decade, the technology will be able to answer many more than 30,000 calls simultaneously, the present limit on 900-number calls, and computerized voice messages will be able to provide personalized responses to caller inquiries.

≡ Big Brother Really Is Watching

The past ten years saw an explosion in the variety and volume of marketing data as companies began recording consumer viewing and shopping habits, credit card and coupon usage, product movement, and more. The new media—not to mention the fragmenting old media—require new measurement technology.

The traditional paper diary maintained by 1,200 people that A. C. Nielsen used to measure television viewing was adequate when the three networks accounted for virtually all television. As the number of cable television networks grew, and as advertisers became more interested in smaller population segments (upscale viewers, working women), the diary became inefficient, and Nielsen introduced the People-meter in 1987. With the People-meter, now in about 4,000 households, viewers simply push a button to tell the device they are watching.

People-meters have their problems, however; they do not adequately capture children, teens, or out-of-home viewing (of course, the diaries may not have adequately captured these either). Children and teens are more capricious than adults in recording their viewing. Some sample respondents grow tired of pressing the buttons every time they watch television. Also the People-meters do not capture out-of-home viewing, since TV sets in bars, hotel rooms, and friends' homes do not have the meters.

To solve two of these problems, engineers are working on a passive people meter, a device that will be able to electronically "recognize" the facial images of sample household members and record their viewing. Such a device will record child and teen viewing and, conceivably, will track audiences second by second, so that a marketer can obtain ratings for individual commercials. That still leaves out-of-home viewing under-recorded, and one suggestion is an electronic diary that could register any television set.

Radio audience measurement is moving toward such electronic

diaries. Currently Birch (local/spot radio) and RADAR (national/network radio) use a telephone-recall methodology to measure listening. Arbitron Radio uses a self-administered diary and is testing an electronic diary, a hand-held computer that resembles a personal calculator. Listeners punch in call letters, which the device checks for incorrect entries. Arbitron says that eventually the electronic diary could be scaled down to the size of a credit card and the information downloaded to Arbitron daily.

Magazine readership currently depends on personal interviews and reader memory. Simmons Market Research Bureau uses a "stripped down" version of an issue to jog respondents' memories; Mediamark Research uses cards with magazine logotypes. Both are limited in the number of titles they can measure and depend on human recall.

The Pretesting Company is developing a passive readership recording device—a wristwatch that picks up media usage. For print, publishers would apply a special microscopic chip through the ink to the page. The chip would interact electronically with the wristwatch and so record exposure to each magazine and newspaper page. For television and radio, the broadcaster could include a signal in programs and commercials the watch would automatically record. Theoretically, the watch could record all reading, viewing, and listening.

Furthermore, store cash registers could be equipped to interact electronically with the watch. This would permit marketers to record the respondent's purchases and correlate them directly with specific media usage habits. Other than having to wear the watch all the time (which may be a serious qualification) respondents would not have to do anything except return the watch periodically to The Pretesting Company to have the data downloaded.

Whether publishers, broadcasters, and marketers adopt the watch technology or something else, companies realize the value of capturing the consumer's media consumption and product purchases to see how one influences the other.

Because marketers want to know whether (and when) their ads appeared, commercial recognition technology today electronically identifies and measures both television advertising and programs. The machine records television transmission electronic patterns and compares them to a database library of previously stored and identified patterns. If the computer does not find that transmission pattern, it records it for later identification, and in this way creates, market-by-market, a database of time-stamped commercials and programs. VCR engineers might use a version of this idea to screen out commercials the consumer has already seen.

Universal Product Code labeling streamlined supermarket checkout as clerks simply wave products over laser scanners, while simultaneously making it possible to record household purchase information. A number of companies, of which Citicorp POS is perhaps the most famous, are attempting to record consumer behavior at the cash register and to build a database that documents what people buy together with who they are—demographically, psychographically, and socioeconomically. In the Citicorp system, shoppers present an ID card at the checkout that the clerk scans or keys in along with purchases. The computer saves the entire purchase transaction for later use. In another system, a panel of shoppers scan their own purchases at home using a small wand. Both methods give marketers purchase tracking and household behavior information.

There's no reason why what's being done for Kraft/General Foods or Campbell or ConAgra to record consumer purchases in the supermarket today can't be done for Dart Drugs or Sears' Auto Stores or whatever. We see these new data-collection and -measurement technologies spreading from packaged goods into other areas, and we see them spreading more quickly with a higher transmission level than new technologies spread in the past. In the 1950s it probably took ten years for other companies to catch on to what packaged goods companies were doing; that pace will necessarily accelerate in the 1990s.

Not only will researchers be recording media consumption and shopping behavior, but traditional market research will be evolving. We suspect there will be a move away from personal interviews to even more research done over the telephone. We will see more interactive research. For example, researchers might contact people by telephone and ask them to tune to, say, Channel 45 that evening. That evening, these viewers would be taken through an electronic questionnaire, pushing buttons on a box to answer the questions. At the interview's conclusion, they would be asked to press the "end" button, and the hardware and software combination that sits beside the VCR or cable junction box would automatically download the responses and communicate the information by telephone to the research firm. The answers to a national survey could be available overnight.

But with the new media options and new measurement technology, come even greater problems in turning data into information.

≡ Expert Systems: Bright, Dependable, Inexpensive Consultants

Even though services like the Nielsen Marketing Research, Arbitron, and Information Resources are currently providing a wealth of potentially more useful information than marketers ever had before, most marketers aren't using the information because they're overwhelmed by it. Companies need some system to help managers manage the information explosion, systems able to extract what's significant from the mass and boil it down to a simple story that marketers and their managements can easily understand.

The only way researchers and marketing management will be able to cope with the data deluge of the 1990s will be with the help of expert computer systems. These are interactive computer programs that apply a variety of knowledge elements such as facts, rules, and models in a manner that supports and enhances problem-solving in specific fields. Those in the field often refer to them as *knowledge-based systems* because how they perform depends on how well they represent and manipulate knowledge.

To imagine how they work, think of how physicians make a medical diagnosis. They apply their accumulated expertise selectively and by trial and error, testing for one thing, then another as they rule out possibilities. They ask patients questions based on their past experience, run the tests that seem indicated, consult with other physicians, and refer to textbooks to uncover additional information. Out of this comes a diagnosis.

Expert systems typically follow a similar process. The systems represent knowledge in symbolic form, with numeric values reflecting the subjective probability of the likelihood, or the truthfulness, of the information. The expert system's general reasoning strategies (the so-called inference engine) are separated from the domain specific trial-and-error attempts, models, and facts (the so-called knowledge base). The domain-specific knowledge includes some combination of facts ("All shipments to Europe originate from our New York office"), rules ("If the marketing objective is to stimulate primary demand, then the advertising objective is to stimulate category need"), and models and their interrelationships ("To calculate sales-response coefficients, first run a regression of sales on marketing variables").

This separation between inference and knowledge allows the system to use knowledge in a variety of ways. It can tap into particular elements of the knowledge base and request additional information to solve a specific problem. An expert system can explain the reasoning behind its questions and recommendations by reporting the trials it has attempted and the facts it used to investigate hypotheses and draw conclusions.

We believe that expert systems will lead to expert marketing managers, managers who will lead the way to exceptional marketing programs. An expert system is like having a consultant beside the desk, one smarter than most consultants, more expert than most consultants, and one who doesn't charge $3,000 a day. Perhaps the best known, if fictional, expert system, was HAL, the on-board computer of Stanley Kubrick's *2001: A Space Odyssey*.

Expert systems employ artificial (AI) or automated intelligence to do their thinking. By *AI*, we mean computers or computer programs that think, or seem to think, the way humans do. By *expert systems,* we mean programs that clone, or seem to, the knowledge, experience, and decision-making ability of an expert in a particular field (see Fig. 13.1).

Think of AI as general intelligence while expert systems represent specialized intelligence in a particular field such as geology, neurology, philosophy—or marketing. An expert system depends on an artificial intelligence subsystem to do the thinking for it. But the AI subsystem, here labeled an intelligent program, needs to be integrated with the knowledge of an expert or experts and, often, with specialized databases as well. A whole new class of engineers called *knowledge engineers* captures the knowledge of the expert—the doctor who makes the diagnosis or the marketing executive who makes the plan. The knowledge engineer's contribution is to reflect in a computer program the knowledge, experience, rules of thumb, insights, and judgment of an expert in a particular field.

A good expert system thinks through a problem or question—given the available intelligent program, expert knowledge, and database—to arrive at a solution, an answer, or a decision. In expert systems, as in real life, the higher the intelligence of the experts, the greater the expert's knowledge, and the more sophisticated the databases available, the better the solution, answer, or decision.

Such a system can use two forms of intelligence: the form that has dominated artificial intelligence thus far is called *artificial intelligence,* while our own term, *automated intelligence,* describes an alternate approach. The difference between the two is similar to the orthodox

Figure 13.1 *An Expert System*

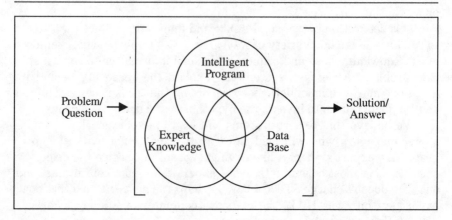

ethological distinction between human and animal thinking. Until recently, it had been almost universally held that humans think creatively. We reason. We make choices. Animals, on the other hand, cope with the challenges they face solely by following imprinted genetic behavioral instructions. Humans think, the argument goes; animals follow complex command structures.

Artificial intelligence programs operate like human thinking processes. They seem to reason. They employ logical rules to manipulate words and phrases in languages such as "Lisp" and "Prolog."

Automated intelligence programs, on the other hand, can follow complex orders. They do what they're told to do. But no reasoning is involved. They manipulate numerical characters, using algorithms and equations written in mathematical languages such as PL-1 and C.

DIFFERENCES BETWEEN ARTIFICIAL AND AUTOMATED INTELLIGENCE

Characteristics	Artificial intelligence	Automated intelligence
Simulates	Creative thinking	Flexive reacting
Manipulates	Nonnumeric symbols	Numerical values
Based on	Rules of logic	Algorithms, equations
Program languages	AI natural languages	Contemporary languages

Although there has been enormous interest in expert systems in marketing, relatively few examples currently exist. Some smart programs are available, however, that employ automated intelligence technology to make the market researcher's job easier—programs, for example, that help a researcher design a conjoint study or aid in the interviewing or analytical process. While today's smart programs do their assigned chores efficiently, displaying a modest level of intelligence, they show little or no marketing expertise. They are not expert systems.

In 1985, we developed a program called "Robot Researcher," designed to work with an IBM mainframe and a marketing research database. It was designed to write the first draft of a research report, a tedious, repetitive kind of report such as one based on an awareness tracking study, a copy test, or a sales analysis. Robot Researcher selects the appropriate statistical model, integrates it with preprogrammed text with words and phrases randomly modified the way any good analyst would do, and prints the report using a word processing package. Robot Researcher generates such a report in a few hours; research departments across the country typically take between six to fifteen days to develop one.

In 1988 Information Resources Inc. introduced "CoverStory," a software product that assists consumer packaged goods marketing executives to investigate, analyze, and present IRI's syndicated scanner data. CoverStory automatically analyzes the data and writes an English language memo such as, "During the four weeks ending June 26, 1988, volume in the Total Frozen Pizza category stood at 31.1 million consumer units—up 0.7 percent from the prior year. Pillsbury's share of the category was 29.1, which is an increase of 5.7 share points from last year but a loss of 3.1 points since last period."

Developed by Professors John Little of MIT and Leonard Lodish of Wharton, CoverStory extracts the most important information, as defined by the user, from the IRI database and delivers it in memo format, supported by tables and graphs. For a specific product category, CoverStory produces headlines for category volume and trends, describes how the company's brands are doing with respect to sales and share, while extracting and presenting major geographic shifts in brand performance. It identifies shifts in price, merchandising, and distribution associated with share gains and losses. It also identifies competitors that are gaining and losing share.

Dr. Little says that consumer packaged goods manufacturers purchase 1,000 times more syndicated data than they have in the past. Although fourth-generation computer languages and workstation software solve the basic problem of easy retrieval and analysis of information, CoverStory is the first software to automatically search for the key news items in a scanner database, report them in easy language on the screen, and produce them in presentation-quality copy. CoverStory reports provide a coherent picture of who's gaining, who's losing, where, and why.

Nielsen Market Research planned to release a similar program in the near future. This will be an update of ScanFact, which provides specific sales and marketing information from 3,000 stores in fifty markets in a matter of minutes but which, unlike CoverStory, does not analyze the data. As one user remarked, "ScanFact is just a way to get data in front of you—there's no assembly, no interpretation, like there is with CoverStory. It's just numbers on the screen."

Presumably the new program will address these concerns. Nielsen says that while user interface and reporting are on a personal computer, the data is stored on and the computational processing takes place on the mainframe. The Nielsen Performance Exception Review claims to use a true expert system inference engine. It evaluates a product's performance with causal explanation, reports category volume performance, finds and explains exceptional market performance, and finds and reports segment shifts (for example, sizes and flavors) for both the category and the product. The new program evaluates the product's performance relative to competitive merchandising activity and deduces generalized conclusions for the product across all markets or similar markets. It produces graphs, and combines text, graphs, and tables to help users visualize what's happening.

We suspect that most of the marketing systems introduced during the 1990s will be based on automated intelligence technology. We've yet to find very many good applications of traditional artificial intelligence. That's why many of the artificial intelligence firms founded during the 1980s are dying or have died; they could not find the market or the application for their product. Automated intelligence, however, is another story. Any area in which professional people spend a lot of time working on a problem is an area where expert systems technology will show promise.

There may be, of course, certain areas of human activity where this technology may not work at all—creativity, for example. Will an expert system ever be used to create an effective television commercial or write a persuasive advertisement? Maybe not, although two Wharton professors have been working for a number of years on a system that helps design advertising copy.

The system helps the agency and company make decisions like: Should your ad just talk about your product, or compare it to the competition? Should it be a one-sided or a two-sided presentation? Should it be an emotional appeal or a reasoned appeal? They have programmed research study results, so conceivably the system could give the agency suggestions about a company's message strategy and ideas about how to execute the strategy: For example, use a famous personality and testimonial-type television program to talk about the new car's safety model without comparing it to any past models or to competitive cars.

But if an expert system will never actually create, it can be extraordinarily helpful in environmental scanning, targeting, positioning, product design, pricing, advertising—all the decisions that marketers routinely make. One can imagine a time toward the end of this decade when marketing managers will routinely use expert systems to make marketing decisions.

≣ Expert or Not, Does the System Help Make Decisions?

Recently, we sat through a day of media advertising planning with one company. It was alarming. The company was not sure its target market—executives in high-tech industries—watched television or actually read the specialized business publications in the field. The advertising agency had rough estimates of cable and network television reach for this group, but they had only circulation—not readership—figures for the twenty top trade publications they were considering. They did have readership scores that are roughly comparable for *Business Week* for some of the general audience publications, such as *Time, Esquire,* and *GQ.* In other words, they had incomplete data, and what they had was not comparable.

We found it appalling that in 1991 executives of a major advertising agency were leafing through loose-leaf research books to find cross-tabs of media exposure patterns for men, forty years of age and older, in high technology industries. By now, one ought to be able to sit at a computer and tell it, "I have a budget of $25 million. My target group consists of these kinds of people. Give me a profile of the media these folks watch, read, and are exposed to." Then answer the machine's questions: "How many times do you have to reach a person each month to be successful? Do you have one campaign going or several?"

Once it asked its questions, such a machine would analyze its databases and produce a recommendation. A relatively primitive expert system could provide a recommendation. But if companies buy media in terms of eighteen- to forty-nine-year-old women or heavy buyers instead of buying more subtle target groups, like people most responsive to the firm's marketing efforts, even a primitive expert system is probably overqualified.

The last five years have seen tremendous growth in computerized marketing decision support systems (MDSS) that are outgrowths of corporate sales databases. The latest technology matches near real-time sales tracking information, which means that the marketing executives obtain sales data almost as fast as the sales occur, with sophisticated market modeling. For the first time, we are able to study marketing input-output relationships in depth.

The complaint of most practitioners who are struggling with implementing a marketing decision support system is that they are drowning in data, and they have no information. Companies are creating artificial intelligence, or automated intelligence, or expert systems on top of the MDSS systems to absorb the huge data stream pouring into corporate databases, winnow through the data to find the critical trends and advertising sales effects, and emerge with recommendations for action.

Tools now exist, some in the form of expert systems, that vary considerably in terms of sophistication. A device that simply takes a load of data and analyzes it to ferret out the key findings is a primitive version of automated intelligence technology. But the fact that a technology may be primitive does not make it uninteresting or useless. Something may be very useful without requiring a great deal of technological polish.

The most advanced of these programs incorporates the best thinking of inspired analysts with the tireless patience of the computer. In the future, these systems will use sophisticated modeling and decision rules to identify marketplace opportunities, such as local competitive vulnerabilities, long-term share-gain opportunities, or optimal pricing and dealing tactics. Once researchers understand these effects, they can model them.

As we discussed in Chapter 9, evolving expert systems such as Litmus are being used with great success on an experimental basis to actually create marketing plans for new consumer products. Work with such systems suggests much promise as the model-generated plans routinely beat the ones prepared by marketing managers by 15 percent or more. The following table shows one case where a system-created plan achieved the same share objectives (approximately 14 percent) with a $19 million investment as did the manager's plan with a $27 million investment.

FOOD PRODUCT OPTIMIZATION

	Manager-prepared plan	Model-generated "optimal" plan
Cost of plan	$27 million	$19 million
Forecasted share of market	13.7	14.2
Expected losses (end of year 1)	-7.9 million	+.2 million
Payout period	38 months	16 months

In the near future, it will be possible for most brands to "parse out" the effects of short-term sales promotions and local store activity to uncover direct short-term effects of advertising. For those who take a longer-term view, the promise of single-source panel data is the ability to track the longer-term effects of advertising on purchasing loyalty and deal sensitivity.

Not only will these expert systems work with the data that exists, they will permit human managers to study the world that could be. They will integrate marketing science modeling, automated-intelligence technology, historical marketplace relationships, and marketing mix models. These systems will take the mathematics and merge it with the knowledge of marketing experts: the experience, the rules of thumb, and the insights experienced marketing practitioners now use.

True single-source data, which merges household media exposure information with sales data for the same household, is increasingly available. Many companies are merging this new data source into their overall structure for evaluating advertising and, in the process, fundamentally changing the advertising evaluation system.

Some marketing people react to these changes by (metaphorically) throwing up their hands and burying their heads in the sand. They say, in essence, "So what? I don't need more and faster data. I don't know what it tells me anyway." If they don't know what the data tells them, and if they're not willing to learn, then they're right. They don't need more data; they need compassion.

If a company is an astute, smart, and aggressive competitor, and its managers take the time to understand and use these new information systems—especially while its competitors are sitting back and saying, "So what?"—they can gain a tremendous competitive advantage.

We've learned working with Litmus, especially in exercises designed to optimize a marketing plan, that over time the level of superiority of "machine" over "manager" goes down. The more people use the system, the smarter they become. The more they use an expert system, the more they become expert managers.

So we do not really believe the day will arrive when a computer can become a marketing department in a box. The world, human beings, and reality, will remain too complex.

We do believe, however, that an expert manager guided by an expert system will be a formidable competitor. Companies that adopt this emerging technology early will enjoy an edge over competition, an edge that will be difficult to overcome. Perhaps total product failure rates, on average, will remain the same. But they will certainly decline for the firms employing expert managers and systems, as they will increase for the companies that do not.

Have no doubt, the age of the thinking machine is coming, and the time for expert systems in marketing is close at hand.

WHAT CURRENT SMART SYSTEMS NOW DO FOR YOU

- Write draft research reports quicker and more accurately than analysts.
- Analyze scanner data to produce memos, tables, and graphs.
- Report exceptions and evaluate product performance.
- Provide data and some information but display no great intelligence.

WHAT EXPERT SYSTEMS *WILL* DO FOR YOU

- Put the combined knowledge of marketing experts at your marketing manager's fingertips.
- Organize the mountain of consumer information available into an information database to make marketing recommendations:

    1) Help in environmental scanning.
    2) Evaluate hundreds of thousands of targets in terms of profitability.
    3) Help in the creation of advertising messages and the measurement of advertising effectiveness.
    4) Engineer new products through computer-aided design.
    5) Simulate marketing plans to answer questions about media weight and schedules, pricing, couponing, shelf-facings, and other issues.
    6) Eventually actually design, launch, and track the performance of marketing programs.

14

THE MARKETING
REVOLUTION IS HERE

The material conditions for the revolution are present. Consumers are changing. Companies are under extraordinary pressure. And the tools are available.

Consumer values and lifestyles are undergoing a seismic change as people streamline their lives, seek to reduce risk, and hold business accountable for its failures. People are dramatically reordering their spending priorities, which means that much of what we knew (or thought we knew) about market segments five years ago is probably wrong today.

Consumers are overwhelmed by product choices. Cereal marketers introduced more than 150 new brands in the 1980s. Companies introduced 1,239 new bakery products in 1990 alone, including such products as Oat Bran Sahara Bread, Oat Bran & Nut Bagel Chips, and Less Oat & Fiber Bread. Is there any consumer who feels America does not have enough pizza shops, hotels, shoe stores, or quick lube spots? Are there consumers who want *more* variety among shampoos, computers, toothpaste, automobiles, paper towels, microwave entrées, soft drinks, soups, or nuts? Shakeout seems inevitable.

Companies therefore are under extraordinary pressure. There is not enough time, money, or people to do everything. They introduce new products and watch them fail. They reposition failing products and watch them continue to slide into oblivion.

Similar tremors are evident for those businesses that market to other businesses. Consumers consuming is the engine, and when that engine has a governor on it, businesses that supply consumer businesses and those that serve other industrial marketers feel the ripple effects. People do not check changed values—which emphasize moderation, new priorities, and more restraint in spending—at the door when they go to work at nonconsumer businesses.

Yet to grow, companies must innovate. They need to create new products and services and successfully reposition and restage established ones. Above all, they need to invest their marketing dollars wisely. Stockholders, boards of directors, and top management will not sit idly by in the 1990s and watch million-dollar, hundred-million-dollar, and, in some cases, billion-dollar marketing and advertising investments being made foolishly. They will demand accountability, demand a fair return on the marketing investment just like any other kind of investment, and demand an end to death-wish marketing.

Death-wish marketing, as we have stated before, is undertaken when the marketing manager has a secret desire to kill a brand, product, service, or even an entire company. It is marketing based on myth (e.g., "the *highest* quality products and service maximize profitability") and ignorance (low marketing IQs).

As we discuss this topic, we sometimes feel like those early twentieth-century scientists who were debunking the ether theory in physics. The concept of ether (also called luminiferous ether and not to be confused with the chemical compounds of the same name) originated with the Greeks, but it really came into its own in the nineteenth century. Early in the 1800s, French and English scientists successfully proposed the wave theory of light. But if light were a wave—like sound through the air or mechanical motion through an iron bar—it seemed self-evident that something must carry the waves. Space must be filled with something, and that something was ether—weightless, transparent, frictionless, undetectable chemically or physically, and literally permeating all matter and space.

Until late in the century, virtually every knowledgeable scientist believed in ether, even as the theory had to stretch to explain more and more inconsistent experimental evidence. For example, the famous Michelson-Morley experiment of 1881, designed specifically to detect the motion of Earth through the ether, demonstrated there was no such motion. The concept of ether was finally destroyed in 1905 with the publication of Einstein's first paper on the special theory of relativity. Nevertheless, scientists (and writers about science) continued to write about ether well into the 1920s since it was an easier concept to understand than Einstein's theory. There may still be people who believe in ether, just as there are those who still claim to believe in a flat Earth.

Similarly, the world of marketing is filled with people who believe in myths such as "Heavy buyers" (also known as "heavy users," "high rollers," "big spenders," etc.) "are the best target for most marketing programs, including consumer and industrial products and services." Or common among business-to-business marketers, "Your best prospects 'look just like' your best current customers."

As we've tried to show, myths like the heavy buyer myth are simply not true, but these commonly held assumptions cost marketers billions of dollars each year.

Ether does not exist. The sun does not revolve around Earth. Earth is not flat. And much of what people believe to be true about marketing is not true, including the belief that most marketing and advertising programs produce a return on investment.

≡ The End of Death-Wish Marketing

There is an alternative to death-wish marketing: marketing intelligence. Executives who work with marketing intelligence recognize the myths of marketing. They do not make judgment calls, do not use their competition as guides to their actions, do not seek short-term results. These executives know manufacturing costs and understand the relationship between all costs, revenue, and return on investment.

Top executives who want to see their organizations thrive in the 1990s, in what is already a difficult decade, will ask their marketing executives the hard questions. They will attack marketing myths when someone casually uses one at a meeting: "Oh, let's go with the concept—IBM *and* Apple compatible—because it generated the highest 'top box' scores!" Or "According to our focus group research, this is the best way to position our brand."

The age of myth and ignorance in marketing is coming—must come—to an end.

Marketing, no matter what practitioners thought in the past, is more science than art. It is no longer necessary to rely on hunch, hope, mythology, and experience or on creative breakthroughs and divine illumination. The data and the tools currently exist to dramatically improve a company's marketing programs for new and established products and services. All that's required is the will to use them.

And that, we acknowledge, requires a revolution in management thinking. It requires top managers who have made it their business to know enough about marketing and who have the will to ask the hard questions. It does not mean that the CEO has to be a marketing expert. It does mean that the CEO knows when a product is truly in the red or in the black.

A CEO doesn't have to understand how conjoint analysis or simulated test marketing works to know that both are *far, far more useful* marketing research tools than focus groups, gap analysis, and concept tests. Top management doesn't require a course in scientific sampling procedures, but *it must realize that small strange samples of people roaming shopping centers is a poor basis for multimillion dollar decisions.* Top managers don't have to know exactly *why* so much market research is flawed (although it helps) as long as they can spot the good stuff when it's presented to support a marketing plan.

In our experience, too much marketing floats free from any reasonable constraint. We *can* measure marketing performance, and performance should be measured against clear objectives. A clear objective is not, "We want to improve our brand recognition" or "We expect product trial to be up significantly as a result of this campaign." A clear marketing objective is, "We will increase our market share by two points in the next twelve months"; or "increase sales per square foot by 15 percent in the next year"; or "sell every Saturn we bring into our showrooms during the next 100 days"; or, better yet, "increase Clorox's bottom line by 20 percent during the next year."

Objectives should be specific, realistic, and measurable. We don't promise more than we can deliver, and we know when we've delivered what we promised. Marketing decision makers should also remain in the job long enough to be rewarded for their success or held accountable for the failure.

Effective marketing takes time. As rapidly as the world is changing, a company must go through every step we've described. *Those who recognize and accept the coming revolution will adopt the notion of clean-slate marketing we discussed in Chapter 2.* Before a single dollar is invested in annual marketing programs, marketing managers will be challenged to demonstrate the profit-directed thinking that went into each critical decision in the plan and the anticipated return on the investment of the plan as a whole. Starting with a *perfectly clean slate*, it must analyze the environment, the target, the positioning, the product design, pricing strategy, advertising, market test, and campaign tracking. To skip or abbreviate any one step risks the entire project.

But while marketing takes time, the computer can dramatically speed up many of the routine marketing tasks. The computer can analyze billions of alternatives to find the optimal plan before it's too late to do anything about it.

Remember that for each decision in the marketing mix (targeting, positioning, product design, pricing, distribution, advertising, etc.) there are many alternatives to choose from—in some cases thousands, hundreds of thousands, even millions. *And each of these alternatives can be—should be—evaluated in terms of criteria related to profitability.*

The time is *over* for choosing

- Target groups because they are frequent buyers,
- Positioning strategies because of meaningless "gaps" or even more meaningless focus groups,
- Product designs because they produce the highest "top box" scores,
- Ad executions because of high recall scores,
- Message strategies that communicate a myriad of different attributes and benefits,
- Media plans based on experience at roulette tables,
- Pricing levels based on neither strategy nor research,
- Consumer service levels based on the intent to satisfy everyone,
- Marketing plans based on picking one out of 14 billion possible plans out of a hat and launching them only to watch them fail.

American industry can no longer tolerate such a waste of our economic resources. American industry will no longer accept marketing management-led cavalry charges into oblivion as the order of the day.

≡ We Need an Annual Marketing Audit

One sign of the marketing revolution is that top managers will institutionalize in their organizations an annual marketing audit. The annual marketing audit is similar in terms of its potential for corporate diagnosis and prognosis to financial audits and product service quality audits reflected in the national competition for the Baldrige Award. The marketing audit will cover

1) An assessment of key factors that impacted the business for good or for bad during the past year. This assessment should emphasize an evaluation of marketing "surprises," the unanticipated competitive actions or changes in the marketing climate that affected the performance of the marketing programs.
2) An assessment of customer satisfaction based on research undertaken among key target groups.
3) An assessment of distributor, vendor, and intermediary satisfaction undertaken among key stakeholders.
4) An assessment of marketing knowledge, attitudes, and satisfaction of all executives involved in the marketing function.
5) An assessment of the extent to which the marketing program was marketed internally and bought into by top management, marketing, and nonmarketing executives.

6) An assessment of the extent to which each decision in the market-ing mix—e.g., targeting, positioning, pricing, advertising, etc.—was made correctly after evaluating many alternatives in terms of profit-related criteria.

7) An assessment of the performance of advertising, promotion, sales force, and marketing research programs with an emphasis on return-on-investment issues.

8) An overall assessment of whether the marketing plan achieved its stated financial and nonfinancial goals and objectives.

9) An autopsy of all aspects of the plan that failed to meet objectives with specific recommendations for improving next year's perfor-mance.

10) An assessment of the current value of brand equity for each brand in the product portfolio.

This marketing audit will help bring accountability to the marketing function. It will help lay the foundation for the clean-slate marketing ori-entation that is essential if we are to overhaul marketing from the bot-tom up and from the top down.

≣ Closing Thoughts

American industry is in trouble. Our markets are growing slowly, and foreign competition is becoming more intense. Financial wheeling and dealing and manufacturing wizardry, searching for divine inspiration under the veil of "creative license" or "management judgment," employee satisfaction and productivity programs, 100 percent customer satisfaction and zero defect product goals have all had their day in the sun. It's time for CEOs to recognize the overwhelming, overarching potential power of marketing. As Peter Drucker has said, the way to grow a business is through marketing: "Because its purpose is to create a customer, the business enterprise has two—and only two—basic func-tions: marketing and innovation. Marketing and innovation produce results: all the rest are 'costs.'"

The transition of this potential into reality will occur during the com-ing revolution in marketing. Top management will begin to truly compre-hend marketing's significance to their companies' future and drive this new thinking through their firms. The marketing revolution, we are con-vinced, will enable its advocates to dominate the marketplace in the 1990s. There will be companies that fade from the scene, as a result of oversupply *and* having been outmarketed.

Developments are occurring in marketing that are changing the fabric of industry, pushing back the frontier of what we know and what we want to know, separating winners from losers. The exceptional marketer is an organization that keeps abreast of these developments, capitalizes on new thinking and new discoveries, and stakes out the frontier as its own. The exceptional CEO and marketing manager is a professional who not only knows about these developments, trends, and ideas but plays a leading role in their implementation. The logical result of exceptional people leading exceptional companies is exceptional marketing programs —programs that take us to the bank, not to oblivion.

≡ INDEX